Ideas and Ideologies
General Editor:
Eugene Kamenka

Ideas and Ideologies

Already published:

Law and Society:
  The Crisis in Legal Ideals
  Edited by Eugene Kamenka, Robert Brown and
  Alice Erh-Soon Tay
  Robert Brown, Gordon Hawkins, Eugene Kamenka,
  W. L. Morison, Alice Erh-Soon Tay

Human Rights
  Edited by Eugene Kamenka and
  Alice Erh-Soon Tay
  Christopher Arnold, Stanley I. Benn,
  Nathan Glazer, Eugene Kamenka, John Kleinig,
  K. R. Minogue, J. G. Starke, Alice Erh-Soon Tay,
  Carl Wellman

Bureaucracy:
  The Career of a Concept
  Edited by Eugene Kamenka and Martin Krygier
  Robert Brown, Eugene Kamenka, Martin Krygier,
  Alice Erh-Soon Tay

Intellectuals and Revolution:
  Socialism and the Experience of 1848
  Edited by Eugene Kamenka and F. B. Smith
  Leslie Bodi, Tony Denholm, J. H. Grainger, Eugene Kamenka,
  G. A. Kertesz, R. B. Rose, F. B. Smith

Justice
  Edited by Eugene Kamenka and
  Alice Erh-Soon Tay
  Brian Barry, Ferenc Feher, Agnes Heller, Eugene Kamenka, Wieslaw Lang,
  J. A. Passmore, Julius Stone, Alice Erh-Soon Tay

Titles in Preparation:

Community
  Edited by Eugene Kamenka
  S. I. Benn, Eric Cohen, Israel Getzler, Tony Honoré,
  Eugene Kamenka, George L. Mosse, R. B. Rose

Imperialism
  Edited by Eugene Kamenka

Law and Social Control

**Edited by Eugene Kamenka
and Alice Erh-Soon Tay**

St. Martin's Press
New York

©Edward Arnold (Publishers) Ltd 1980

Library of Congress Cataloging in Publication Data
Main entry under title:
Law and social control.
    Includes bibliographical references and index.
    1. Sociological jurisprudence—Addresses, essays, lectures.
I. Kamenka, Eugene.   II. Tay, Alice Erh-Soon.
K376.L357   340'.115   80-18305

ISBN 0-312-47546-2

Printed in Great Britain

Contents

Introduction

'The sabbath was made for man, and not man for the sabbath.' The conflict between Jesus and the Pharisees, as Christians have understood it, was a conflict not just over the sabbath, but over the Law—even if Jesus took up, in the end, a fundamentally ambiguous position. Today the conflict has gone far beyond the realms of religion. It is a fundamental conflict of our time. The rejection of traditional, external authority, of an authority of origins, was an important theme of Protestantism and then, more nakedly, of the French Enlightenment and the French Revolution. It has been followed more recently by a further rejection of the abstract, impersonal rule of law, of the authority, that is, of abstract and impersonal laws, elevated by nineteenth-century thinkers and societies. The call now is to 'humanize' and 'demythologize' law and legal relations, to make law a servant and not a master, to set up over it and against it the values and demands of 'man', 'society', 'the people', or the 'rational' pursuit of 'rational' goals. Not 'law and order', but 'steering society', 'promoting equality and community', planning for the future, providing scope for creativity, 'self-expression' and the natural life, protecting the environment and averting ecological disaster are the popular catch-phrases of today. They represent and bear witness to a remarkable strengthening and increasing popularity of socialist and sociological critiques of law. These, of course, have a long pre-history. Today, they have so much gained in strength and public appeal as to constitute what we called, in the first volume of this series, a crisis in law and legal ideals. In that volume, and in a number of others within and outside the series, we and other contributors have sought to explore various aspects of that crisis. In this volume, we seek to approach the problem in its most general theoretical terms, while still emphasizing both detail and the practical experience and 'contradictions' of contemporary society.

Without question, the new critical attitudes to law and legal ideals have done much not only to alleviate particular injustices but to raise the critical standard of legal thinking and legal discussion. Law, in English-speaking countries, is no longer universally seen as an art, or more accurately as a craft or technique that makes no wider intellectual demands on its practitioners.

In these countries it is now much more generally recognized, as it has long been on the continent of Europe, that law is a central field in social science, social administration, social thinking. The newer disciplines of anthropology and sociology, whose findings are presented in this volume by Martin Krygier and Klaus Ziegert, have immeasurably deepened our understanding of the nature and function of law through studying it in a wide range of social settings. Our increasing awareness of the problems and concerns of communist, socialist and developing societies has had the same effect. The proliferation of new legal areas, in the Common Law world and outside it, has perforce produced new legal attitudes and new views of the function and appropriate procedures of law, as well as a new sense of its limitations (emphasized in this volume by Klaus Ziegert, Robert Simpson and Martin Partington). We have therefore thought it appropriate to arrange the contributions to this volume in two parts. Part One re-examines critically some traditional conceptions of the role of law in society and, in the final contributions by P.H. Partridge and Shlomo Avineri, draws our attention to a growing weakness or even a wider crisis in the doctrines of consensus and obligation that held sway in modern democratic societies until the late 1960s. Part Two turns to newer conceptions of the role of law in society and to the way that law and lawyers have grappled with specific problems of social control in modern times. Chapter 6 seeks to bring out these conceptions; Chapters 7, 8, 9 and 10 present a series of case studies, as it were, from which the reader may wish to draw further conclusions.

What parades in many quarters today as the 'radical critique' of law has its strident and unintelligent extremes—extremes that call forth counter-reaction and a retreat to old positions. The demand for law and order is not dead and is not often accompanied by a subtle appreciation of problems and distinctions. The crisis in law and legal ideals does not consist in a simple switch from one set of attitudes to another—that would simply be change or confrontation. The crisis consists in a polarization of attitudes, at least in words, at the ideological level, that threatens workable conceptions of consensus, obligation and legitimacy and that is accompanied by a characteristically agitational, anti-theoretical, conflation and confusion of contradictory purposes, attitudes and beliefs. The elevation of the demands of 'man', 'community', 'society' and 'reason' against the traditions, institutions and procedures of law may have produced a more critical understanding of the latter, though it has also led to much naive and unintelligent discounting of law. It has not been accompanied by a willingness to do genuinely critical social theory, to examine with the same sharp and jaundiced eye the concepts of 'man', 'community', 'society' and 'reason'. In these areas, the elevation of sociology over analytical philosophy has led to a woolliness of language and an incapacity for self-criticism that have made the new critical approaches to law much less interesting and effective than they should be. There was, after all, a Jewish answer to Jesus. That answer was, 'It is not true that man is made for the law and it is not true that the law is made for man'. The law, said and say the more intelligent rabbis, is made to make man, to change him, to strengthen one side of his constitution, behaviour and activities against others. Those who preach confidently that the law must serve man in practice have few inhibitions for legislating what man ought to be, how he ought to live, what is a proper or 'real' community, society, human relationship. Such concepts and moral presuppositions cry out for examination as much as does the operation of law and it may well be that legal experience and legal traditions have something to teach us about them.

In August, 1975, in an attempt to benefit from and further encourage serious and critical consideration of these questions, the Department of Jurisprudence in the Faculty of Law in the University of Sydney and the History of Ideas Unit in the Research School of Social Sciences of the Australian National University arranged a three-day seminar, held in Canberra, on the theme 'A Revolution in Our Age? The Transformation of Law, Justice and Morals'. That seminar was attended by historians, philosophers, political scientists, social theorists, lawyers and students of modern literature. It considered and discussed some 30 papers dealing with law, legal ideals and legal and moral attitudes in the contemporary world. One theme proposed to the seminar, which we elaborate further in this volume, was the suggestion that a variety of developments, both ideological and 'material', were undermining the classical contractual or *Gesellschaft* paradigm of law and elevating against it both *Gemeinschaft* and bureaucratic-administrative conceptions. This process, the editors of this present volume argued, was leading to most significant transformations in conceptions of law, justice and morals, at least in relation to the classical liberal concepts of law and the rule of law. Not all those present, as Oliver MacDonagh's paper to that seminar, printed in this volume, shows, accepted the idea that we were witnessing a profound transformation, or something very new, but all shared a keen interest in the multiplicity of new attitudes and tasks that confront law today. Some of the papers presented to that seminar have been published in Kamenka, Brown and Tay (eds.), *Law and Society* (this series, 1978) and in Tay and Kamenka (eds.), *Law-making in Australia* (Edward Arnold, Melbourne, 1980). Two more of those seminar papers, those by MacDonagh and Simpson, and a new paper by another participant, J.D. Heydon, are published here.

The Canberra Seminar in 1975 was followed in August, 1977 by a World Congress of the International Association for Philosophy of Law and Social Philosophy (IVR), held in Sydney and Canberra and attended by some 300 legal and social thinkers from 35 countries, spanning most of the world's social and legal systems. The Congress theme 'Law and the Future of Society' produced much further thought on the questions raised in our original seminar and in this volume. The papers by P.H. Partridge and Shlomo Avineri were presented at the Congress public symposium on 'Law and Internal Peace'; our own chapter 'Social Traditions, Legal Traditions' has drawn on A.E.-S. Tay's contribution as opening speaker in that symposium. We owe much to the University of Sydney and the Australian National University for the support they gave to the initial seminar and to the World Congress, as we owe much to all those who participated and to those contributors—J.D. Heydon, Martin Krygier, Martin Partington and Klaus A. Ziegert—who have accepted invitations to write chapters especially for this volume. The German Academic Exchange Service and the Max-Planck Institute for Foreign Private and Private International Law in Hamburg offered us generous hospitality and support from January to September, 1979 when we were working on this and other volumes. Miss Marion Pascoe and Mrs E.Y. Short have assisted us in checking manuscripts. Mr Roger Wilkins read the proofs and prepared the index.

Canberra,   Eugene Kamenka
January, 1980.   Alice Erh-Soon Tay

Part One

Law in Society

1

Social traditions, legal traditions

Eugene Kamenka and
Alice Erh-Soon Tay

I

Ever since Rudolf von Ihering poured scorn on the Platonic heaven of juristic concepts and proclaimed the jurisprudence of interests, there has been a
growing trend in Western societies toward so-called legal realism, toward
discounting the internal coherence and historical integrity of law, its claim
to mould society and to represent specifically legal traditions, procedures
and ideals. Court decisions have been studied to bring out the extent to
which they allegedly are not and cannot be derived from legal maxims, so-
called principles of law, statutes or precedents, but reflect wider, social, conflicts and interests. The operation of law has rightly been recognized to
extend far beyond the courtroom dramas recorded in law reports and case-
books — positively in the operation of that 'living law' internalized in a community's customs, expectations and ways of behaving, negatively in the use
and abuse of threat, negotiation and extra-legal power that precede or
replace the courtroom appearance. The trend has been to de-intellectualize
law, to pit life against what is written in the law books, to demolish the
fences that an earlier generation had put up to distinguish law from custom
and from the legally irrelevant. We now insist, above all, that law stands
neither above nor outside society, but within it, and that it does not make its
own history. All this, of course, is true. When we go on to argue that law
should be a neutral, flexible and totally characterless instrument responsive
to or serving uncritically elevated goals and needs alleged to have logical
priority over the law, that is another matter.

More recently, as Martin Krygier and Klaus Ziegert show in the chapters
that follow, anthropology and sociology have combined to strengthen this
trend. If law is a method of settling disputes in a regularized, predictable
way, then what past Western theorists called 'law' is only one possible
method among the many practised by different societies. Anarchic and
violent self-help, or utter lawlessness, are not the only alternatives to a centralized, state-sanctioned codified legal system. Hobbes's social defence
theory of law is clearly wrong, both logically and historically. Societies have
rules, and quite sophisticated rules and procedures, without having a

sovereign, codes, courts and constables. It may be, indeed, that the elevation of state-centred law, of the will of the sovereign and of a complex machinery devoted to producing stability and justice, is in inverse proportion to the authority of other norms: religion, custom and sheer fellow-feeling and neighbourliness. Some theorists, like Dr Ziegert below, make this point by saying that law is only one form of domination or social control and not necessarily the most important or the most admirable; others reject altogether the claim that law is produced by or controlled on behalf of society. They insist that law stands not above but within class conflict or other social conflict — that law is the will of the ruling class, of notables or elites, and seeks to organize social life in the interest of one group at the expense of another. What the eighteenth and nineteenth centuries did to religion — showing that there were *many* religions, and that they were all made by men, reflecting different climates, periods, values, and aspirations and much dastardy and cynicism — the twentieth century is doing to law.

Ludwig Feuerbach — the nineteenth century German philosopher who was one of the sharpest critics of metaphysical religion, who insisted that man had made God in his own image — declared nevertheless that the transcendence worshipped in religion was real and not a mere fantasy. Religion elevated what man elevated — his hopes for the future, his longings and ideals, his admirations and values. To destroy the metaphysical *form* of religion was to liberate its empirical *content* and that content, Feuerbach believed, was valuable. (He took a different view of law, of course, regarding it as a pious wish — backed by the executioner — that others behave the way I behave, a wish that refuses to notice the difference in our circumstances and falsifies the evidence by killing or putting away those who, through need, behave differently.) The critique of law is in many respects in the Voltairean rather than a Feuerbachian stage of the critique of religion. Even those who seek to use law for what they see as new goals and purposes are first concerned to humble it. Because the rule of law in its modern sense was very much a product of nineteenth century liberalism and the individualist and *laissez-faire* ideology that stood behind it, it is now increasingly discredited, at least in talk if nowhere near as much in action. Law is proclaimed to be undemocratic in its complexity and intellectualism, a form of alienation in its abstraction and formalism, an expression of authoritarianism, or even of violence, in its imposition of rules and obligations, in its ultimate reliance on the threat of coercion.

Elsewhere, we have sought to draw attention to various 'material' factors that have helped to discredit or at least inhibit enthusiasm for the liberal model of law.[1] The free, autonomous individual engaged in transactions with other individuals on the basis of equality and equivalence had reality, at

[1]Eugene Kamenka and A.E.–S. Tay, 'Beyond Bourgeois Individualism — The Contemporary Crisis in Law and Legal Ideology' in Eugene Kamenka and R.S. Neale (eds.) *Feudalism, Capitalism and Beyond* (Canberra and London, 1975), pp. 127–44.

least for some, in the society of comparatively small-scale production, consumption and distribution, of owner-managers and of the manufacture and exchange of discrete and identifiable objects as the most significant productive activity of mankind. Now, we wrote:

> The scale of property has become so vast, the sources from which it draws its wealth so multifarious and pervasive, and its social effects and ramifications so great, that modern man is having increasing difficulty thinking of property as private, as the concretization of an individual will reifying itself in land or objects, as a walled-in area into which others may not enter. There is, in other words, a shift of attention from the property whose paradigm is the household, the walled-in or marked-off piece of land, the specific bales that make up a cargo or consignment, to the corporation, the hospital, the defence establishment, the transport or power utility whose 'property' spreads throughout the society and whose existence is dependent upon subsidies, state protection, public provision of facilities, etc. In these circumstances, a view of society and a view of property as a collection of isolated and isolatable windowless monads that come into collision only externally and as a departure from the norm become untenable. Property becomes social in the sense that its base and its effects can no longer be contained within the framework of the traditional picture. The major sphere of social life passes from the private to the public, not merely in the sense that more and more activity is state activity, but in the sense that more and more 'private' property becomes public in its scale and its effect, in the sense that the oil company is felt to be as 'public' as the state electricity utility, the private hospital and the private school, with their growing need for massive State subsidies, as public as the municipal hospital and the state school.[2]

The distinction between the private and the public is indeed breaking down as the central, organizing principle of legal and political theory, which rested so strongly on the paradigm of property as the expression of private power and private will, of an area of independence and inviolability. Contracts dictated from above, loss distribution and social insurance, ever-increasing state regulation and inhibition of unequal bargaining, the felt need for frank judicial policy to meet new circumstances and take account of new dangers — all are combining to undermine the traditional liberal conception of private law and its centrality in the legal system and legal tradition.

Roscoe Pound, who predicted many of these developments and called them the New Feudalism, nevertheless, like the Marxists, fitted them into an evolutionary scheme of social and legal development. Law, he believed, progressed through stages, emphasizing a particular task at each stage and then turning to a new one as the earlier problem was solved. 'Primitive' law, he wrote, established the idea of a peaceful ordering of the community. The next stage, the stage of 'strict' law, added the idea of certainty and uniformity in that ordering. A third, that of equity and natural law, introduced the notion of good faith and moral conduct based on reason; a fourth — that of individualism — the idea of individual rights. The current stage is

[2]*Op.cit.*, pp. 132–3.

concerned with securing social as opposed to individual interest in the sense of seeking to satisfy the sum total of human demands. It drives us back from contract into status. Even if we reject completely the notion of an evolutionary order, we could hardly doubt that Western law at various times has exhibited each of these concerns especially strongly and that Pound has correctly characterized an overwhelming shift from one concern to another in the course of the present century. The implications of that concern have produced, as new concerns are wont to do, a far-reaching reappraisal of legal history, of the legal systems of other societies and of the very concept of law itself, even if the reappraisal is only in its opening stages.

The underlying truth of evolutionism, of course, lies in the fact that the achievements of each of these so-called 'stages' (more correctly 'moments', reaching the peak of their development at different times) are in principle, as a theoretical resource, now available to us. What is overlooked by the eclectic or the enthusiast for any particular stage or moment is the extent to which these moments stand in necessary tension with each other and have done so throughout the history of law, making it possible for different people to see the essence of law quite differently.

II

As idols fall, others rise in their place. The depreciation of law as an autonomous concept has been accompanied by the uncritical elevation of even more complex and suspect concepts: 'man', 'society', 'welfare'. The critical examination and merciless debunking to which these latter concepts have been subjected in the history of thought has been forgotten or deliberately ignored, as has the moral and intellectual wealth that has been poured into the Western legal tradition. Ideologists find it hard to have more than one thought at a time. Yet one outstanding characteristic of our age, as the contribution by Professor Partridge reminds us, is our vastly increased awareness of others in our own society, in other societies, in other times. We have a greater range of knowledge, and a richer variety of intellectual models and paradigms of social and legal organization to draw on than any age before us. One of the effects of that situation, no doubt, has been to sap our confidence, to promote moral and intellectual uncertainty and cultural relativism and to make us believe that we can be all things at once. The very variety of social arrangements that has come within our ken has made us more uncertain than ever of the very definition of law, or of the way that that term is best defined for at least some purposes. Our very purposes, indeed, threaten to become as confused as our conceptions. But if knowledge is a burden best assumed by stages, it is also an opportunity. We are in a position today, in a better position than ever before, to look critically and comprehensively at the concept of law and of a legal tradition and at the way they have functioned and can function in society.

Dr Krygier, in the chapter that follows, repeats the warning against

'Bongo-Bongoism' — the tendency of the knowledgeable but narrow student of society to dismiss conceptions and ideas because he cannot use them for, or does not find them to apply to, his special neck of the woods. Definitions of law and characterizations of the legal tradition are all too easily dismissed in this way. If they are useful, they pick out features for a specific descriptive or explanatory purpose. They always fail to settle some border disputes, to take account of other features or to provide satisfactory starting points for somebody else's very different concerns. Definitions come at the end and not at the beginning of an enquiry and are to be understood in the light of that enquiry. There is no useful point, therefore, in beginning a book on Law and Social Control with a definition of those two terms or with an examination of the different ways in which theorists have used them for what almost always turns out to be quite different purposes. What is 'Law' for one purpose, in the theoretical sense, is not 'Law' for another; sometimes it is important to distinguish law from morality and custom for instance, or from voluntary submission to arbitration or even from regulation; at other times, it is essential to see them as part of one set of normative interactions. But the principal theoretical problem in talking about law and social control in modern industrial and post-industrial societies is the problem of seeking to isolate and grasp that *specific* Western conception of law, time- and space-bound as it may be, and seeing in what ways it is being confronted and to some extent overwhelmed by alternative traditions. To understand Western law is to grasp a tradition, not to propose a concept. Bongo-Bongo may be interesting for itself, but it is not a significant competitor. In what follows, drawing rather loosely on two great figures in the history of sociological theory — Ferdinand Tönnies and Max Weber — we shall be suggesting that the modern developments in law and the modern crisis in legal ideals consist of a half-conscious confrontation between three great paradigms of social ideology, social organization, law and administration — each of them representing a complex but potentially coherent view of man, social institutions and their place in society. These paradigms we call the *Gemeinschaft* or organic communal-familial, the *Gesellschaft* or contractual commercial-individualistic, and the bureaucratic-administrative paradigms. The contrast between *Gemeinschaft* and *Gesellschaft*, or between what those terms stand for, formed a fundamental theme in Marx's conception of alienation and in the ideology and reality of burgeoning nineteenth-century capitalist society, which elevated contract against status, abstract right against all-embracing custom, individualism against the bonds of kinship, locality and collectivity. These contrasts entered quickly into the new sociology of the later nineteenth century through the work of Herbert Spencer and Sir Henry Maine; they were elevated into the fundamental concepts of 'pure sociology' by the German sociologist Ferdinand Tönnies (1855 – 1936) in his classic *Gemeinschaft und Gesellschaft* (*Community and Society*, first published in 1877) and (much later) reinforced, in one way or another, by more than 50 years of empirical studies of differences between kinds of group cohesion, bases of legitimacy and exercise of authority. At the same time as Tönnies, another of the great founding fathers of modern sociology, Emile Durkheim, was making similar points in his studies of the division of labour and of suicide — developing the concept of *anomie* to explain what appeared to be a greater incidence of helpless despair in urban, industrialized societies. Much of the contemporary use of the concept of alienation, even by a radical Western or 'critical' Marxist, has nearly 100 years of sociological thinking after the death of Marx amalgamated with his conceptions.

Elsewhere,[3] one of us has been critical, in certain respects, of alienation as a philosophical category and we have some doubts about its blanket use as a sociological one. But no one who looks at Marx's use of the concept can fail to note how neatly it brings out a major shift in ideology and in the understanding, legitimization and structuring of social institutions and social relationships symbolized politically by the French Revolution and made, to a substantial degree, a social reality by the development of nineteenth-century *laissez-faire* capitalism. That shift is above all a matter of contrasts and those contrasts, allowing for some of the theoretical infacilities of formulation produced by the period, are still best brought out in Tönnies's concept of *Gemeinschaft* and *Gesellschaft*.

Tönnies takes his departure from the subtle differences between the two German words. Both can mean a society, an association, a community, or a fellowship. But *Gemeinschaft* tends to be used of an association that is internal, organic, private, spontaneous: its paradigm is the *Gemeinschaft* of marriage, the *communio totius vitae*. *Gesellschaft* — comparatively new as a word and as a phenomenon — usually refers to something external, public, mechanical, formal, or legalistic. It is not an organic merger or fusion but a rational coming together for ends that remain individual. The 'secret' of the *Gemeinschaft*, for Tönnies, lies in the household and the concept of kinship, in the ties of blood, friendship, and neighbourhood. The 'secret' of the *Gesellschaft* lies in commerce and the concept of contract, its ties are the ties created by the transaction between (abstract) persons, its measure for all things is money. The *Gemeinschaft*-type of society we find in the village and the feudal system based upon the village. Here,

> the idea of a natural distribution, and of a sacred tradition which'determines and rests upon this natural distribution, dominate all realities of life and all corresponding ideas of its right and necessary order, and how little significance and influence attach to the concepts of exchange and purchase, of contract and regulations. The relationship between the community and the feudal lords, and more especially that between the community and its members, is based not on contracts, but, like those within the family, upon understanding.[4]

---

[3] Eugene Kamenka, *Marxism and Ethics* (London, 1969), esp. chapters II and III, pp. 4–30.
[4] Ferdinand Tönnies, *Community and Association (Gemeinschaft und Gesellschaft)*, translated and supplemented by Charles P. V. Loomis (London, 1955), pp. 67–8; also published (with slight variations) as *Community and Society* by the Michigan State University Press and Harper and Row (New York, 1957, paperback), p. 59. In the account that follows, we have

On the other hand,

> The theory of the *Gesellschaft* deals with the artificial construction of an aggregate of human beings which superficially resembles the *Gemeinschaft* in so far as the individuals peacefully live and dwell together. However, in the *Gemeinschaft* they remain essentially united in spite of all separating factors, whereas in the *Gesellschaft* they are essentially separated in spite of all uniting factors. In the *Gesellschaft*, as contrasted with the *Gemeinschaft*, we find no actions that can be derived from an *a priori* and necessarily existing unity; no actions, therefore, which manifest the will and the spirit of the unity even if performed by the individual; no actions which, in so far as they are performed by the individual, take place on behalf of those united with him. In the *Gesellschaft* such actions do not exist. On the contrary, here everybody is by himself and isolated, and there exists a condition of tension against all others. Their spheres of activity and power are sharply separated, so that everybody refuses to everyone else contacts with and admittance to his sphere; i.e., intrusions are regarded as hostile acts. Such a negative attitude towards one another becomes the normal and always underlying relation of these power-endowed individuals and it characterizes the *Gesellschaft* in the condition of rest; nobody wants to grant and produce anything for another individual, nor will he be inclined to give ungrudgingly to another individual, if it be not in exchange for a gift or labour equivalent that he considers at least equal to what he has given.[5]

Gesellschaft, then, in its paradigmatic form, is the bourgeois society of Marx's *Communist Manifesto* in which the cash nexus has driven out all other social ties and relations, in which men have become bound only by contract and commercial exchange. Where *Gemeinschaft* is associated with the village, the household, and agricultural production directly for use, the *Gesellschaft* is associated with the city, the factory, and commodity production for exchange.

> The head of a household, a peasant or burgher, turns his attention inwardly toward the centre of the locality, the *Gemeinschaft*, to which he belongs; whereas the trading class lends its attention to the outside world; it is concerned only with the roads which connect towns and with the means of transit. This class seems to reside in the centre of every such locality, which it tends to penetrate and revolutionize. The whole country is nothing but a market in which to purchase and sell.[6]

The 'common sphere' of the *Gemeinschaft* rests on a natural harmony, on the ties of tradition, friendship and common acceptance of a religious order; the common sphere of the *Gesellschaft*, in so far as it exists at all, is based on the fleeting moment of contact within the commercial transaction — the moment when the object is leaving the sphere of influence of A but has not

---

drawn on our 'Beyond the French Revolution: Communist Socialism and the Concept of Law', in *University of Toronto Law Journal*, Vol. XXI (1971), pp. 109–40.

[5]Tönnies, *op.cit.*, p. 74; paperback at pp. 64–5.

[6]Tönnies, *op.*cit., p. 90; paperback at p. 79.

yet entered the sphere of influence of B. At this moment, for the contact to be successful, the wills of the two individuals need to be in accord, there has to be what the law of contract calls 'a meeting of minds'. It is a meeting which takes place only in connection with an offer and holds good only in return for a consideration. As Professor Avineri puts it below, while making a similar contrast between *Gemeinwesen* and individualism, the organic *Gemeinschaft* is based on relationships, the contractual *Gesellschaft* on rights.

The distinction between *Gemeinschaft* and *Gesellschaft*, for Tönnies, is intimately associated with the distinction between two kinds of will, each characteristic of one of the two societies. The *Gemeinschaft* is based on the *Wesenwille*, the natural or integral will in which a man expresses his whole personality, in which there is not developed differentiation between means and ends. Against this type of will stands the *Kürwille*, the rational but in a sense capricious or arbitrary will developed in the *Gesellschaft*, the will in which means and ends have been sharply differentiated and in which Max Weber's *zweckrationale* behaviour prevails. Tönnies emphasizes and develops this distinction in his paper 'Zweck und Mittel im sozialen Leben' (1923)[7] and illustrates its application to property in his short pamphlet *Das Eigentum* published in Vienna and Leipzig in 1926. Property which is the object of the natural will is so closely bound to the essential nature of the person that any separation from it necessarily produces unhappiness. The property of this kind and the person tend to fuse together, it becomes part of him, loved as his own creation; it is not a commodity. Men tend to behave thus toward living things which they own, to their house and yard, to the 'sod' that they and their forefathers have worked for generations, and toward other persons who are the objects of their direct affirmation, of love, of trust, or of feelings of duty. In the relations that result from the natural will there is no sharp dichotomy of pleasure and pain, of satisfaction and dissatisfaction; there is rather a complex unity of feelings in which satisfaction and dissatisfaction, enjoyment and trouble, happiness and sorrow, right and duty, feeling honoured and feeling burdened are all bound together. The rational will, on the other hand, finds its paradigmatic expression in the relation to money, to property that is expressed as credit or debit in a ledger, to goods and commodities that one acquires with no other aim but to be rid of them, as quickly as possible, at a profit. The ultimate consummation of the rational will and its attitude to objects is found in the commercial *share*, which can be held by a man who has never even seen the property it confers on him and who has no interest in it whatsoever except as an item of credit. In such relations joy and sorrow, satisfaction and dissatisfaction, are sharply differentiated: profit is *plus*, joy, satisfaction; loss is *minus*, sorrow, dissatisfaction. Everything is abstracted, torn out of its living context, subsumed under an

[7]Published in Melchior Palyi, editor, *Hauptprobleme der Soziologie, Errinerungsausgabe für Max Weber*, vol. 1 (Munich, 1923, photographic reprint New York, 1975), pp. 235–67.

inviolable end. It is in its character as a *Gesellschaft* system of law, even within feudalism, that the Common Law has insisted on seeking to reduce all claims to financially expressible claims, leaving all other remedies, originally, to religion, Equity or state regulation. The distinction between Tönnies's two kinds of will is indeed central, though not explicit, in Marx's concept of 'free' labour as opposed to *forced* labour, to labour performed under the domination of need or of the desire to *have* rather than to enjoy and to the conception that law cannot produce morality, but only the semblance of it.

   Gemeinschaft and *Gesellschaft* for Tönnies are not close, accurate descriptions of two different existing kinds of societies. They are rather what he calls *Normalbegriffe*, a forerunner of Max Weber's concept of ideal types and of the modern concept of models. They are two opposed sets of connected presuppositions, two ways of seeing social reality and human relations, on which societies can be based. They are, in short, mental constructs, but constructs derived from observable reality, suggesting hypotheses and lines of investigation in dealing with that reality. In an 'ideal type' or *Normalbegriff* some aspects of that reality are selected and accentuated in defining the type, because of their apparent interdependence and theoretical importance. However, ideal types are not classifications. No actual society will conform completely to such a type. Tönnies himself likened the concepts '*Gemeinschaft*' and '*Gesellschaft*' to chemical elements that combine in different proportions and he made it clear, as his former student and son-in-law Rudolf Heberle has stressed, that there was no question of treating even an institution like marriage as simply a *Gemeinschaft* institution. The point was to ask of a particular marriage or of a particular type of marriage-institution, to what extent it approximated to the *Gemeinschaft* ideal and to what extent to the *Gesellschaft* ideal. No one who has observed contemporary changes in family law and relations can fail to see that those are fruitful and revealing questions to ask or that the moral choice between *Gemeinschaft* and *Gesellschaft* relations is not a simple and obvious one.

   Tönnies's inspiration was unquestionably historical. The product of a rural community, he was struck by the enormous changes produced, in Europe, by the growth of commercialism and individualism and the emphasis on abstraction and quantification — even of public opinion — that accompanied this growth. Like Marx, he was conscious of the civil society postulated by Hobbes and elevated by Adam Ferguson and the Scottish political economists; its contractual presuppositions were borne in upon him even more strongly through his detailed work on Hobbes, culminating in a classical three-volume study of Hobbes's life and thought. In his earlier work, Tönnies unquestionably historicized his fundamental concepts, treating the world as going through a fundamental shift from a feudalism that approximated to *Gemeinschaft* toward a commercial industrialized society, with large 'world-cities' that approximated more and more closely to the *Gesellschaft*. Man was passing from the primacy of the social unit, custom, tradition, and religious order to the primacy of the abstract individual, of trade, calculation, abstract law, and the arithmetical summation of 'public opinion'. Others have called this the 'post-historical society' and seen the United States as its paradigmatic expression. Ultimately, Tönnies hoped, the world would move toward a socialist community, in which *Gemeinschaft* relations would be re-established but on the basis of equality, not of hierarchy. In the early 1930s in protest against the Nazi misuse of his conception in their attack on Western, Jewish and capitalist decadence, he joined the Social Democratic Party.

Marx would not have cared for Tönnies's tendency to idealize the agrarian community or for the positive emphasis that Tönnies placed on the role of a sacred tradition and an accepted hierarchy within the *Gemeinschaft*. Above all, Marx would have rejected the view that *Gesellschaft* and *Gemeinschaft* are the two primary categories in terms of which society is to be understood. The *Gemeinschaft* of feudalism for Marx was a totally different thing from the *Gemeinschaft* of communism, and the intensified alienation of capitalism, its creation of the *Gesellschaft*, was, for Marx, a necessary step in the development from the *Gemeinschaft* of bondage to the *Gemeinschaft* of freedom. Marx and Engels themselves do not use the word *Gemeinschaft* to contrast their concept of a *community* with the state or the *bürgerliche Gesellschaft* (civil society) of capitalism; in its place they use the allied (but less hierarchical) word *Gemeinwesen*, as Shlomo Avineri does in a later chapter. Nevertheless, Tönnies has portrayed quite accurately, in his account of the *Gesellschaft*, those features and presuppositions of modern capitalist society which struck Marx and strike so many socialists as being its essential and alienating , inhuman, features. Socialists, in the first half of the nineteenth century, *were* deeply conscious — as were Marx and Engels in *The Communist Manifesto* — of an intensification of alienation, abstraction and atomization produced by the fully developed bourgeois-commercial society; they *did* contrast this (unfavourably) with the community life of traditional feudal-agrarian society. Marx and Engels themselves rejected, quite bluntly, what they scathingly called 'feudal socialism'; as socialists, they had to dissociate themselves from that backward-looking romantic and conservative elevation of the feudal community, so prominent in the work of Carlyle, and to stress that the feudal community was a community in *bondage*. Nevertheless, those who predict the future draw on the past; a strong nostalgia for an idealized version of the social relations found in the village *Gemeinschaft* is characteristic of the anarcho-communist strain in socialism and forms part of the vision of communism that we find in the work of Marx and Engels.

In Tönnies's later work, including the substantially revised editions of *Gemeinschaft und Gesellschaft* he brought out at frequent intervals between 1912 and 1936, and certainly in subsequent sociological reception of his thought, *Gemeinschaft* and *Gesellschaft* become more and more de-historicized as ideal types, preserved as polar opposites in a community-society continuum in which not only societies, but all sorts of specific human institutions and relationships, take up their positions. Tönnies's evolutionism appeared dated; so did his insistence on reducing social institutions to manifestations of will. The cohesion of his two central concepts was to some extent challenged as attempts were made to 'operationalize' these concepts in empirical social research. The American sociologist Talcott Parsons broke them down into four 'pattern variables' that are polar opposites facing each social action with a dilemma of choice: *affectivity* (immediate self-gratification) versus *affective neutrality*; *specificity* (narrowness of relationships, e.g. between shop-assistant and customer) versus *diffuseness* (breadth, as between husband and wife); *universalism* (action in terms of generalized standards) versus *particularism* (action governed by a reference scheme peculiar to the actors in the relationship); and *ascription* (status-based evaluation of persons) versus *achievement*. For empirical studies, Pitirim A. Sorokin and Howard Becker devised an eleven-point linear scale, embodying a dozen or so variables, for locating social systems in the *Gemeinschaft-Gesellschaft* continuum — work that brings out, as one might expect, the complexity of actual societies and systems and their failure to conform strictly or approximate evenly to the ideal type.

Outside the operational concerns of American sociology, critics such as Raymond Aron have rightly stressed the extent to which the *Gesellschaft* of capitalism, even in its heyday, was humanized and made bearable by an infinite number of *Gemeinschaften* contained within it, and that the *Gemeinschaft* of feudalism in feudal Europe was based, as Max Weber saw, on a fundamentally contractual view of the relationship of fealty and service and on the politically central concept that liberties granted by the king were in principle rights and charters, not gifts, and therefore maintainable against him. It is this which provides a central and crucial distinction between 'contractual' European feudalism and bureaucratic, service-based Islamic and Oriental 'feudalism', in which there was nothing comparable to these contractual rights, to the pluralism of church, king and barons or to the social importance of Roman and Common Law. Many serious students would hold that the emergence of capitalism in Europe and its failure to emerge in an initially technically and scientifically more sophisticated East was connected with this pluralist contractual nature of European feudalism. Anthropologists at the same time have brought out the strength of 'contractual' reciprocal relations — of gift exchanges and the like — even in comparatively uncomplex, 'primitive' communities and the extent to which the much vaunted mediation procedure of the *Gemeinschaft* works successfully, as it often does in the modern family, only when there is economic interest or economic dependence lurking behind.

The categories or ideal types put forward by Tönnies, then, have to be treated with caution and sophistication; they are, as Marx earlier said of his own categories, no substitute for detailed knowledge and work. But they can be used, we believe, to make the concept of alienation more than a mere literary concept, or a way of promoting an unattainable utopian ideal, and to help illuminate some fundamental concerns of our time. It is true that all law incorporates and is based upon a relation of domination and submission, whether to persons, customs, principles or rules. If all such domination is called alienation then law is always a form of alienation and the argument that it can nevertheless be replaced by uncoercive, spontaneous social regulation that represents the will of everybody is, in our view, totally implausible. But if we treat alienation as a term that brings out the formal and in principle intense abstraction and individualization of the *Gesellschaft* as an ideal type, then we are able to give specific rather than utopian content to the socialist conception, partly taken up and partly inspired by Marx, that the deficiencies of bourgeois law lie in its being a particularly intense and virulent form of alienation. We might bring out this point best by distinguishing, on the basis of Tönnies's work, between *Gemeinschaft* and *Gesellschaft* conceptions of law — alienation in principle being a characteristic of the latter and formalized direct suppression or social pressure, subsuming mediation, being much more characteristic of the former. Then we could say, as we have said elsewhere,[8] the following:

Sociological analysts of actual legal systems have tended to stress that law performs three different if perhaps related and relatable functions in society.

1   Law seeks to establish and maintain what even Lenin called certain simple fundamental rules of living together. Lenin and many others have thought that these were known to all ages and were something which, in the proper conditions, all rational persons of goodwill could agree upon. In fact, it is not easy to separate these so-called basic requirements of social life from historically specific conceptions of social aims and social goods and of particular social orders, with their fundamental constitutions, class and power structures, social and moral conceptions and taboos, protected by legal or customary sanctions with a degree of implied and actual force.

2   Law provides principles and procedures for conflict resolution between individuals and groups within a society, at least in so far as those individuals and groups accept a version or aspect of a common social order that includes submission to law.

3   To varying degrees at various times and in different places law both guarantees and protects existing productive relationships and ways of distributing resources and provides the means for active intervention by the sovereign or state, for whatever reasons or at whatever behest, to actualize new principles and policies for resource allocation and to enforce and supervise the carrying out of these.

These three functions of law — the peace-keeping and social harmonizing function, the conflict-resolution function and the resource-allocation

---

[8]A.E. – S. Tay and Eugene Kamenka, 'Editors' Introduction: Law, lawyers and law-making in Australia', in Tay and Kamenka (eds.) *Law-making in Australia*, (Melbourne, 1980) and Eugene Kamenka, 'What is Justice?' in Kamenka and Tay (eds.) *Justice*, (London, 1979).

function — have all been recognized in and given varying emphasis by different theories or alleged types of law and justice. The peace-keeping and social harmonizing function is much emphasized, as we might expect, in theories of law and justice that elevate its connection with the social organism or whole, with determining the 'proper' place of individuals, activities and institutions in a structured totality free of destructive conflicts. Such a view of justice is especially strong in traditional, pre-modern, organic pre-capitalist societies (communities), i.e. in the *Gemeinschaft*. In the *Gemeinschaft* type of social regulation, punishment, and resolution of disputes, as Tönnies saw, the emphasis is on law and regulation as expressing the will, internalized norms, and traditions of an organic community, within which every individual member is part of a social family. Here there tends to be no sharp distinction, if there is any formal distinction at all, between the private and the public, between the civil wrong and the criminal offence, between politics, justice, and administration, between political issues, legal issues, and moral issues. There is no theory of law as a distinct, autonomous social institution. The village is ruled by custom, the city — in its *Gemeinschaft* character — by religion and authority. There is little emphasis on the abstract, formal criteria of justice. The person at the bar of judgement is there, in principle, as a whole man, bringing with him his status, his occupation, and his environment, all his history and his social relations. He is not there as an abstract right-and-duty-bearing individual, as just a party to the contract or as owing a specific and limited duty to another. Justice is thus substantive, directed to a particular case in a particular social context and not to the establishing of a general rule or precedent. Its symbols are the seal and the pillory. The formalisms of procedure in this type of justice, which can be considerable, are linked with magical *taboo* notions, are emotive in content and concrete in formulation; they are not based on abstract rationalistic concepts of justice and procedure. Punishment, as Michel Foucault has stressed, is public, is a social drama, symbolizing the awesome power of the social unity. The almost overwhelming strength of this *Gemeinschaft* strain in traditional Chinese legal procedure, with its emphasis on the emperor and the magistrate as the father of his people, and in popular Chinese concepts of the political order, justice, morality and the place of the individual in society, is widely recognized; it was very much the medieval world-picture in Europe, it was also characteristic of proceedings before the early English jury and in the Russian peasant *mir*, especially as envisaged in the 1497 *Sudebnik* of Ivan III, where men were to be freed or convicted not as a result of investigating the specific crime they are accused of, but on the basis of their general reputation in the community, to which the jury testifies. It remains characteristic of aspects of justice in Communist societies, with their emphasis on the general social behaviour of the accused, and in Moslem community and revolutionary courts and tribunals.

The *Gemeinschaft*, as we have said, is not a description of an actual existing society in all its aspects; it describes a dominant or strong *moment* (in the Hegelian sense) or tendency of a society; it is a Weberian ideal type, linking actual institutions and the historical ideologies or perceptions on which they rest and which they mould, and showing how these presuppose and tend toward a particular view of man and society and the relations between them. There are in any society countervailing trends to the dominant world-view, institutions that do not fit, beliefs that do not square — sometimes very powerful or important institutions or beliefs. The King's Common Law in feudal England was one such institution that, in certain respects, quite fundamentally did not square and stood in contradiction with baronial justice. So were elements of Roman private law (as opposed to Roman public law) in the Republic, the Principate and the Empire, even if the concept of *ius* was backed by the *Gemeinschaft* philosophy of the Stoics. For the *Gemeinschaft* as *Gemeinschaft* does not have, as we have seen, a specific legal tradition. It brings together law, justice and morality and fuses them with politics and administration. The countervailing trends, Roman law, for example, and even the Greek codes, are strikingly the product of commerce and cities, of the need to provide for justice between citizen and foreigner — those inside the *Gemeinschaft* and those outside it — and of class struggles within the *Gemeinschaft* in which the lower classes demanded guarantees and settled procedures in place of the patrician conception of justice as custom, *their* customs.

The *Gemeinschaft* conception of justice, then, in its general assumptions or trend is a particular conception of justice rather than a universal one, though it has universal pretensions. It elevates social harmony and subordinates both conflict-resolution and resource-allocation to a conception of the total social order. In doing so, it does not simply neglect conflict-resolution or resource-allocation; it takes a different view of them — emphasizing a sharp dichotomy of reconciliation or total outlawry, of *li* or *fa*, in conflict, elevating relationships, status, 'merit' generally and such concepts as the non-contractual 'just price' and 'just reward' in resource-allocation. But it is true that the *Gemeinschaft* conception of justice is above all the conception of the *justitia communis*, in which universal principles of justice and both commutative and distributive justice are reconciled as mere parts of the whole and in which law, too, is seen as only an instrument. The content of this *justitia communis* tends to be provided by custom, tradition and a conception of a religiously sanctified order, or, in modern conditions, by social ideology and its policies. Behind them, of course, lurk historical accident, power and interest. In so far as the *Gemeinschaft* conception of justice may be said to have contributed something comparatively timeless to the conception of justice, or to display a common feature with other conceptions of justice, it has done so by elevating in its conception of justice the element of moral reciprocity — of rights and privileges as involving duties to others and not just by others, i.e. as a moral and not a logical matter. This is what Confucius does in taking the five relationships (four of them asymmetrical) — of governor and governed, parents and children, elder brother and younger brother, husband and wife, friends — as models for the social order. He elevates *relationships*. The *Gemeinschaft* is not clear — in fact, it is systematically unclear — about what is often taken to be a fundamental characteristic or even definition of law or justice in modern positivist thought: as action according to rule. It elevates the situational ethic against the ethic of rules and principles.

Today, there is in many quarters, as there is in Marx, considerable enthusiasm for a new secular *Gemeinschaft* — an organic community in which all persons and all activities are seen and judged as part of an organic whole, but without recourse to status, structured hierarchies or religious or customary taboos. The evidence so far is that status, structure, hierarchy and a strong quasi-religious ideology meant to provide social direction and cohesion emerge quickly when the experiment is on a national scale — but again the conception of justice that is elevated (if one is elevated at all) is that of the *justitia communis*, with its discounting of law and legal rights, its belief that justice is not to be seen as primarily or distinctively a legal matter, as application of rules, but as a matter of assessing ('understanding') the total man and the total situation, a matter of morals and politics, or of distribution of resources.

The *Gesellschaft* type of law and legal regulation is in all respects the very opposite of the *Gemeinschaft* type. It arises, as we have seen, out of the growth of individualism and of the protest against the status society and the fixed locality; it is linked with social and geographical mobility, with cities, commerce, and the rise of Protestantism and the bourgeoisie. It assumes a society based on external as opposed to internal links, made up of atomic individuals and private interests, each in principle equivalent to the other, capable of agreeing on common means while maintaining their diverse ends. It emphasizes formal procedure, impartiality, adjudicative justice, precise legal provisions and definitions, and the rationality and predictability of legal administration. It is oriented to the precise definition of the rights and duties of the individual through a sharpening of the point at issue and not to the day-to-day *ad hoc* maintenance of social harmony, community traditions and organic solidarity; it reduces the public interest to another, only *sometimes* overriding, private interest. It distinguishes sharply between law and administration, between the public and the private, the legal and the moral, between the civil obligation and the criminal offence. Its model for all law is contract and the *quid pro quo* associated with commercial exchange, which also demands rationality and predictability. It has difficulty in dealing with the state or state instrumentalities, with corporations, social interests, and the administrative requirements of social planning or a process of production unless it reduces them to the interests of a 'party' to the proceedings confronting another 'party' on the basis of formal equivalence and legal interchangeability. The *Institutes* of Justinian already elevate this conception of 'private' law as concerned with the individual. The American Constitution and Bill of Rights and the French Declaration of the Rights of

Man and the Citizen, as we have said, are the fundamental ideological documents of the *Gesellschaft* type of law, which reached the peak of its development in the judicial attitudes of nineteenth-century England and of German Civilians, and in the actual legal system of the United States. It is enshrined, at least in part, in the concept of the *Rechtsstaat* and the rule of the law, i.e. of a specifically legal conception of the foundations and core of the operation of justice and legitimacy in society. It is at home with the social contract theory of society, with individualism and abstract rights. This view again elevates a specific, historically shaped conception of law and justice, closely linked with individualism and a specific legal tradition grounded in the private law of the Romans and focusing on law and justice as conflict-resolution according to broad general principles and rules applying to all persons in that situation. But while this view of justice, too, elevates one particular function — that of conflict-resolution — it has its characteristic views of the social ordering and resource-allocation functions. It assimilates the former, as far as possible, to the minimum framework necessary for orderly and effective pursuits — i.e., to the rules of the road or the basic regulations of buying and selling necessary to make a market possible. Resource allocation it leaves to the efforts of individual enterprise, at least in principle. (In fact, of course, no society has been a pure *Gesellschaft* and no relations or institutions have ever been based solely on the cash-nexus or individual interest.) But the *Gesellschaft* conception of law and justice is especially suspicious of the attempt to derive these from the social whole; it sees the state as resting on law and serving the pluralism of private interests, rather than imposing a superior and independent universal interest or conception of justice.

Whether we treat individualism and the ideology of *Gesellschaft* relations as preceding and facilitating, or following and reflecting, the development of bourgeois capitalist society (and the former view is more plausible), there is no doubt that Tönnies's contrast helps to dramatize and illuminate (show what is involved in) the social revolution that overtook Europe after the industrial revolution. It helps especially to bring out sharply the conflict between classical liberalism and early socialism, explaining the nature of their confrontations and of their sympathies, the basis of their enmities and alliances. Nor is there any doubt that the *Gemeinschaft* strain has remained strong in the socialist and other critiques of capitalism and liberalism, that it is an active force today.

Nevertheless, the contraposition of *Gemeinschaft* and *Gesellschaft* as the two fundamental social traditions smacks unmistakably of the nineteenth century. It ignores the ever-increasing scope and power of the state and its bureaucracies, that have become so evident in the twentieth century. It ignores the increasing emphasis on bureaucratic rationality, on planning and administration within the capitalist firm itself, and the widespread impact that planning goals and values elevated by research and development have had on modern society. That phenomenon, not much noticed by Tönnies, constituted a fundamental theme in the work of Max Weber and much earlier, through the scientific optimism of the French Enlightenment and the technocratic interests of the Saint-Simonians, had become a central part of socialism as the ideology of rational planning. For socialism, and for that matter much wider social sentiments today, do not represent mere attempts to bring into being a new secular *Gemeinschaft*. We are foward-looking where the *Gemeinschaft* was backward-looking, progressive where it was traditional, rational and scientific where it was emotional and familial. The opposed paradigms of *Gemeinschaft* and *Gesellschaft*, then, require a third distinct paradigm, that of the bureaucratic-administrative society and 'legal' system. It is within that paradigm, indeed, that the conception of law as social control, as a means of general administration, receives its fullest development. Where *Gemeinschaft* elevates community and common tradition, religion or ideology, human relationships and organic bonds, where *Gesellschaft* elevates the abstract individual and his abstract rights and duties in a social contract and a system of abstract and impersonal law, the bureaucratic-administrative elevates what the Soviet legal theorist E. B. Pashukanis called the socio-technical norm — the rational requirements of a social province, field or activity, the implications of a policy, the regulations required to alter consciously a society and its ways of living, in short, its concept of law. Where the *Gemeinschaft* thinks of justice as the *justitia communis*, oriented to particular cases in a particular social context, where the *Gesellschaft* sees justice as commutative, determining rights and duties on abstract, impersonal and universal principles of law, independent of status, the bureaucratic-administrative society elevates the concept of legality, of action according to regulations to which human beings are subject, by which their status and their consequent rights and duties are determined.

Gemeinschaft-type law, we have said, takes for its fundamental presupposition and concern the organic community. *Gesellschaft*-type law takes for its fundamental presupposition and concern the atomic individual, theoretically — for the purposes of law — free and self-determined, limited only by the rights of other *individuals*. These two 'ideal types' of law necessarily stand in opposition to each other, though in any actual legal system at any particular time both strains will be present and each type may have to make accommodations to the other. In the *bureaucratic-administrative* type of regulation, the presupposition and concern is neither an organic human community nor an atomic individual, it is a non-human ruling interest, public policy, or on-going activity, of which human beings and individuals are subordinates, functionaries, or carriers. The (*Gesellschaft-*) law concerning railways is oriented toward the rights of people whose interests may be infringed by the operation of railways or people whose activities may infringe the rights of the owners or operators seen as individuals exercising individual rights. (*Bureaucratic-administrative*) regulations concerning railways take for their primary object the efficient running of railways or the efficient execution of tasks and attainment of goals and norms set by the authorities and taken as given. Individuals as individuals are the object of some of these regulations but not their subject; they are relevant not as individuals having rights and duties as individuals, but as part of the railway-running process and its organization, as people having duties and responsibilities. Such people are seen as carrying out roles, as not standing in a 'horizontal' relation of equivalence to the railway organization or to all their fellow-workers, but as standing in defined 'vertical' relations of subordination and sub-subordination. The relation of the bureaucratic to people as subjects and not objects is never direct but mediated through the policy, plan or regulations that purport to have human needs as well as technical requirements for their foundation. Hence the appeal against bureaucracy as bureaucracy is always to politics, which replaces the judge. The distinction between *Gesellschaft* law and bureaucratic-administrative law or regulation accords with a traditional distinction common lawyers have made between law and administration, courts and tribunals, judges and commissioners. The lawyer has often had to serve in both capacities but he has distinguished the *Gesellschaft* conception of law, oriented to dispute-resolution and conflicts that can be expressed as conflicts between parties, that sees judicial hearings as adversary proceedings, dominated in the first instance by the parties stating their case, concerned with actual past occurrences or the immediate likelihood of such occurrences, providing remedies and not planning the future. Those many departments of social life, or specific problems, that require investigation of a wider kind, assessment of the possible effect of social policy, considerations of a whole area or province or set of likely future developments, or even arbitration in the light of the arbitrator's independent investigation, the common lawyer sees as the proper task for a commission or tribunal which may function under quasi-judicial rules but whose 'essence' or task is not fundamentally judicial, or rights-oriented, but investigative and administration-oriented. To the *Gesellschaft* court, indeed, the bureaucratic-administrative society opposes the Star Chamber, exhibiting and applying to specific cases predetermined political policy, the commission, charged with determining the right policy, and the tribunal established to mediate, conciliate or investigate. (The well-known investigative role of continental European courts under the civil law system bears witness to the strength of the continental state, to the extent that law there was instituted from above and that the *Gesellschaft* system of civil law has come to bear strong bureaucratic-administrative traits.)

Bureaucratic-administrative regulation, thus, is quite distinct from both *Gemeinschaft* and *Gesellschaft* law, but it does not stand in quite the sharp uncompromising opposition to them that they do to each other: pursuing different aims, it nevertheless finds points of contact and affinity with each of the other forms. The bureaucratic-administrative emphasis on an interest to which individuals are subordinate, on the requirements of a total concern or activity, brings it to the same critical rejection of *Gesellschaft* individualism as that which is characteristic of the *Gemeinschaft*; it gives it a similar interest in maintaining harmonious functioning, in allowing scope for *ad hoc* judgement and flexibility, in assessing a total situation and the total effects of its judgement in that situation. This is why the growth of corporations has produced *Gemeinschaft*-like features in the internal direction of the corporation, even while the corporation maintains *Gesellschaft* relations with its external counterparts. At the same time, bureaucratic-administrative regulation is a phenomenon of large-scale, non-face-to-face administration, in which authority has to be delegated. As the scale grows, bureaucratic rationality — regularity and predictability, the precise definition of duties and responsibilities, the avoidance of areas of conflict and uncertainty — becomes increasingly important. This requirement of bureaucratic rationality in the bureaucratic-administrative system stands in tension with *Gemeinschaft* attitudes, unless they are strictly limited in scope. It finds a certain common ground with the distinguishing features of *Gesellschaft* law in the emphasis on the universality of rules and the precise definition of terms, in the important role ascribed to the concepts of intra and ultra vires, in the rejection of arbitrariness and of the excessive use of *ad hoc* decisions to the point where they threaten this rationality. In the Soviet Union, the bureaucratic-administrative strain has been very strong indeed, imperfect as the execution may often have been. While earlier Soviet theoreticians saw law being replaced by the revolutionary consciousness of justice, which would strengthen the *Gemeinschaft* side of socialism, in fact the influence of plan and of bureaucratic requirements in the Soviet Union has been notably in the direction of strengthening the presuppositions of bureaucratic rationality and of thus strengthening, at least to some extent, the respect and need for *Gesellschaft* law. This point, of course, is of crucial importance for assessing future development in China, where the prospects of *Gesellschaft* law are intimately associated with the elevation or non-elevation of bureaucratic-administrative features and requirements and the consequent growth or retardation of interest in bureaucratic rationality. That is what is involved in the struggle between Chairman Hua (or more accurately Deng Xiao-ping) and the Gang of Four (more accurately the Gang of Five, since Mao was a member).[9]

---

[9]The demarcation between *Gesellschaft* law and bureaucratic-administrative regulation has been partly obscured by that bureaucratic rationality which gives them some common elements and features. It is made even more complex in western societies, especially in the British Commonwealth and the United States, by the extent to which *Gesellschaft* law has shaped social attitudes and expectations and has made respect for the legal rights of those involved an important condition for successful bureaucratic direction and administrative control. Common Law judges, indeed, have been strong in providing common law remedies for administrative abuse of power and have influenced and indeed helped to produce new *Gesellschaft*-type legislation.

III

Much of the argument in jurisprudence has been concerned with judging the merits of competing prescriptions for the use of the term 'law', though the dispute has rarely been purely verbal. There is a strong tradition which wants to reserve the word 'law' for use in a narrow sense (as in 'the rule of law') to refer to what we have called the *Gesellschaft* type. Others would say that *Gemeinschaft* law is also law and some use the word 'law', at least in one sense, broadly enough to include bureaucratic-administrative regulation, even in its pure ideal type form, as well. *Domination-submission*, however, is clearly extra-legal and supra-legal in that it neither implies nor requires a structured system of regulation incorporating certain values and moral or socio-political assumptions; gangsters can and do rule by terror and the imposition of force and they need not ideologize their pretensions. Domination-submission therefore does not inevitably confront the *Gemein-schaft*, the *Gesellschaft*, and the bureaucratic-administrative form as a fully blown rival pattern of a social structure or value-system; it can, to some extent, live above or within all of them, modifying or shaping the conditions in which they operate. It is also, to some extent, implied by each of them. The ideas of *Gemeinschaft*, in their classic formulation, incorporate domination-submission in so far as it can be plausibly presented as voluntary exercise of 'parental' responsibility and voluntary submission to 'parental' will. As such, they are particularly susceptible to degeneration into naked relations of personal domination and helpless or hopeless submission. The French Revolution and the ideals of the *Gesellschaft* were, in fact, a protest against precisely this sort of degeneration, an attempt to create a political and legal system that was by its very nature inimical to the institutionaliza-tion of status, of dependence, of relations of personal dominance and sub-mission. It was an attempt to replace the government of men by the govern-ment of law. *Gesellschaft* law as a pure ideal type is indeed inimical to the recognition of social hierarchies; it does presuppose the equality and equiva-lence of all the parties before it and it operates best when those parties are in fact equal and do not stand, one to the other, in a relation of pervasive depen-dence or subordination. (The elevation of the — abstract — rights of women and rights of children is an attempt to turn the family into a *Gesellschaft* and not a *Gemeinschaft* institution recognizing implicity the bias of *Gesellschaft* law toward freedom and equality and against status-dependence.) The bureaucratic-administrative form, on the other hand, lends itself much more readily to an institutionalization of domination-submission. In communist countries, including China, the domination-submission relation has been institutionalized, or at least ideologized, in the doctrine of the leading role and historical infallibility of the communist party and in the proclamation of 'democratic centralism'; a vast range of legal and extra-legal measures have been taken to ensure that the domination remains secure. The over-whelming basis of domination is, in the narrower senses of law, extra-legal.

Though *Gemeinschaft* attitudes and bureaucratic-administrative structures are more easily manipulable in the interest of domination than *Gesellschaft* attitudes and structures, *Gemeinschaft* can produce a dangerously uncontrollable popular enthusiasm or resistance through its implicit elevation of fellowship, of popular participation and non-impersonal relations, and its stress on the mutual ties between rulers and ruled. On the other hand, bureaucratic rationality can produce attitudes highly critical of irrational bases for domination and 'inexpert' personnel in control. The history of the Soviet Union in the past sixty years confirms all of these points: the Soviet régime has been able to manipulate all three of the ideal types in the interest of its domination, but it has also been confronted by limited challenges from each. The Soviet government, indeed, has not committed itself exclusively to any of the three types. It has kept all the options open and has quite skilfully balanced *Gemeinschaft* and bureaucratic-administrative attitudes and procedures with appeals to socialist legality and limited but patent *Gesellschaft* guarantees and assurances.

The state-imposed laws of imperial, traditional China, where they are not primarily rules of bureaucratic organization, as they so largely were, may be seen in either of two ways. They presuppose and seek to maintain the social life of the *Gemeinschaft* and even the emperor's seemingly arbitrary exercise of judicial and punitive powers is taken to be part of his parental function. In this sense, they are the laws of a *Gemeinschaft* concerned with a whole man and an organic society. At the same time, the dominant Confucian tradition with its strong internalization of *Gemeinschaft* values had to insist that rigorous punitive intervention by the state and its magistrates was a sign that social harmony had been breached, that the *Gemeinschaft* had been broken. It thus presents state law, not as a product of the *Gemeinschaft* but as an attempt to restore the *Gemeinschaft* through a basically external intervention, through the iron-fisted exercise of power relations, of domination and submission. The external intervention was justified or ideologized in so far as its aim was to restore the *Gemeinschaft* and in so far as it was based on the emperor's recognition of his duties as *parens patriae*, but the punitive laws themselves could be seen, in this context, as terroristic interventions, as resting immediately if not ultimately on bare domination and submission. Imperial China, indeed, went much further than this; it enforced and symbolized, in the *kowtow*, the institutionalized acceptance of total imperial power, the citizen's complete prostration before the emperor and the magistrate. At the same time, its remarkably complex (by the time of the Ching) Great Code of Laws, with over 4,000 provisions, had no conception of private law. It was a Code of Punishments and of regulations addressed to officials.

This aspect of terroristic intervention, of total domination and submission, is stressed by the theorists of totalitarianism and in Professor Wittfogel's theory of the hydraulic society and its agro-managerial despotism. It cannot be counterposed, as a 'native' Chinese tradition, to the

Marxist-Leninist view of state administration and judicial or extra-judicial punishment. The systematic use of legal and extra-legal terror as an exercise of naked domination has played an important role in the development of all communist states; it is given ultimate ideological foundation, but no coherent legal or ideological form, by the doctrine of the leading role of the party and of the necessarily ruthless dictatorship of the proletariat. It is best understood, however, in relation to the *Gemeinschaft* concept or aspirations that strive to give it legitimacy, for even a heavily terroristic government, especially in modern conditions, will seek to legitimize its despotism and conceal its arbitrariness; it will argue that terror is used to restore or create a *Gemeinschaft* and applies only to the violator who has put himself outside it. There is thus a complex intertwining of traditional and foreign themes, of universal problems and trends which emerge just as clearly in other communist societies and are as much Marxist-Leninist as Chinese. The use of terror in the pre-1949 Red Areas of China and the further developments since bring this out clearly; they also indicate the care that the Chinese communist party has taken to limit the application of terror, at any particular time, to a specifically circumscribed section of the population small enough to be treated as standing outside the *Gemeinschaft* and to limit the duration of any specific terror-campaign in such a way as not to threaten the underlying *Gemeinschaft* legitimation of the party. This is the aim and significance of the important distinction re-emphasized by Mao Tse-tung in his famous 1957 speech on contradictions between the (*Gemeinschaft*) ways of handling contradictions among the people and the (domination-submission) use of coercive terror in handling contradictions between the people and its enemies. The latest developments in China, of course, constitute a renewed elevation of bureaucratic-administrative and limited *Gesellschaft* conceptions of law and of administration, with the fundamental communist ideology and claim to legitimacy still protected by the ruthless use of force and of law as a political instrument.

IV

It may be tempting to some to see our presentation of the *Gemeinschaft*, *Gesellschaft* and bureaucratic-administrative paradigms as an alternative statement of the Marxist belief in the passage from feudalism through capitalism to socialism — especially since an intelligent reading of Marx makes it clear that he used the terms 'feudalism' and 'capitalism' also as paradigms or ideal types and not as actual descriptions of any single existing society at any particular time. But that is not out intention, even if we would say that each of Marx's three stages elevates one of our paradigms more strongly than the others. But *Gemeinschaft*, *Gesellschaft* and bureaucratic-administrative features, as we have argued, are all present in both Western and socialist societies today, were present in capitalism and feudalism (think only of the Tudor Poor Law or consider Professor MacDonagh's contribution to this book) and existed in developed forms in what Marxists choose to call slave-owning societies. There is no reason to suppose that they are entirely absent from much less differentiated societies. But our concern with the paradigms is as a means of understanding the present — the crisis in western legal ideology, the remarkable similarity of legal developments and legal problems in modern industrial and post-industrial societies and the striking elements of legal convergence, the abandoning of doctrines of the withering away of state and law and of the revolutionary consciousness of justice, between communist and non-communist modernizing societies. The debate in the Soviet Union over the concept of economic law replacing or supplementing civil law is closely parallelled by discussions in Western societies, especially the Federal Republic of Germany, where the concept of an economic offence has also emerged as something distinct from the *Gesellschaft* conceptions of crime and tort. The conversion of the law of matrimonial offences into family law and all it implies has proceeded rapidly in the West; the accompanying institution of the informal Family Court is being experimented with in Poland. (The Polish decision to have assaults within the family dealt with within the Family Court represents a consistent extension of the *Gemeinschaft* ideology enshrined in the concept of family law; interestingly, those who promote women's and children's rights in Western society particularly want such assaults dealt with by the ordinary courts on *Gesellschaft* principles.) So are the new concerns with and provisions for facilitating the citizen's interest in vindicating his 'new property' — claims to state benefits and allocations which are not strictly rights in a *Gesellschaft* system of law. No one looking at legal discussion and the strident criticisms of law and the legal profession today can fail to note the extent to which the confrontation is between a *Gesellschaft* legal ideology and new or revitalized *Gemeinschaft* and bureaucratic-administrative ideologies. Nor can one account for the slightly more than lip service that communist constitutions and codes pay to *Gesellschaft* conceptions of law except by seeing the strength of the Western legal tradition and the extent to which bureaucratic-administrative conceptions in modern times are forced to build on it and seek some alliance with it. The three paradigms we have put before the reader do not exhaust or cover all forms of social administration or ideology, nor is it necessary to define law in such a way as to limit the use of the word to one or other of the paradigms. But the paradigms do help to illuminate the centrality and coherence of Western legal ideology, to exhibit its strengths and its limitations, to show why Pashukanis thought that law reached its apogee only with the bourgeoisie, which consummated law as a material force, as a judicialization of social relationships. Today, as we shall see in the second part of this volume, it is becoming more fashionable to speak of law as a form of steering society, or as a neutral instrument for achieving specific non-legal tasks. But the *Gesellschaft* conception of law, with the *Gemeinschaft* and bureaucratic-administrative conceptions, has its own ideology, its own demands to make on the rest of society, including, we believe, a bias toward freedom and equality and against arbitrary coercion. Only the *Gesellschaft* conception of law has a conception of the specificity of legal procedures, legal institutions and legal values. That they are not suited for all purposes, that they cannot deal with all problems, that they can give rise to inequity while seeking to do justice is apparent enough and is perhaps becoming even more apparent in modern conditions. But theoretically, we will not further understanding by simply dissolving the concept of law into policy, administration or social control and practically we will find both the *Gemeinschaft* and bureaucratic-administrative regulation unbearable unless tempered by a central and continuing elevation of the social role of *Gesellschaft* law and *Gesellschaft* legal ideology. Once that is recognized, there are, of course, other important tasks — above all, perhaps, that of determining, in specific areas and for specific purposes, the optimal mix of *Gemeinschaft*, *Gesellschaft* and bureaucratic-administrative arrangements and procedures, whether combined, as Dr Ziegert suggests, in the concept of the legal programme, developed in Sweden, or achieved through a differentiation of rules and roles.

2

Anthropological approaches*

Martin Krygier

Legal anthropology has a distinguished and moderately long 'prehistory', but rather a brief period of real history. In the earlier stage, writers trained in law — Bachofen, McLennan, Maine and Morgan — were of great importance in the development of anthropology generally, and they and historical jurisprudes, such as Maitland, Pollock, Seebohm and Vinogradoff, were particularly interested in historical and contextual studies of law. Comparative jurists such as A. H. Post and Josef Kohler collected and compiled what were taken to be the legal rules of a vast range of societies. Durkheim put law at the centre of his analysis of the organization of societies primitive and modern.

What was particularly lacking from speculation and evolutionary theorizing about 'law' in societies with which anthropology has traditionally been concerned — technologically simple, non-industrialized, and usually quite small-scale societies — has been an adequate empirical base. The ethnographies available to nineteenth and early twentieth-century theorists and comparativists were rarely compiled by anthropologists, and few of them have proved of enduring value. Detailed and reliable ethnographic accounts of the law of small-scale societies only began to appear with the publication in 1919 of Barton's study of the Ifugao in the Philippines, and in the 1920s with Kroeber's work on the American Yurok Indians, the German missionary Gutmann's study of the Chagga of Mount Kilimanjaro and one of the best known of all anthropological accounts of law, Malinowski's brief, lively and deliberately iconoclastic account of 'law' among the Trobriand Islanders of New Guinea.[1]

Even after these works had appeared, anthropologists tended not to focus

*I am indebted to Peter Lawrence, Professor of Anthropology in the University of Sydney, for his valuable comments on an earlier draft of this chapter, comments from which I have sought to benefit.
[1]R.F. Barton, *Ifugao Law* (Berkeley, 1919); A.L. Kroeber, *Principles of Yurok Law* in *Handbook of the Indians of California* (Washington, DC, 1925); B. Gutmann, *Das Recht der Dschagga* (Munich, 1926); B. Malinowski, *Crime and Custom in Savage Society* (London, 1926). Cf. also R.S. Rattray, *Ashanti Law and Constitution* (Oxford, 1929).

on law; it is still not uncommon to find those who work in this area drawing attention to, and often bemoaning, the novelty and scarcity of such work. In 1934, Malinowski complained that 'the problem of primitive law, so fascinating theoretically, so fundamental in all practical applications of anthropology, has been neglected to an extent which the layman would find unbelievable and which the specialist realizes with a shock.'[2] More recently, Pospisil has written of

> A 'legal 'vacuum in the ethnological literature which, with the noteworthy exception of Barton's (1919) and Malinowski's (1926) writings, persisted into the middle of the present century. Otherwise outstanding ethnographic studies, which described in great detail even the most obscure aspects of tribal cultures, systematically failed to account for their most fundamental part — their law.[3]

Similarly in 1964 Bohannan could still observe, correctly, that 'the literature in legal anthropology is small and almost all good — neither claim can be made for very many other branches of the subject';[4] the bulk of the literature to which he was referring had been written in the preceding ten years. Since then, anthropology of law has taken part in the Parkinsonian expansion of almost every branch of social science, and there is now a large literature in the area, which includes many works of high quality.[5] However, legal anthropology still remains a rather discrete and specialized sector of activity, both among anthropologists and lawyers. This is unfortunate because each discipline could afford and benefit from more than nodding acquaintance with the other.

I   Law, Social Control and the Variety of Political Systems

Society, according to Thomas Hobbes, is impossible without a politically omnipotent sovereign whose commands constitute the law. In the pre-legal and therefore pre-social state of nature, people are condemned to a war of all against all and life is 'solitary, poor, nasty, brutish and short'. In this analysis, Hobbes fuses two distinct types of claim. One of these claims is

[2]Introduction to H.I. Hogbin, *Law and Order in Polynesia* (London, 1934), p. lxi.

[3]Leopold Pospisil, 'E. Adamson Hoebel and the Anthropology of Law', *Law and Society Review* VII (1973), p. 537.

[4]Paul J. Bohannan, 'Anthropology and the Law' in Sol Tax, (ed.) *Horizons of Anthropology* (London, 1965), p. 199.

[5]Good reviews of this literature, written by and primarily for anthropologists can be found in Laura Nader, 'The Anthropological Study of Law' in Laura Nader, (ed.) *The Ethnography of Law*, Supplement to *American Anthropologist* LXVII (1965), pp. 3 – 32; S.F. Moore, 'Law and Anthropology', *Biennial Review of Anthropology, 1969*, edited by B.J. Siegel, (Stanford, 1970). pp. 252 – 300, reprinted in her *Law as Process* (London, 1979), pp. 214 – 56; Laura Nader and Barbara Yngvesson, 'On Studying the Ethnography of Law and its Consequences' in John J. Honigmann, (ed.) *Handbook of Social and Cultural Anthropology* (Chicago, 1973), pp. 883 – 921; Jane F. Collier, 'Legal Processes', *Annual Review of Anthropology*, IV (1975), pp. 121 – 44. The first introductory book on legal anthropology is Simon Roberts, *Order and Dispute* (Harmondsworth, 1979).

about the *function* of law: for Hobbes, this is essentially the maintenance of order. The other has to do with the structural or institutional prerequisites for the existence of law: a centralized, unified political sovereign. Hobbes was both equating anarchy or lawlessness with disorder and also specifying the institutions necessary for a legal order to be said to exist. It was an order only slightly caricatured in Malinowski's well known and oft repeated phrase, one with 'central authority, codes, courts, and constables'.

This conception of sovereignty, of the State 'as the sole bearer of *Imperium* within its own territories, all other corporations and organizations being allowed to exist only with its permission'[6] had begun to crystallize in Europe only at the beginning of the seventeenth century. However, already in Hobbes we find the historically quite specific institutions on which the conception was based becoming fused with allegedly universal *functions* of law. This fusion profoundly influenced subsequent Western political philosophy and jurisprudence. In particular, it encouraged nineteenth century legal positivists to attribute far broader significance than now appears warranted to a particular phenomenon — the rise of centralized, 'sovereign', states — which was itself relatively novel in European history and unparallelled in much of the rest of the world.[7] According to Jeremy Bentham, for example,

> we know what it is for men to live without government, for we see instances of such a way of life — we see it in many savage nations, or rather races of mankind; for instance, among the savages of New South Wales, whose way of living is so well known to us: no habit of obedience, and thence no government — no government, and thence no laws — no laws, and thence no such things as rights — no security — no property: — liberty, as against regular control, the control of laws and government — perfect; but as against all irregular control, the mandates of stronger individuals, none. In this state, at a time earlier than the commencement of history — in this same state, judging from analogy, we, the inhabitants of the part of the globe we call Europe, were; — no government, consequently no rights: no rights, consequently no property — no legal security — no legal liberty: security not more than belongs to beasts — forecast and sense of insecurity keener — consequently in point of happiness below the level of the brutal race.[8]

In anthropology, this historical and geographical parochialism has, we shall see, not been without effect, either on those who suffered from it or on those

[6]Quentin Skinner, *The Foundation of Modern Political Thought*, Volume II (Cambridge, 1978), p. 352.

[7]Cf. Martin Krygier 'State and Bureaucracy in Europe: The Growth of a Concept' in Eugene Kamenka and Martin Krygier (eds.) *Bureaucracy: The Career of a Concept* (London, 1979). pp. 1 – 33, and M.G. Smith, 'The Sociological Framework of Law' in H. Kuper and L. Kuper (eds.) *African Law* (Berkeley and Los Angeles, 1965), pp. 24 – 48.

[8]'Anarchical Fallacies' in *Works*, [edited by] J. Bowring (11 vols, Edinburgh, 1843), II, pp. 500 – 1.

afflicted with the 'seductions of negative ethnocentrism'[9] common among anthropologists.

A second and related concern of English jurisprudence, also emphasized by Bentham, has been to distinguish law from other means of regulating conduct, legal institutions from non-legal ones and legal matters from other matters. The assumption that such distinctions can sensibly be made is, indeed, implicit in the title of this volume; the conviction that law and social control are at the same time functionally related and conceptually distinct gives it its point. Usually, legal positivists have sought to link their concern with authoritative public institutions to this concern with finding the distinguishing marks of law, by developing what Dworkin calls 'tests of pedigree' for law. For Bentham and Austin, following Hobbes, any positive law, as distinct from rules of custom, morality, etiquette etc., is the command of a legally unlimited sovereign to his habitually obedient subjects. For Salmond, Holmes and Cardozo, the 'pedigree' of a law lies in its recognition by the courts.

Whatever the adequacy of any particular test of pedigree, there is at least good sociological sense in seeking to identify such distinctions in societies such as our own, where law has clearly distinguishable institutional 'carriers'. Moreover, there is no objection in principle to attempts to distinguish analytically between types and components of institutions and activities in other societies, even where they appear, or are, indistinct. There may be, and I believe there are, particular historical reasons for this essentially philosophical task being taken up at all, or in one way rather than another, or at certain times and places more than at others. But these matters of the genesis of analytical distinctions are irrelevant to their validity or usefulness. On the other hand, if such distinctions are made to depend on contingent institutional features of a writer's world, then the writer should at least be aware that there are significant geographical and historical limitations on the weight which the features he chooses can bear. Accounts of law which assume not only that law can be distinguished from other forms of regulation, but also that the distinction can be made by invoking a discrete and authoritative institutional source, face and create problems in relation to societies where both assumptions are, at the very least, problematic.

One of the first things which strikes a neophyte on reading ethnographic literature is the vast range of political and legal systems consistent with the existence of social order. Of course, these political and legal mechanisms and structures never exist in a social or economic vacuum; they are intimately linked with, in some societies indistinguishable from, social and economic forms. It is not my intention in this chapter to *account* for the various political and legal systems which exist, nor can I discuss them all. But important among the distinctions to which legal anthropologists have drawn

[9]Richard L. Abel, 'A Comparative Theory of Dispute Institutions in Society', *Law and Society Review* VIII (1974), p. 305.

our attention are those between Western industrialized states, states in non-industrialized and somewhat less differentiated societies, especially in Africa, and 'stateless' societies.

In the industrialized West, as Dr Ziegert emphasizes in the next chapter, and as Marx, Weber and Durkheim also emphasized, there is a high degree of differentiation between familial, political, legal and economic institutions, actors and relationships. There is often, as Marxists never tire of observing, considerable overlap of spheres but only a very vulgar Marxist would today deny that such distinctions exist and are, at least until 'the last analysis', significant. Confining our attention to law: in industrialized Western societies, legal institutions are structurally differentiated from other institutions, and within legal institutions measures are taken, if not always with uniform success, to distinguish the responsibilities and authority of one sort of legal office-holder from those of another. Within legal institutions, occupants of specific publicly defined roles, and only they, have authority to legislate. Their legislative acts are legally binding on citizens. Occupants of other publicly defined roles have authority to adjudicate disputes among citizens and between the State and citizens, and the adjudicators' decisions are also legally binding. The legal system in general is 'worked' by large numbers of professionals trained to operate with legal techniques. There are, finally, special rules which enable one to distinguish in large part 'the law' from other modes of regulating people's conduct, even if, as Ronald Dworkin emphasizes, the 'institutional autonomy' of law which 'insulates an official's institutional duty from the greater part of background political morality' is incomplete.[10]

Differentiation of a 'legal' realm, in ways analogous to the above over-simplified sketch, is not confined to Western or industrialized societies. In Africa, for example, there were a number of large states, some in the nineteenth century including over a million persons, which possessed political and legal institutions, administrative structures, and courts which were also highly differentiated, if less than our own. For example, the Lozi (or Barotse) society of Zambia, studied by Max Gluckman, 'has had for at least two centuries a governmental political organization including a hierarchy of courts which had power to enforce their decisions'.[11] The Soga of Uganda similarly possessed a state structure 'comprising a ruler and a hierarchy of chiefs with great authority, who were also the judges'.[12] Though many African chieftainships — including the Lozi and the Sotho of Lesotho, as Ian Hamnett's *Chieftainship and Legitimacy* (London, 1975), shows — combined executive and judicial functions in the manner of early European

[10]Ronald Dworkin, 'Hard Cases' in *Taking Rights Seriously* (London, 1978) p. 101 *et seq.*
[11]Max Gluckman, *The Judicial Process among the Barotse of Northern Rhodesia* (Manchester, 1955; second edition, 1967), p. 2.
[12]Lloyd A. Fallers, *Law without Precedent* (Chicago, 1969), p. 331. See also his 'Administration and the Supremacy of Law in Colonial Busoga', in Ian Hamnett (ed.), *Social Anthropology and Law* (London, 1977), pp. 53–76.

monarchs, judicial institutions and activities among the Soga were clearly separated from political and administrative ones. Indeed, according to Fallers, the Basoga had a highly whiggish commitment to the 'rule of law'. In the Soga context this meant that

> the chiefs and headmen are subject to the same courts and law as other Basoga and that when they shirk their duties or exceed their authority they may, upon complaint by an ordinary citizen, be tried by the regular courts, rather than being simply disciplined administratively . . . . Basoga may well have been surprised (and pleased) to discover that British administrators were subject to judicial restraint. They cannot, however, have found the idea novel, for there is every indication that they and their ancestors shared it.[13]

In all African chieftainships of this sort, there were rulers who possessed judicial, administrative and, though there is little anthropological literature on this, legislative authority, which could levy armies and mobilize labour. There were also traditional kingdoms and chieftainships in Polynesia, Fiji and Southeast Asia.

Most societies which anthropologists have studied, however, have not possessed obviously distinguishable institutions of this sort. These are the stateless societies. Nomadic hunting and gathering groups, for example, including Australian aborigines, many American Indian and African tribes and Eskimoes were usually small. It is now generally believed that few had centralized governmental institutions or indeed any 'offices' which continued after outstanding individuals, who might have influence for a time, lost that influence or died. This of course has not prevented Europeans from 'discovering' such institutions. Hiatt nicely summarizes fluctuating European analyses of Australian aboriginal government thus,

> . . . observers in the middle of the last century denied that Aborigines had governmental institutions but did not indicate satisfactorily how affairs were conducted despite the lack. Observers later in the century asserted that Aborigines had governmental institutions but did not explain in any detail how these functioned. Observers in the first half of the present century described Aboriginal government as gerontocratic, but the evidence they themselves supplied indicates that the old men had little authority outside the sphere of ritual. Finally, in recent years Meggitt and I found no governmental institutions in two different areas and have described how, nevertheless, the people organized and controlled their activities.[14]

Many other societies were also found to be 'stateless'. The works of Fortes on the Tallensi of then French West Africa, and Evans-Pritchard on the Nuer of southern Sudan[15] greatly influenced later studies of African societies

---

[13]Fallers, 'Administration and the Supremacy of Law . . .', in Hamnett (ed.), *op.cit.*, pp. 66–7.

[14]L.R. Hiatt, *Kinship and Conflict* (Canberra, 1965), p. 147.

[15]See esp. M. Fortes, *The Dynamics of Clanship among the Tallensi* (London, 1945), E.E. Evans-Pritchard, *The Nuer* (Oxford, 1940) and M. Fortes and E.E. Evans-Pritchard editors, *African Political Systems* (Oxford, 1940). See also J. Middleton and D. Tait, editors, *Tribes without Rulers* (London, 1958).

which had highly intricate principles of kinship, locality, marriage and descent, but no legislative, judicial or administrative institutions. In such stateless societies

> power is diffused rather than concentrated. A relatively orderly existence is secured by the alliance of groups of various sizes, each alliance being roughly balanced by rival alliances. Cross-cutting systems of organization ensure that a man's friend in one context may be his enemy in another; in any quarrel there are some who are friends of both sides . . . . [There exist] . . . fundamental differences between states, where power is centralized or concentrated, and stateless societies, where it is diffused or dispersed and where, as it were, there is no sovereign.[16]

According to Fortes and Evans-Pritchard, though there was no government in such societies, one could point to a political system based upon principles of patrilineal descent. Later work in Africa has drawn attention to stateless societies where principles of unilineal descent are not the exclusive or even the central principle of political organization,[17] or do not apply. Some writers have suggested that earlier work on lineage-based systems might have overemphasized the political importance of unilineal descent and underemphasized the importance of other relationships, such as cognatic and affinal ties, age-sets, locality, and of overlapping and cross-cutting ties.[18] In New Guinea, the tendency of early postwar ethnographers to follow Fortes and Evans-Pritchard in isolating and emphasizing patrilineal descent has proved misguided. In the New Guinea Highlands, for example, 'the dogma of descent is absent or is held only weakly',[19] and in Papua New Guinea societies generally, as Lawrence has argued, it is impossible to identify any single mechanism which can be distinguished as political. Rather, 'descent and/or local groups, on the one hand, and the cognatic and affinal networks that link them, on the other, have potentially equal importance . . . . As [Laura] Bohannan says of the Tiv of West Africa, every intragroup, intergroup and interpersonal relationship has political consequence at some time.'[20]

The existence of societies such as these has led anthropologists to reflect upon the two common assumptions of pre-anthropological legal theory to which I have referred: the assumption that social order is necessarily

---

[16]J.A. Barnes, 'Law as Politically Active' in G. Sawer (ed.), *Studies in the Sociology of Law* (Canberra, 1961), p. 171.

[17]See E. Colson, 'Social Control and Vengeance in Plateau Tonga Society', *Africa* XXIII (1953), pp. 199 – 212; P.H. Gulliver, *Social Control in an African Society* (London, 1963), V.W. Turner, *Schism and Continuity in an African Society* (Manchester, 1957).

[18]E. Colson, *op.cit.*, pp. 210 – 11; J.A. Barnes, 'African Models in the New Guinea Highlands', *Man* LXII (1962), p. 9.

[19]J.A. Barnes, *op.cit.*, p. 6; P.H. Gulliver, *Neighbours and Networks* (Berkeley and Los Angeles, 1971), pp. 4 – 27 and 237 – 9.

[20]Peter Lawrence, 'Introduction' to Ronald M. Berndt and Peter Lawrence (eds.), *Politics in New Guinea* (Nedlands, Western Australia, 1971), p. 15. See Laura Bohannan 'Political Aspects of Tiv Social Organization' in J. Middleton and D. Tait (eds.), *op.cit.* p. 65.

dependent on the existence and sway of 'law' of a particular kind, and the assumption that law can readily be distinguished from 'non-law'.

Anthropologists have responded in several different ways to the jurisprudential problems which their researches revealed. One simple verbal solution, of which Austin would doubtless have approved, and Salmond explicitly did, is to deny that 'law' exists in some primitive societies. Thus, on the basis of Roscoe Pound's definition of law as 'social control through the systematic application of the force of politically organized society', Radcliffe-Brown explained that 'in this sense some simple societies have no law, although all have customs which are supported by sanctions'.[21] Similarly, Evans-Pritchard argued that

> In a strict sense Nuer have no law. There are conventional compensations for damage, adultery, loss of limb, and so forth, but there is no authority with power to adjudicate on such matters or to enforce a verdict. In Nuerland legislative, judicial, and executive functions are not invested in any persons or councils. Between members of different tribes there is no question of redress; and even within a tribe, in my experience, wrongs are not brought forward in what we would call a legal form, though compensation for damage (*ruok*) is sometimes paid.[22]

In these examples, and many others which could be cited from early twentieth-century anthropological and jurisprudential writing about law, the English concept is simply not called upon to work overtime or away from home. If in the societies studied, structural analogues exist for European legal institutions, then there is law; if not, not.

Another tradition in legal anthropology, however, does attempt to enlist familiar concepts and the learning of jurisprudence for comparative purposes. According to E.A. Hoebel, one of the pioneering figures of modern legal anthropology, all societies have legal norms — that is, norms whose

> neglect or infraction is regularly met, in threat or in fact, by the application of physical force by an individual or group possessing the socially recognized privilege of so acting.[23]

Since this is the case, Hoebel argued, an anthropologist was justified in using 'the basic tools of the student of Western jurisprudence' for the analysis of primitive law. The tools he chose were Hohfeld's 'fundamental legal conceptions', which he considered applicable to legal relations in every society. Pospisil purports to derive four universally present attributes of law from cross-cultural research, on the basis of which law can be identified in any society, and also, he argues in every functioning subgroup of society.

> I conceive of law as principles of institutionalized social control, abstracted from

[21]A.R. Radcliffe-Brown, 'Primitive Law' reprinted in *Structure and Function in Primitive Society* (London, 1971), p. 212.
[22]*Op.cit.*, p. 162.
[23]E.A. Hoebel, *The Law of Primitive Man* (Cambridge, Mass., 1954), p. 28.

decisions passed by a legal authority (judge, headman, father, tribunal, or council of elders), principles that are intended to be applied universally (to all 'same' problems in the future), that involve two parties locked in an *obligatio* relationship, and that are provided with a sanction of physical or non-physical nature. Since this concept, defined by its 'form' and the four attributes, is applicable to the Western concept called law, I am adopting this term for my cross-culturally derived category of phenomena of authoritative (but not necessarily authoritarian) social control, rather than coining another term. Adoption of this analytical concept of law enables me to make cross-cultural analysis of law for comparative purposes.[24]

The applicability of Pospisil's conception, and particularly of the attribute of 'authority', to stateless societies is highly controversial.

Gluckman, in *The Judicial Process among the Barotse* . . ., was also searching for universal features of judicial process and legal reasoning. He claimed, for example, that

my study of the Lozi judicial process, which is akin to our own judicial process, faithfully depicts modes of reasoning which are probably found wherever men apply norms to varied disputes.[25]

The Lozi, he argued, had a special word for law (*mulao*) which had many of the different senses of the English word. They distinguished legal questions from moral and other ones, and they used 'the norm of the reasonable man', 'the man who conforms reasonably to the customs and standards of his social position' as a crucial tool in adjudication. The reasonable man was, Gluckman asserted elsewhere, 'the dominating presence . . . in all Barotse court trials . . . the standard figure against which, both in cross-examination and in judgment, the councilors assessed the behaviour of the disputing parties' and Gluckman went on to attempt to demonstrate that the concept existed in the law of acephalous, segmentary societies.[26] The influence of *The Judicial Process among the Barotse* . . . was not confined to other anthropologists; because of its highly lawyerlike concerns, it influenced lawyers as well. A.L. Goodhart, who wrote the forward to the book, was moved to criticize 'the Austinians' and 'the neo-Austinians' for adopting 'the remarkable view that early law was not law at all'. He explained that 'it is now realized that no clear line can be drawn between early law and the fully developed legal system of a modern state, and that the latter has not only sprung from the former but is identical in nature with it.' The parallels which Gluckman drew were made easier by the fact that the Lozi, as we have seen, had a highly differentiated state, law and court system; they were also assisted, as Moore points out, by Gluckman's definition of 'judicial process'. The Barotse had used ordeals and divining in pre-colonial times,

---

[24]Leopold Pospisil, *The Anthropology of Law* (New York, 1971), p. 95.
[25]*Op.cit.*, p. 33.
[26]Max Gluckman, 'Reasonableness and Responsibility in the Law of Segmentary Societies' in H. Kuper and L. Kuper (eds.), *op.cit.*, p. 120 and *passim*.

but Gluckman writes of old Barotse 'magico-religious methods of arriving at the truth in disputes' as 'extra-judicial' and says 'here there was no judicial process'.[27]

Gluckman was heavily criticized for importing ethnocentric assumptions into his analysis, and while on many matters he defended himself vigorously and often, he admitted in a reappraisal published at the end of the second edition of *The Judicial Process among the Barotse* . . . that

> I realize now that it would have been better had I merely stated the similarities and the differences without coming to the overall assessment that similarities outweighed differences . . . . So much emphasis has been placed by many authors (jurisprudents, anthropologists and others) on the differences between modern and tribal law that I was to some extent carried away by my demonstration of the similarities in the judicial process. (*Note*: not in the whole of law) (p. 375)

In a later work, *The Ideas of Barotse Jurisprudence* (New Haven, 1965), Gluckman uses Barotse substantive law not to show similarities with modern European law, but to bring out differences from it. These differences, however, were of quite a special kind, enlisted to show that 'tribal' law bore close similarities to early European law, and to bear out Maine's belief that the evolution of law had been from status to contract.

More recently, and less ambitiously, Fallers has adopted Hart's view of law as a combination of primary and secondary rules in order to make useful distinctions between societies, including our own and the Basoga, which do, and those which do not, make use of what he calls 'the legal mode of social control'. In this usage the legal mode

> requires that values with respect to human conduct be reduced to normative statements which are sufficiently discrete and clear so that it may be authoritatively determined *whether or not* in a particular case a particular rule has been violated.[28]

In this deliberately limited sense, it is perfectly conceivable that there will be societies without law and there will be great variation, even in societies which do have it, in the extent to which it is relied upon.

A third tradition, often in direct reaction to the two discussed above, follows Malinowski's injunction that in primitive communities law should be defined 'by function and not by form'. Thus, Koch among many others is impatient with the perennial controversies in legal anthropology over whether simple societies have 'law'. He observes that

> No one has ever disputed the universal existence of something we call economy. Australian aborigines knowing no metal or pottery and living solely on edibles gained in exploitative hunting and gathering have economy in spite of their primitive technological inventory and their simple system of transfer of goods

[27]Sally Falk Moore, 'Archaic Law and Modern Times on the Zambezi', *International Journal of the Sociology of Law* VII (1979), p. 7.
[28]Fallers, *Law without Precedent*, p. 11. For another application of Hart's concept of law, see Stuart A. Schlegel, *Tiruray Justice* (Berkeley and Los Angeles, 1970).

and services. If economy has to do with 'how people make a living', law — for me — has to do with 'how people make living a relatively ordered social existence'. And if one can have an economy without a decimal system of accounting, without money, and without banks, I suppose one can have, or even must have, law without codices and courts. As soon as we begin to be curious about the *ways* in which people attempt to settle disputes, resolve conflicts, and control violence, these traits of our own legal system (courts, codes) become examples, not standards, of cultural experimentation in the legal domain.[29]

A further, and currently popular, move in this functionalist line of argument is to try to rid legal anthropology of concern with 'law' or lawlike institutions in small-scale societies, and replace it with investigation of mechanisms of 'social control'. Roberts' introduction to legal anthropology, *Order and Dispute*, for example, distinguishes sharply between two traditions in legal anthropology. One tradition, which Roberts rejects, and which includes authors such as Maine, Llewellyn and Hoebel, Gluckman, Fallers and Pospisil, shows 'a continuing determination to pursue the study of how order is maintained and disputes are settled in these [small-scale, stateless] societies within the framework of Western legal theory, despite the patent lack of close institutional counterparts to our own arrangements' (p. 13). The other tradition, which he endorses, 'disregards or even explicitly rejects' (p. 184) Western jurisprudence, says little or nothing about 'law' in small-scale societies and is 'concerned with problems of order and conflict, rather than that segment of the subject which could be identified with the "legal" (significantly, the word "law" is rarely used in many of these works)' (p. 198).

Instead of an ethnocentric concern with 'law' or law-like institutions, we should, according to Roberts, come with an open mind to examine the 'control mechanisms we find elsewhere' (p. 13). It is with these control mechanisms, whatever shape they take, and the ways in which, and extent to which, they contribute to the maintenance of order and settlement of disputes, that we should be concerned.

The question of what word to use is on its own, as Humpty Dumpty taught us, not a very interesting one. It is not as important as it has been prominent in anthropological debates. Ethnocentrism about institutions and concepts is, as I have suggested above and all anthropologists know, a continual danger in anthropology. If anthropologists feel that the excision of 'law' from their vocabulary helps them to avoid this danger, then, while few have found it easy to do so consistently, no great damage is done. There is much to be said for at least limiting the concept in ways such as those suggested by Fallers, among others. But, whether or however one uses the word, nothing necessarily follows about the relevance of Western law and jurisprudence to an understanding of other societies. Acquaintance with and

---

[29]Klaus-Friedrich Koch, 'Law and Anthropology: Notes on Interdisciplinary Research', *Law and Society Review* IV (1969), p. 12.

consideration of one's own laws does not *have* to lead to ethnocentrism. It might simply make anthropologists as aware of cross-cultural similarities as they are of differences. That would not be a negligible achievement in this field.

In any event, it is not obvious to me that in choosing to investigate 'social control' rather than 'law', Roberts and the many anthropologists whose views he endorses in fact liberate legal anthropology from as many stereotypes as they believe. Roberts contrasts the narrowness of focus of those who concentrate on 'law' with the alleged expansiveness of an approach geared to understanding 'other people's control institutions' (p. 29) in their own terms. But while a study of 'order and dispute' might broaden the range of *institutions* one studies, it does not broaden — if anything it narrows — the range of *functions* that one looks for. In this crucial respect, anthropologists who choose to replace the search for law with investigation of the operation of 'control mechanisms' still seem to me to suffer from the Austinian, 'imperativist', constriction of view which afflicts many jurists and sociologists of law.

If an anthròpologist were to investigate our own society, he would find that law is used for control but he would also find, if he looked, that it is used for many other purposes as well, purposes not at all well characterized as 'social control'. Writing in 1951, David Riesman assured us that:

> the anthropologist is not likely to harbour the naive assumption that the law, or any other institution, serves only a single function — say, that of social control — and that any other functions which in fact it serves are excrescences or 'contradictions'. The concept of ambivalence is part of his equipment; he tends to search for latent functions, transcending the ostensible.[30]

In fact, the bulk of work in legal anthropology, as in other areas of social science, has proceeded on the basis of just this 'naive assumption'. As Laura Nader has pointed out several times,

> ... the law does not function solely to control. It educates, it punishes, it harasses, it protects private and public interests, it provides entertainment, it serves as a fund-raising institution, it distributes scarce resources, it maintains the status quo, it maintains class systems and cuts across class systems, it integrates and disintegrates — all these things in different places, at different times, with different weightings. It may be a cause of crime; it plays, by virtue of its discretion, the important role of definer of crime. It may encourage respect or disrespect for the law, and so forth. We have assumed that there was probably a cross-cultural difference in the content and form of a legal system, and at the same time we have ignored the variety of functions (sometimes referred to as extralegal, latent, or unintended) that a legal system may or in fact does have.[31]

[30]'Toward an Anthropological Science of Law and the Legal Profession', reprinted in *Individualism Reconsidered* (New York, 1954), p. 445.
[31]Laura Nader and Barbara Yngvesson. 'On Studying the Ethnography of Law and its Consequences', *op.cit.*, p. 909. See also Laura Nader, 'The Anthropological Study of Law', *op.cit.*, pp. 18 ff.

Anthropologists are well placed to enlighten us about the range of functions that legal or other mechanisms serve (or, for that matter, fail to serve). They might be helped in doing so by a broader understanding of law. It was, after all, not an anthropologist but the jurist H.L.A. Hart in his *The Concept of Law* (Oxford, 1961), who awakened us to the importance in legal systems of 'power-conferring rules', for which the Austinian 'analogy with orders backed by threats altogether fails, since they perform a quite different social function . . . . Such laws do not impose duties or obligations. Instead, they provide individuals with *facilities* for realizing their wishes, by conferring legal powers upon them . . .' (p. 27). The mystique of social control is so strong that even Hart conventionally refers to law as 'a means of social control'. His own work suggests that it is either loose or misleading to rest with such a label. Apart from controlling, facilitating and distributing services, law is, as Summers has observed, 'a means of "doing justice and equity" between individuals, too'.[32] Performing such a function might *involve* social control, but one caricatures what it amounts to if one simply reduces it to social control. More generally, Colson is pointing to something profoundly important about law and comparable normative arrangements in all societies, when she comments that 'rules do not solve all problems; they only simplify life'.[33] Of course, as Kafka knew, not all rules do simplify life, but a central reason for the existence of rules and norms, whether articulated or not, is precisely the simplification to which Colson draws our attention. This, too, involves but is more than and different from control. A clearer understanding of the roles of law in our own society might sensitize anthropologists among others to a wider array of functions — not, of course, necessarily the *same* functions — which fall to be performed, there and elsewhere.

II Issues of Method and Substance: The Proper Field of Study

In their now classic monograph, *The Cheyenne Way* (Oklahoma, 1941), the American legal realist Karl Llewellyn and the anthropologist E.A. Hoebel distinguished 'three roads into exploration of the law-stuff of a culture' (p. 20). One, which they called 'ideological', is concerned with "rules" which are felt as proper, for channelling and controlling behaviour'. A second, the 'descriptive' road, 'explores the patterns according to which behaviour actually occurs' (p. 21). The third road, which they favoured and made famous, involves searching 'for instances of hitch, dispute, grievance, trouble; and inquiry into what the trouble was and what was done about it' (p. 21). The history of legal anthropology is marked by periods in which each of these roads has been favoured, and by continual controversy over

---

[32]R.S. Summers, 'Naive Instrumentalism and the Law', in P.M.S. Hacker and J. Raz (eds.), *Law, Morality and Society* (Oxford, 1977), p. 123.
[33]Elizabeth Colson, *Tradition and Contract: The Problem of Order* (Chicago, 1974), p. 53.

which should receive most attention. These methodological choices and disputes are particularly revealing, for what anthropologists discover in the field is to a large, though not exclusive, extent, a product of what they choose to look for. This in turn is deeply influenced by their notions of the nature and function of law: the ways in which they believe law or 'control mechanisms' work in general, or at least in the societies studied, the extent to which rules are believed to be clearly articulated and generally obeyed, and whether the prime function of law is taken to be to prohibit illegitimate or to channel legitimate behaviour. Frequently, and unfortunately, one or other of these 'roads' has received exclusive attention, and our understanding of the societies discussed has suffered accordingly.

Before the ethnographic revolution brought about by Malinowski and his contemporaries, what ethnographies there were dealing with law took statements of rules gleaned from informants as the 'laws' of the societies studied, and gave scant attention to the ways in which, or indeed whether, these rules affected people's lives. This was not an absurd procedure for writers confident that 'primitive' peoples did not break the law, that, as Sidney Hartland put it, 'the savage is far from being the free and unfettered creature of Rousseau's imagination. On the contrary, he is hemmed in on every side by the customs of his people, he is bound in the chains of immemorial tradition . . . . These fetters are accepted by him as a matter of course; he never seeks to break forth'.[34]

It was such views that Malinowski sought to dispose of in *Crime and Custom in Savage Society*. This was not the first or the only work that Malinowski wrote about the law of 'savage' societies,[35] but it is certainly the best known and most influential. Prominent among Malinowski's aims was 'to urge the great need for more theory in anthropological jurisprudence, especially theory born form actual contact with savages' (p. x), and the book raised serious and interrelated theoretical questions as to the substance of, and appropriate ways of studying, primitive law. Methodologically, Malinowski insisted that one could not gain any understanding of the law of primitive peoples by merely collecting statements of rules from informants: rules often conflicted with other rules, or with people's strong preferences or attachments, and the only way to discover 'the discrepancy between the ideal of law and its realization, between the orthodox version and the practice of actual life' (p. 107), is to pay close and extended attention to the latter.

> To give an illustration, reversing the role of savage and civilized, of ethnographer and informant: many of my Melanesian friends, taking at its face value the doctrine of 'brotherly love' preached by Christian Missionaries and the taboo on warfare and killing preached and promulgated by Government

[34]Sidney Hartland, *Primitive Law* (London, 1924) p. 138. Quoted in part, and derided, by Malinowski in his introduction to H.I. Hogbin, *op.cit.*, p. xxii.

[35]See I. Schapera, 'Malinowski's Theories of Law', in Raymond Firth, (ed.), *Man and Culture: An Evaluation of the Work of Bronislaw Malinowski* (London, 1963), pp. 139–55.

officials, were unable to reconcile the stories about the Great War, reaching — through planters, traders, overseers, plantation hands — the remotest Melanesian or Papuan village. They were really puzzled at hearing that in one day white men were wiping out as many of their own kind as would make up several of the biggest Melanesian tribes. They forcibly concluded that the White Man was a tremendous liar, but they were not certain at which end the lie lay — whether in the moral pretence or in his bragging about war achievements (p. 83).

If one followed his prescriptions and actually *observed* the way 'savages' behaved, Malinowski breezily and engagingly assured his readers, one would quickly be disabused of most of the fashionable myths about savage law: that 'the savage — so runs today's verdict of competent anthropologists — has a deep reverence for tradition and custom, an automatic submission to their biddings' (pp. 9 – 10); that savages were ruled by undifferentiated rules of custom and that 'with the description of crime and punishment the subject of jurisprudence is exhausted as far as a savage community is concerned' (p. 56). Against what he thus characterized, and in several respects caricatured, as the conventional wisdom, Malinowski insisted that 'whenever the native can evade his obligations without the loss of prestige, or without the prospective loss of gain, he does so, exactly as a civilized business man would do' (p. 30); that nonetheless, even without 'central authority, codes, courts, and constables', savages did have rules of law which stood out from other customary rules 'in that they are felt and regarded as the obligations of one person and the rightful claims of another' (p. 55),[36] and that far from being primarily retributive or penal, as Durkheim among others believed, 'civil law, consisting of positive ordinances, is much more developed than the body of mere prohibitions . . . a study of purely criminal law among savages misses the most important phenomena of their legal life' (pp. 30 – 1).

Malinowski's emphasis on the need to study law 'in action' rather than simply to collect rules has been shared in the bulk of legal anthropology written since. However, whereas Malinowski was in effect advocating 'the study of the obligatory aspect of all social relationships,[37] much subsequent legal anthropology has sought to carve out a more discrete focus for study. The first important programmatic innovation in this area was Llewellyn and Hoebel's *The Cheyenne Way*. The most influential legacy of the book was the method of investigation which it exemplified and recommended: the analysis of 'trouble cases'. This method, Llewellyn and Hoebel freely admitted, was

grounded in the American System of case law in which we root; especially in the

---

[36]This is not Malinowski's only definition of law, even in this book. See his 'A New Instrument for the Interpretation of Law — Especially Primitive', *Yale Law Journal* LI (1942), pp. 1237 – 54 and I. Schapera, *op.cit.*, *passim*.

[37]Sally Falk Moore, 'Law and Anthropology' *op.cit.*, p. 220.

modern treatment of cases at law as being not only crucial tests of the meaning of rules of law, but also as exhibits of law's processes and techniques, and of the interaction of the legal system and the legal craft-specialists with the social, economic, political, and indeed individual aspects of the society concerned (p. ix).

Unlike some of their followers, Llewellyn and Hoebel did not deny that one should investigate 'rules' or general behaviour, but they reiterated time and time again that 'the trouble-cases, sought out and examined with care, are . . . the safest main road into the discovery of law. Their data are most certain. Their yield is richest. They are the most revealing' (p. 29). Llewellyn and Hoebel did not observe the cases which they discussed, but 'reached through [informants'] memory or hearsay, and through an interpreter' (p. 29) cases which had occurred between about 1820 and 1880. It was not until Gluckman's *Judicial Process among the Barotse* . . . that an anthropologist provided a book based on detailed examination of cases which he had actually witnessed. In 1957, Bohannan published the first book dealing with observed cases of dispute settlement in a stateless society, *Justice and Judgement among the Tiv* (London, 1957), and this was followed shortly afterwards by Pospisil's analysis of dispute cases among the Papuans, *Kapauku Papuans and their Law* (New Haven, 1958).

The arguments for their method developed by students of 'trouble cases' are based on reflection about the behaviour of law in general and especially in the small-scale, technologically simple societies with which most of their work has been concerned. Pospisil, typically, regards 'the function of the exercising of social control' as the central function of law, and he rejects 'emphasis on abstract rules as a form of law, because

> . . . an abstract rule need not exercise the function of social control when it is believed to be outdated, obsolete, or regarded as an ideal which in actual life either cannot be realized or can only be approximated. We speak about dead rules which, since they are never applied in deciding legal cases, simply clutter many of the legal codifications (p. 250).

Over fifty per cent of the cases studied by Pospisil were decided in ways which diverged from the stated rules. As Malinowski, not to mention Jerome Frank, emphasized some time earlier, these comments are fairly generally applicable, both in states of whatever kind and in stateless societies. But in small-scale societies a focus on rules is complicated by a number of special problems. First, some societies appear to rely less on clear and articulated norms than others. Thus, according to Llewellyn and Hoebel,

> if one takes as his main road (the others being feeders) the road of felt or known 'norms', he meets in some cultures with bafflement on the part of the informant. A Comanche, or a Barama River Carib, does not like to think that way. He finds trouble in reducing such general 'norms' to expression or in stating a solution for an abstract or a hypothetical case (p. 22).

Moreover, where there are effective and discernible norms, in the least differentiated societies, they rarely apply impersonally or across the board. Epstein, for example, reports that judges in Zambian urban courts could explain at length points which had arisen in cases they had heard, but had more difficulty in discussing hypothetical situations. He attributed this:

> to the fact that their mode of legal thinking was particular rather than abstract; the rules of law they administered were not conceived as logical entities; they were rather embedded in a matrix of social relationships which alone gave them meaning . . . . One implication of all this is to suggest that the study of rules needs to be tackled, at least initially, through the examination of the way they are invoked and applied in the context of disputes.[38]

The study of cases provides a researcher with a great deal of otherwise inaccessible information about the nature of disputes that come to be processed, the content and effectiveness of applicable norms and the style of and parties to the process. And disputes are not merely convenient arenas in which putative law is put to test. As Bailey has observed, disputes play a strategic role in their own right:

> Crisis situations have a diagnostic value. In disputes an established rule may be proclaimed, publicly stated, and uttered as a warning to would-be deviants: but a dispute may also proclaim that an established rule of behaviour can now be flouted with impunity . . . , it may encourage other would-be deviants, and it may announce that a particular type of relationship or allegiance is no longer an effective means of gaining one's end.[39]

Despite the obvious need to study cases, however, it seems to me that to concentrate on disputes and their management, as so many legal ethnographies have done, puts one in constant danger of presenting systematically skewed findings. As all new law graduates learn, some to their joy, others in dismay, there is a great deal about the behaviour of law in their own society which they did not learn and could not have gleaned from the fullest case reports. Even the experienced lawyer, one of whose main jobs is to keep clients out of institutions of dispute settlement, sees a rather weighted sample of law-related and affected behaviour. He sees far more than courts, and especially higher courts, do of what Malinowski called 'the law of order and maintenance, the law which is positively primed and baited'.[40] But he sees far less of such law, and the way it affects those who generally observe it, than a sociologist needs to in order to understand the role played by law in ordinary life. If his only experience of the law were to come from watching court proceedings, he would see even less.

Given the importance of what one does learn from trouble cases, it is also important to realize what one is unlikely to learn from them. First of all, trouble cases are not a random sample of disputes in our society or any other.

[38]A.L. Epstein, 'Introduction' in A.L. Epstein (ed.), *Contention and Dispute*, (Canberra, 1974), p. 7.
[39]F.G. Bailey, *Tribe, Caste, and Nation* (Manchester, 1960), pp. 15 – 16.
[40]'A New Instrument for the Interpretation of Law — Especially Primitive', *op.cit.*, p. 1250.

They are not socially random, because some categories of people make more consistent and successful use of them than others;[41] many people choose not to report or seek institutional intervention in a dispute or grievance, but rather choose to 'lump it'[42] and some categories of people are more often prosecuted than others. They are also not *legally* random. As Holleman has argued, an ethnographer can rarely see an adequate sample of trouble cases in his period in the field, and, more important,

> there are, in probably every society, certain avenues of social and economic activity in which the passage of legal traffic and transactions takes place regularly but with very few known cases of litigious collision . . . in a field of the law in which litigation is rare, a field-worker relying mainly on a case-method focused ˜upon actual trouble-cases may get a skewed idea of the accepted principles and regularities in this particular field.[43]

Finally, in many societies what comes before a court may both represent a minority of disputes and not expose the real issues which are in dispute in the particular case. Thus Cohn reports that in colonial India

> It was evident that courts did not settle disputes, but were used either as a form of gambling on the part of legal speculators . . . or as a threat in a dispute. There is apparently no quicker way of driving an opponent into bankruptcy than to embroil him in a law suit. Most people would go to any length to avoid going to court. It is likely that most of the cases that went into courts were fabrications to cover the real disputes.[44]

Moreover, quite apart from whether one sees a representative sample of disputers or disputes in trouble cases, the fact remains that it is only disputes that one sees. But, without entering here into whether disputes are normal or aberrant in social life, it is clear, it may indeed be necessarily true, that they do not occupy the whole of it. And the way in which disputes are handled, by the disputants *or* third parties, may not tell us much about the role of laws, or for that matter of 'social control', where disputes are not occurring.

In his well-known and influential *Justice and Judgement among the Tiv*, Bohannan sought to demonstrate the unimportance of norms in dispute processing among the Tiv of West Africa. According the Bohannan,

> The decision [of a *jir* or court] seldom overtly involves a point of law, in the sense that we think of a rule or a law. . . . The purpose of most *jir* [cases] is, thus, to

---

[41]See Marc Galanter, 'Why the "Haves" Come Out Ahead: Speculations on the Limits of Legal Change', *Law and Society Review* IX (1975), pp. 95 – 160, for the distinction between legal 'one-shotters' and 'repeat-players'.

[42]For 'lumping it' as a means of 'processing' a dispute, see William L.F. Felstiner, *op.cit.*, p. 81.

[43]J.F. Holleman, 'Trouble-cases and Trouble-less Cases in the Study of Customary Law and Legal Reform', *Law and Society Review* VII (1973), p. 592 and p. 599.

[44]Bernard S. Cohn, 'Some Notes on Law and Change in North India', reprinted in Paul Bohannan (ed.), *Law and Warfare* (New York, 1967), p. 154.

determine a *modus vivendi*, not to apply laws, but to decide what is right in a particular case. They usually do so without overt reference to rules or 'laws'. (p. 19)

Bohannan's account has been criticized and re-analysed by several writers who argue that norms play a greater role in Tiv dispute settlement than he allows, and that it would be impossible to understand how a Tiv case could be settled without knowledge of the norms on which settlement and procedures for settlement were based.[45] On the whole, I find these criticisms persuasive. But even if Bohannan's account of the role of norms in Tiv dispute settlement were adequate, we would not, on that basis alone, necessarily know much about their role in other contexts. Gulliver has also been criticized by Gluckman and others[46] for emphasizing the 'normlessness' of dispute settlement among the Arusha of Tanzania. But while his account and his reiterated emphasis on the primary importance of studying disputes might be questioned, at least Gulliver is clear that what he finds there is not the whole of the story:

> . . . among the Arusha there are, as in any society, commonly enunciated and accepted norms of behaviour. . . . These norms are well known, and each is similarly enunciated everywhere in the country. . . .
>
> While it would be incorrect to say that an agreed settlement of a dispute never wholly conforms with the relevant, socially accepted norms, it is true to say that such precise conformity is the exception. . . . After beginning to appreciate Arusha concentration on compromise, which would provide an initially acceptable resolution of a dispute, I was almost inclined to describe them as cynical opportunists. If by that is meant 'unprincipled', it is a wrong description of the Arusha in these matters. Clearly they recognize norms and they hold them in great respect. . . . They are, then, guided by their principles of right behaviour, and they use them as the basis of claims to rights; but they accept an imperfect world in which an individual does not and should not expect to gain all the ideal rights prescribed by the approved norms. But equally, men hope to be able to avoid some of the obligations implicit in those norms.[47]

Where norms do play an important role in dispute settlements one may miss them if one merely examines cases, for, as Hamnett points out, 'in a relatively homogeneous society, these norms and expectations do not need authoritative exposition by formal courts'.[48] Moreover, what *is* emphasized in such institutions need have little to do with broader values or even with the values and interests of the litigants. Marilyn Strathern explains that in New Guinea

[45]See Max Gluckman, Preface to the Reprint of the second edition of *The Judicial Process among the Barotse* (Manchester, 1973), pp. xxvii – xxxii; J. van Velsen, 'The Extended-case Method and Situational Analysis' in A.L. Epstein (ed.), *The Craft of Social Anthropology* (London, 1967), pp. 137 – 8; Geoffrey MacCormack, 'Procedures for the Settlement of Disputes in "Simple" Societies', *The Irish Jurist* XI (1976), pp. 186 – 7.

[46]Max Gluckman, 'Limitations of the Case-Method in the Study of Tribal Law', *Law and Society Review* VIII (1973), pp. 611 – 41; Ian Hamnett, *Chieftainship and Legitimacy*, pp. 19 – 21.

[47]P.H. Gulliver, *Social Control in an African Society* (London, 1963), pp. 241 – 2.

[48]Hamnett, *Chieftainship and Legitimacy*, p. 21.

[Mount] Hagen *kots* place relatively little emphasis on statements of norms. This is not to say that there is no normative framework — indeed speeches are shot through with references to how people ought to behave, and the introduction of 'outside' issues depends on the recognition of specific values. But, as such, norms are not much argued over. What standards of and expectations about behaviour apply in the various circumstances which a trouble case brings to light will be treated largely as 'understood'. Litigants are certainly blamed and castigated for what they have done, and motives and circumstances are considered, but what one could call the oratorical focus of a *kot* hearing often lies elsewhere. . . . The point is that the *kot* context, in appearing to endow him with authority, provides the big man with a further set of roles he can add to his portmanteau . . . it is no accident that it should be matters of procedure on which dispute settlers concentrate (rather than, say, increasingly subtle interpretations of general norms). When they draw attention to procedure they are drawing attention to the manner in which *kot* are conducted, and in doing this they are acting as big men have constantly to act in order to keep themselves in people's minds: they are drawing attention to themselves.[49]

What in particular is underemphasized by focusing on trouble cases are the normative sources of regularity and predictability in social life, those things which keep most people, most of the time, within the law and away from dispute settlers. It is true that Llewellyn and Hoebel stressed that, besides its 'peculiar job of cleaning up social messes when they have been made' law has 'as one of its main purposes to make men go round in more or less clear ways' (p. 20). In fact, however, as Malinowski complained, 'throughout the book the "messes" predominate'.[50] This comment applies, as we shall see, to much recent legal anthropology where the focus has remained on disputes. There has been a considerable refinement of techniques of studying disputes, and a great extension of the range of *praxis* which is considered, but trouble has remained more popular than lack of it.

A number of anthropologists, several of them colleagues of Gluckman, have sought to study the development of disputes through *time*, rather than simply when settlement is attempted, in order to observe the genesis and consequences of the dispute. This method has been variously dubbed the 'extended case method', 'situational analysis', or by Stanner in a review of one of the earliest uses of this approach 'the relentless case method'.[51] The advantage of this method over concentration on dispute settlement is that disputes are set in context and that one's investigation is not constrained by artificial limits, which might hide the point of a Bemba saying, that 'a case never ends'.[52] Thus, Victor Turner in his *Continuity and Schism in an*

[49]A.M. Strathern, 'Managing Information: The Problems of a Dispute Settler (Mount Hagen)' in A.L. Epstein (ed.), *Contention and Dispute* pp. 315–6.

[50]Bronislaw Malinowski, 'A New Instrument for Studying Law — Especially Primitive', *op.cit.*, p. 1252.

[51]W.E.H. Stanner, 'Continuity and Schism in an African Tribe — A Review', *Oceania* XXIX (1959), p. 208.

[52]Cited in A.L. Epstein, 'The Case Method in the Field of Law' in A.L. Epstein, (ed.), *The Craft of Social Anthropology*, p. 230.

African Society (Manchester, 1957) studies what he calls the 'social drama' as it runs through four stages, taking what he calls 'processional form': first, 'breach of regular norm-governed social relations occurs'; second, 'a phase of mounting crisis'; third, 'in order to limit the spread of breach certain adjustive and redressive mechanisms, informal or formal, are speedily brought into operation by leading members of the relevant social group'; and fourth, though not necessarily finally, 'reintegration of the disturbed social group or . . . the social recognition of irreparable breach between the contesting parties' (pp. 91 – 2). According to Turner, the special point and advantage of studying the social drama is that it

> is a limited area of transparency on the otherwise opaque surface of regular, uneventful social life. Through it we are enabled to observe the crucial principles of the social structure in their operation, and their relative dominance at successive points in time (p. 93).

This approach was part of a more general move in anthropology away from description or construction of static structures, illuminated by selected case materials but 'primarily concerned with relations between social positions or statuses than with the "actual relations of Tom, Dick, and Harry or the behaviour of Jack and Jill" (Radcliffe-Brown)'.[53] In its place modern anthropologists have directed attention to social processes. 'Situational analysts', for example, insist that

> . . . it is necessary to record, in meticulous detail, the actions of certain specified individuals over a period of time. When such a series of related case material is later presented in the analysis, the As, Bs, and Cs of so many of the situationally isolated 'apt illustrations' will lose their anonymity and, instead, will regain their identity as Tom, Dick, and Harry, or Jack and Jill: they are now actors in a series of different circumstances who make greater or less use of (i.e. manipulate) an element of choice of norms to suit the requirements of the particular situation (van Velsen, p. 143).

In legal anthropology, this method has frequently involved a shift from looking 'from above' at laws or 'control mechanisms' and discussing their role in constraining or settling disputes to looking from below at individuals or groups as they choose which rules to emphasize and which to ignore, as they plan strategies which take account of and are affected by law, but by many other things as well. In our society we might call this a shift from macro- to micro-anthropology, but this distinction is not always easy to make in small-scale studies.

These recent studies have revealed a great deal more conflict in the small-scale societies than frequently used to be assumed, and a great deal more room for individual strategy and choice. Turner reports that conflict is endemic in Ndembu society, Chowning analyses disputes among the Sengseng and Kove of West New Britain, whom she describes as 'both

53J. van Velsen, *op.cit.*, p. 131.

people with well deserved reputations for being quarrelsome . . . [both] do seem to show a somewhat unusual incidence of quarrels between the closest kinsmen and neighbours.'[54] The Kalauna of Goodenough Island 'tend to enjoy disputation and they accept it as a normative mode of conducting certain social relationships outside the domain of kinship.'[55] Conflicts occur not merely between persons and groups but also, as Malinowski was well aware, between norms. Even where at an abstract level norms do not appear to conflict, their combination, when applied in specific cases, often requires, and therefore allows, individuals or groups in small-scale societies to choose to emphasize some rather than others of the complex range of relevant ties, relationships or norms. Such combinations of norms, often pulling in different directions, may also lead, in a systematic fashion, to individual or group conflict. How this works out, it is argued, cannot be discerned in a static structural analysis, but requires attention to 'embattled actors and actions',[56] and to 'the totality of continuous processes rather than . . . a single, static structure'.[57]

This research provides useful and often vividly portrayed[58] correctives to belief in 'primitive automatism' and valuable descriptions of just how individuals and groups go about rationalizing their actions, selecting and manipulating norms in their favour, building alliances and coalitions and conducting disputes. That such tuggings and pullings should be emphasized is, of course, no accident. As Turner explained in the preface to *Continuity and Schism:*

> That the pervasive theme of the book is conflict and the resolution of conflict arises from my predilection for the views, fast becoming a theory, of that school of British social anthropologists who are coming to regard a social system as 'a field of tension, full of ambivalence, of cooperation and contrasting struggle' [Gluckman]. For these anthropologists a social system is not a static model, a harmonious pattern, nor the conceptual product of a monistic outlook. A social system is a field of forces in which, to quote Fortes, 'centrifugal tendencies and centripetal tendencies pull against one another', and whose power to persist is generated by its own socially transmuted conflicts (p. xxii).

Given these theoretical assumptions, and the trend in many areas of anthropology to concentrate on 'paradox, conflict, inconsistency, contradiction, multiplicity, and manipulability in social life',[59] it is not surprising that disputes should receive the attention which they do in contemporary legal anthropology.

[54]Ann Chowning, 'Disputing in two West New Britain societies: similarities and differences', in A.L. Epstein (ed.) *Contention and Dispute*, p. 152.

[55]Michael W. Young, 'Private sanctions and public ideology: some aspects of self-help in Kalauna, Goodenough Island', *ibid.*, p. 41.

[56]Elizabeth Colson, *Tradition and Contract*, p. 18.

[57]P.H. Gulliver, *op.cit.*, p. 3.

[58]See especially Turner, *op.cit.*; F.G. Bailey, *Tribe, Caste and Nation* and P.H. Gulliver, *Neighbours and Networks* (Berkeley, 1971).

[59]Sally Falk Moore, 'Uncertainties in Situations' in *Law as Process*, p. 37.

As with many other new movements, however, in intellectual life and else-where, partisans of processual analysis occasionally oversell its novelty and insights, and there is an unfortunate tendency to polarize schools of thought and theoretical approaches. Thus, Yngvesson contrasts two views of law in anthropology. There was, she claims, an older school influenced by Durkheim and including Gluckman, which assumed that

> order is based on the commitment of individuals at all levels of the social hier-archy to society in its present form. Social rules are accepted because it is through them that peace and general prosperity are guaranteed. Conflict . . . is perceived to be present but to be dampened by an awareness that it is ultimately against the interest of society as a whole and thus of the individual. To this extent, conflict is perceived as aberrant by anthropologists with this concept of social order.[60]

Against this, Yngvesson explains,

> law is viewed by a number of anthropologists more as a political tool, used by individuals and groups to advance or maintain their own interests vis-à-vis those of other individuals and groups. Ideological systems — legal rules, principles of social organization — are seen as closely linked to material interests, and social values are assumed not to be shared but to be fought over (*ibid*, p. 130).

Apart from the elements of caricature in polarizations of this sort, they also present theoretical difficulties. Of course there are conflicts in which rules are ignored, bent or broken in every society. Equally of course, if one con-centrates on disputes, one is likely to find them. But to discover that people rationalize their actions in disputes, that they seek, often successfully, to choose and manipulate rules for their purposes, is not to prove that these rules are simply resources or political tools. It may be more useful to see law as process rather than structure (though I suspect that it has elements of both), but it is a process which, if used by individuals, is neither simply set up by them nor infinitely plastic in their hands. In most societies, except perhaps twentieth-century industrialized ones, legal processes have served primarily as what Sally Falk Moore calls, in her splendid article 'Uncer-tainties in Situations', 'processes of regularization'. Outside antheaps, such processes never completely triumph. They face competing processes and individual choices, they often compete among themselves and, as Karl Popper has stressed, they spawn unintended effects and cannot cover the field. As a result, 'order never fully takes over, nor could it' (p. 39). On the other hand,

> the options are far from unlimited. . . . An emphasis on the range of manipul-ability within microsituations does not do away with the fact that larger political and economic contexts exist, that common symbols, customary behaviours, role expectations, rules, categories, ideas and ideologies, rituals and formalities

[60]Barbara Yngvesson, 'Law in Pre-Industrial Societies', *Sociological Inquiry* XLVII (1977), pp. 129–30.

shared by the actors with a larger society are used in these interactions as the framework of mutual communication and action. These place real and sometimes merely apparent limits on what is negotiable. By definition this set of social contexts and cultural artifacts affects the form of the interaction, and usually profoundly affects the content and outcome as well (*ibid,*. p. 40).

In this respect, the process of ordinary life bears analogy with skilled musicianship. As visitors to unfamiliar societies and aspiring violinists both know, an ability to improvise successfully is both limited by and *dependent* upon the existence of, and one's awareness of, a large number of 'processes of regularization'.

III Disputes and Dispute Processing

Notwithstanding the reservations which I have expressed, one salutary result of legal anthropologists' concentration on disputes is that we now have a great deal of detailed information about them and about the way in which they are handled in many societies. The range is wide, between and within different societies. Apart from the, in many societies important, use of ritual or occult forms of disputing and settling disputes, variations occur in two major areas: first, in the ways in which, and extent to which, dispute processing is *institutionalized*, and second, in the aims and style of dispute processing. One major institutional distinction is that between societies which do and those which do not have institutionalized third-party intervention in disputes. Even where such intervention occurs, it can take various forms: mediation, where an office-holder such as the Nuer leopard-skin chief, the Ifugao go-between or simply a person of prestige, seeks to aid, but cannot force, the parties to reach settlement; arbitration, where parties agree to accept the judgement of a third-party — non-human, in the case of ordeals or divinations, human in union/management disputes; or adjudication, where a third party has authority to intervene in and decide a dispute, whether or not the parties agree to his intervention or his decision. Logically, and it now appears in fact, distinct from the mode of dispute processing are its aims and style. Black, drawing on much anthropological and sociological research, distinguishes between four styles of law (which for him is simply governmental social control): penal, compensatory, therapeutic and conciliatory. In penal control, certain conduct is prohibited by 'the group as a whole' and prohibitions are enforced with punishment; in compensatory control a victim demands redress or payment. These two forms are both in their pure form

> accusatory styles of social control. Both have contestants, a complainant and a defendant, a winner and a loser. For both, it is all or nothing — punishment or nothing, payment or nothing. By contrast, therapeutic and conciliatory control are remedial styles, methods of social repair and maintenance, assistance for people in trouble . . . the goal of therapy is normality . . . in conciliation, the

ideal is social harmony.[61]

It was common, particularly in evolutionary theories of law, for contrasts of various substantive and procedural sorts to be drawn between 'primitive' and modern law. For Durkheim, the former was essentially 'penal' and collectively enforced; the latter was 'restitutive' (in Black's terms, compensatory) and privately enforced. For Hoebel, the analysis was reversed: 'private' laws preceded 'public'. Many writers, including Maine and Pound, have contrasted the individualism of modern law with the alleged emphasis on group responsibility in primitive law.

Such contrasts have been highly influential, but they are rather gross. The so-called 'penal' societies lay great stress on conciliation of disputes; their 'private' disputes threaten to escalate to include the whole society; their non-individualist law puts individuals under the constant surveillance of their associates and under the terrible threat of expulsion. The 'individualistic' law of modern, highly bureaucratized societies relies heavily on rules which in effect shift liability from individual agents to corporate principals; in our fault-based legal system it is considered extremely progressive to put strict liability at the core of the law of tort and social insurance; our 'accusatory' methods of dispute settlement are not applied to large areas of law-affected behaviour. It has thus become far more difficult to sustain the sorts of distinctions which had traditionally been made between 'primitive' and modern laws, either in terms of content or style. One important reason for such difficulty is that more is known about the ways in which disputes are handled in small-scale societies. Another is that increasing attention has been paid to common modes of dispute processing in industrialized societies, which fit tidily into none of these stereotypes.

In stateless societies, where there are few if any differentiated institutions of social control, there are nonetheless forces of what Nadel called social 'self-regulation',[62] which exert very strong pressures on individuals to act within accepted ranges of behaviour. On the other hand, as Colson has suggested, in the absence of specialized and authoritative institutions, one powerful source of restraint is 'fear of violence that brings more violence':[63]

> it should . . . be no surprise to us if some people live in what appears to be a Rousseauian paradise because they take a Hobbesian view of their situation: they walk softly because they believe it necessary not to offend others whom they regard as dangerous (p. 37).

On the other hand, members of small-scale societies perpetually and inevitably rely on the support of those with whom they have, or can forge, ties, in every field of cooperative endeavour, and they cannot easily evade their scrutiny or judgement. In such egalitarian, face-to-face societies

[61]Donald Black, *The Behaviour of Law* (New York, 1976), pp. 4–5.
[62]S.F. Nadel, 'Social Control and Self-Regulation', *Social Forces*, XXXI (1952–3) pp. 265–73.
[63]Elizabeth Colson, *Tradition and Contract*, p. 40.

social life means the submission of the individual to the constant judgement of peers. . . . Under these conditions a flouting of generally accepted standards is tantamount to a claim to illegitimate power and becomes part of the evidence against one (*ibid.*, p. 58 and 59).

Pressures to conform include socialization, gossip, public criticism, 'shaming', withholding of support, ostracism and, the ultimate sanction, expulsion. As Moore demonstrates, what to Roscoe Pound and other outsiders appears to be primitive collective responsibility for individual actions and grievances is to a *member* of such a society a heavily qualified and contingent matter:

> The penalty of expulsion forces one to consider that a collective obligation, while it may appear altogether collective when viewed from the outside or at a distance, is not so from the inside. . . . In the pre-industrial world, when an individual brings about a situation in which a corporate group to which he belongs is involved in heavy obligation, it may honour his claims wholly or in part, or it may turn him out. Certainly, even if he is given help he may be exhausting his potential claims and bringing himself closer to the point of refusal of expulsion. It becomes part of the history of his relationships with his fellows, a history which will bear on all his future dealings. Within the group he is in this way being held individually responsible for what he did, even though his kinsmen (and/or associates) may bail him and themselves out, and he may not 'pay' them for his act at once . . . there is no doubt that within a group or aggregate bearing collective liability, in the long run individuals are held individually responsible for their actions. Collective responsibility does not exclude or substitute for individual responsibility. Both can and do operate simultaneously at different social levels.[64]

Nevertheless, as we have seen, disputes and infractions of rules constantly occur. In stateless societies, mechanisms of dispute settlement vary greatly, but one common remedy available to an aggrieved person is retaliatory self-help. This usually goes in hand with strong pressures toward conciliation of disputes, at least among closely linked people. Thus, in New Guinea 'self-help has to be maximized. The plaintiff must himself initiate and carry through retaliatory action with whatever support he can get from kinsmen, affines and other associates'.[65] This description would not fill Hobbes with surprise or joy, yet the situation has built-in sources of restraint, and, in certain circumstances, strong pressures to conciliate disputes — stronger than exist in many disputes in modern societies. Order is in general maintained by insistence on reciprocity, and even in retaliation, 'the matter can only be settled by "pay back"; a New Guinean will seek vengeance, not over-kill'.[66] Moreover, in small-scale societies, the *relationship* between the

[64]Sally Falk Moore, 'Legal Liability and Evolutionary Interpretation: Some Aspects of Strict Liability, Self-Help and Collective Responsibility' reprinted in *Law as Process*, pp. 125 – 6.

[65]Peter Lawrence, *op.*cit., p. 20.

[66]A.L. Epstein, 'Introduction' to A.L. Epstein, *Contention and Dispute*, p. 26.

disputants is crucial; it affects both the way the dispute develops, who else will become involved, and what pressures they will bring to bear. As Lawrence has argued, in disputes between closely related persons in stateless societies, the disputants

> should remember that their close tie in the long run represents mutual advantage and should have some sense of moral obligation toward each other. They are of the same political group or network: to cause one another irreparable harm would weaken their position against outsiders. Second, other people likely to be interested in the dispute also belong to this political group or network. Relatively few in number and closely related to both parties, they do not split into two groups, one on each side, but are swayed by the same considerations as described above. If, as sometimes happens, either litigant should lose restraint, they join forces to blanket the dispute and ensure an agreement as soon as they can. (*Op. cit.* p. 21).

Gulliver reports similarly of the Ndendeuli of Tanzania:

> Within the local community a disputant sought to recruit active supporters in his own interest through the kinship relations of the community's network. At the same time he was subject to pressure and limitations exercised by his opponent and the opponent's supporters because of the relations interlinking them and his own supporters in that same closed network.[67]

In disputes between members of different political groups or networks in New Guinea, on the other hand, disputes might erupt into either limited blood-feud — if there are effective neutral kin related to both parties, who can mediate and smother the dispute — or genuine warfare if such restraining pressures are absent.

By no means all stateless societies rely on retaliatory self-help in the sense of physical action. The Arusha, for example, like many African societies, are highly litigious, but they insist that disputes must be taken to one of a range of settlement institutions, to be argued through; direct self-help 'is not only disapproved, . . . it is not in Arusha society an effective technique for dealing with disputes. The proper, but also the efficient, method is to raise the dispute in an assembly or conclave, there to depend on one's associates to support one.'[68] Yet in a weaker sense, self-help is as important among the Arusha as in New Guinea, for it is up to the aggrieved individual to recruit the help of associates throughout the dispute; 'he cannot act without them and there is no established third party to whom he and they can appeal for wider impartial intervention' (p. 222). Though mediators are important, there is a great stress on making settlement emerge through discussion 'from within — that is, from them together' (p. 232) just as among the Tiv, 'for Tiv judges to settle a *jir* [case] by any standards other than the concurrence of the litigants, and eventually of the community, is to settle it "by force" . . . .

[67]P.H. Gulliver, *Neighbours and Networks*, p. 133.
[68]P.H. Gulliver, *Social Control in an African Society*, p. 221.

This is the worst thing that can be said of any *jir*.[69]

Compromise is not sought in all small-scale societies; some seem to enjoy continuing quarrels, others break up as the result of them.[70] But there are obvious reasons why, in a society where no one has authority to enforce decisions, the agreement of the parties and their supporters is necessary for dispute settlement. In chieftainships and states, it is possible for adjudication to occur which overrides the wishes of one or both of the disputants.

Several writers have argued for a connection between the mode of dispute processing and the *style* of settlement. Thus, according to Bohannan, where parties are all roughly equal and have to live in close contact with each other, dispute processing usually emphasizes compromise, and norms tend to be vague and often unimportant in settling disputes. Where institutions exist with the power to adjudicate, to make and enforce a decision binding the parties, norms tend to be more precise and important.[71] Similarly, Gulliver once (but no longer) argued that there was a crucial distinction between two ideal types of dispute settlement: judicial and political. In judicial settlement a third party has the authority and responsibility to make a binding decision, and he does so in accordance with established norms;

> The purely political process, on the other hand, involves no intervention by a third-party, a judge. Here a decision is reached and a settlement made as a result of the relative strengths of the two parties to the dispute as they are shown and tested in social action. . . . In this case the accepted norms of behaviour relevant to the matter in dispute are but one element involved, and possibly an unimportant one.[72]

There is no doubt that law in small-scale societies is 'politically active'[73] to a degree that even Americans, and certainly British and Australians, would find unusual. But Gulliver has conceded that his early dichotomy even seen as two polar ends of a continuum, was 'too simple as well as inaccurate' at both ends: negotiation is more affected by norms, and adjudication is often more 'political' than he originally suggested. He now suggests 'with the greatest of caution' that

> in adjudication there is a greater inhibition by norms and rules. . . . But in negotiations, values, norms and rules are more than merely strategems of ideological appeal. Perhaps, though it appears problematical, they may be used in much the same way as in adjudication.[74]

Some anthropologists would question even this modest distinction.

---

[69]Paul Bohannan, *Justice and Judgement Among the Tiv*, p. 65.

[70]See Ann Chowning, *op.cit.*, 152 – 3.

[71]Paul Bohannan 'The Differing Realms of the Law' reprinted in Paul Bohannan, (ed.), *Law and Warfare*, p. 53.

[72]*Social Control in an African Society*, p. 298.

[73]See J.A. Barnes, 'Law as Politically Active', *op.cit.*, *passim*.

[74]P.H. Gulliver, 'Negotiations as a Mode of Dispute Settlement: Towards a General Model', *Law and Society Review*, VII (1973), p. 683.

A different, though related distinction has been drawn by Fallers. Fallers's concern is not with whether or not rules are applied, but with what *sorts* of rules are applied. He was, as we have seen, concerned with 'law' in a specific and restricted sense and one of the central attributes of law in this sense is that it is a limited, discrete and distinguishable body of norms. Typically, dispute settlers applying law in this sense, like our own courts, are concerned to narrow the issues before the court to extract from them only what is considered legally relevant. As a result,

> the legal mode of assessing situations of conflict may be contrasted with their full moral evaluation. . . . It is characteristic of the legal mode of social control that rules are used to arrive at simple, dichotomous moral decisions — 'yes' or 'no' decisions that in other contexts would seem intolerably oversimplified morally. The legal process does not ask: What are all the rights and wrongs of this situation — on both sides? Rather, it asks: Is John Doe guilty as charged? John Doe may be utterly depraved — may be shown to have treated Richard Doe abominably — but if he cannot be shown to have violated the rule as charged, he (as far as the legal process is concerned) goes as free as if he were a saint (*op. cit.* pp. 12 – 13).

Fallers suggests that this legal simplifying practice is characteristic of our own and Soga law. It is not at all characteristic of Arusha litigations and even the Lozi *kutas* (courts) are 'morally more holistic' than Soga courts. Fallers suggests that 'legalism' in dispute settlement can be linked to functional differentiation of a legal subculture in the society: 'there appears to be a quite clear correlation between the differentiation of the bench, in terms of authority, and the legalism of the proceedings, in the sense of differentiation between law and popular morality' (p. 329). Fallers's hypothesis has been extended by Abel, who has developed an extraordinarily comprehensive theory seeking to link the 'role' differentiation of the intervener' with other characteristics of the dispute process.[75]

Fallers's highly positivist characterization of the 'legal' mode is in several respects overdrawn, even in relation to the practices of superior courts in highly differentiated societies. Yet the distinction he draws is an important one, as much for what 'law' is contrasted with as for the account of the legal mode itself. Even if legalistic tribunals are not as much constrained by the 'legal' mode as Fallers suggests, where it is considered the appropriate one for dispute settlement, it affects or is reflected in proceedings in a manifold range of ways: in the evidence which is admitted; in the definition of the dispute or offence — what is considered to be in issue; in the mode of examination of parties and witnesses; in the conduct expected of them and the dispute settlers, if any; in the goals of proceedings. In some respects Fallers's distinction cuts across Black's list of the different 'styles' of law; in other respects it is very closely related to it.

It is a truism of anthropology that in most small-scale societies a high value is placed upon the conciliation and compromise of disputes, at least where

[75]Cf Richard L. Abel, *op.cit.*, *passim*.

they occur between related disputants. As Lawrence, echoing Gluckman, has frequently stressed, in place of the concept *fiat justitia, ruat coelum,* there is in New Guinea societies 'a clear recognition that the sky must be kept up. In settling a dispute, the aim is to vindicate the consensual ideology: to restore the social order by patching up relationships that have been damaged or broken' (*op. cit.* p. 24). Similar comments can be found in ethnographies of an extremely wide range of small-scale societies. Gluckman's materials are particularly revealing in this regard, just because Lozi processes, unlike those of New Guinea, are so 'legalistic' in so many respects. According to Gluckman, 'in general terms, their courts aim at the same ends as courts in highly developed societies . . . their jurisprudence shares with other legal systems many basic doctrines.'[76] But the central aim of Lozi adjudication between kin is

> to prevent the breaking of relationships, and to make it possible for the parties to live together amicably in the future. Obviously this does not apply in every case, but it is true of a large number, and it is present in some degree in almost all cases. Therefore the court tends to be conciliating; it strives to effect a compromise acceptable to, and accepted by, all the parties. This is the main task of the judges (p. 21).

This task broadens the courts' view of what is properly regarded as being in dispute and what is regarded as relevant and admissible evidence:

> In order to fulfil their task the judges constantly have to broaden the field of their enquiries, and consider the total history of relations between the litigants, not only the narrow legal issue raised by one of them . . . in cases of this sort the court's conception of 'relevance' is very wide, for many facts affect the settlement of the dispute. This applies particularly to cases between blood-kin and between fellow-villagers. The relationship of husband and wife is more ephemeral, and in disputes between them the court concentrates more on the immediately relevant facts. When a contract between strangers, or an injury by a man on a stranger, is involved, the court narrows its range of relevance yet further (p. 21). . . . There is no refinement of pleadings in Lozi procedure to whittle a suit down to certain narrow legal claims so as to present the judges with a mere skeleton of the facts relevant to those claims (p. 51).

Another consequence of this stress on preserving important relationships is that often the status and relationship of the parties is of more concern to dispute settlers than the alleged offence or precipitants of dispute. To adapt the cliché, it is not what you do, but who you are and to whom you do it, that counts. The unconnected atoms of Hobbes's state of nature and of liberal-democratic theory have no place in the law of pre-industrial society.

Gluckman ascribes these characteristics of dispute-settlement to the 'multiplex' nature of social relations in small-scale societies. In differentiated societies, displaying what Tönnies calls *Gesellschaft* characteristics, citizens have single-interest ties with each other, outside the family; in

[76] *The Judicial Process among the Barotse . . .,* p. 17.

Barotse and other small-scale societies, relationships are multiplex, 'nearly every relationship serves many interests'. Since 'no multiplex relationship can survive if the parties insist on their rights only and try to live by the letter of the law' (Gluckman, p. 29) and since 'by virtue of multiplicity, most small-scale societies (and this would include small-scale societies within larger societies) are constantly aware of the possibility that any one act may escalate'[77] the range of people involved in a dispute, there is a general interest in settling intra-group disputes by compromise rather than by war of all against all. Thus litigants will seek and be satisfied by compromise decisions, mediators or courts will seek to restore relationships to harmony, and settlement procedures will be tailored to permit the kind of investigation and remedies appropriate to this end rather than simply to declaring winners and losers.

More recent studies of individuals' options and strategies accept the importance of multiplexity in small-scale societies, but they suggest that multiplexity is neither a sufficient nor a necessary condition for compromise. It is not sufficient because disputants in multiplex relationships can and do choose to ignore or at least accept the damage done to their relationship if the subject matter in dispute is important enough; in particular, if it is scarce. In such circumstances disputants will not be satisfied with compromise. They will try to win.[78] Multiplexity is also not a necessary condition for compromise. All that is needed is that disputants value highly the relationship in which they are involved, for whatever reason. Thus, in Korea, Imperial China, among Hopi Indians, Turkish villagers, expatriates in colonies, and American businessmen in continual dealings with each other, courts tend to be avoided so that disputes can be negotiated in ways that allow the relationship to survive.

Gluckman's attention to the importance of dense social relationships, and the refinements and extensions which his analyses have received, are obviously important for an understanding of pre-industrial societies. But their importance does not stop here. For industrialized societies are not monolithic, and relationships within them are not all 'alienated' or *gesellschaftlich*. In *all* societies, there are relationships which are mutliplex; in all differentiated societies there are many people who choose or are locked into single-interest relationships which they value highly and often depend upon. Recognition of this can help one to avoid the reification of ideal-typical contrasts between primitive and modern, which was such a staple of early evolutionary theories. Brown makes this often overlooked point particularly well:

[77]Laura Nader and Barbara Yngvesson, 'The Ethnography of Law and its Consequences', *op.cit.*, p. 912.

[78]See Laura Nader, 'Forums for Justice: A Cross-Cultural Perspective', *Journal of Social Issues* XXXI (1975), pp. 151–70; Laura Nader and Barbara Yngvesson, *op.cit.*; Laura Nader and Harry F. Todd, 'Introduction: The Disputing Process' in Laura Nader and Harry F. Todd, (eds.), *The Disputing Process — Law in Ten Societies*, (New York, 1978), pp. 1–40.

Western 'state' societies furnish many illustrations of small communities whose proto-legal arrangements are not dissimilar from those of the New Guinea village. They lack total political organization, they have no single identifiable sovereign power to make laws and put them into effect. A few examples of such groups are family and neighbourhood units (especially some of the new planned communities), the social club, the businessmen's association, the place of work. They are as much concerned with achieving group conformity with norms and settling conflicts between members as is the State in its more extensive bailiwick. In the latter case it would be inaccurate to view law as isolated from the other social systems; to treat it that way in the former case would create a false picture.

... the small-group member in our Westernized society engages in self-service justice on rare occasions, especially as he does not live on his solicitor's doorstep. With the New Guinea villager, he shares the profound, not wholly unself-interested, belief that the sky must be kept up. Each recognizes that this economic and general welfare depend on the attitude of the particular community in which he is likely to spend much of his life. The enthusiastic litigant is mistrusted. There are local, often politically fraught, means for maintaining or restoring the *status quo*, and the wronged individual is expected to have recourse to the juridical machinery of the State only in extreme cases. In any homogeneous community, where the emphasis is on cooperative endeavour, the action of taking one's fellow to court may be a head-on challenge to group solidarity.[79]

These parallels can be pushed further, and more deeply in the actual legal systems of differentiated societies themselves. I suggested earlier if the case method were applied to our own legal system, much that is sociologically significant would be missed. In fact, of course, such a method is applied to contemporary legal systems all the time. In Anglo-American law schools it is the basis of almost all law teaching; in jurisprudence and especially in the American jurisprudence from which *The Cheyenne Way* was drawn, it is also a central concern. Dworkin's now highly influential discussion of the nature of law similarly focuses on 'hard cases' decided by the highest courts. These cases are clearly of disproportionate legal and, more arguably, jurisprudential significance. But they are not obviously of the same sociological significance. The vast bulk of law-affected behaviour does not issue in cases; the bulk of legal disputes never reach the courts, in part because lawyer-mediators attempt to settle disputes by compromise; the bulk of those that do are not 'hard' and do not climb very high in the legal hierarchy. Before disputes get to court, there is frequently strong emphasis on conciliation, as there is in many inferior tribunals, which are the only ones with which most disputants have any dealings.[80]

It is impossible, or at least it would be foolish, to deny the importance of

[79]Bernard Brown, 'Outlook for Law in New Guinea', *Oceania* XLI (1971), pp. 244 – 5.

[80]See J. van Velsen, 'Procedural Informality, Reconciliation and False Comparisons', in Max Gluckman (ed.), *Ideas and Procedures in African Customary Law* (Oxford, 1969), pp. 137 – 50, and R.S. Summers, 'Naive Instrumentalism and the Law', *op.cit.*, pp. 129 – 31.

institutions and social and legal arrangements in differentiated societies which find no parallel in small-scale societies. Any social theory must account for such differences as much as for similarities between societies. But to do so effectively one must give close thought to precisely what is being compared. The jurisprudential traditions which anthropologists have chosen either to draw on or reject were often tailored to different purposes than theirs, and have concentrated most on institutions least comparable to those in small-scale societies. To a large extent, this is also true of the great social theorists, such as Marx, Durkheim and Weber, whose prime concern was to account for what was *unique* about the modern world. Any reliance on such writings must be supplemented by a much closer attention to the ways in which, and the *levels* at which, law and legal institutions actually enter people's lives. Such attention might have benefits both for jurists and anthropologists. The former might be led to reflect more than is common among lawyers, on differences between legal matters of sociological importance and those, more familiar to them, of doctrinal importance. Such reflections would be greatly aided by an awareness of some anthropological literature, for, as Malinowski remarked some time ago, 'in the study of communities where law is neither codified nor administered before courts, nor yet enforced by constabulary, certain problems arise which can be easily overlooked in a jurisprudence based on our own formal and crystallized systems'.[81] Similarly, as many anthropologists are coming to realize, an acquaintance with contemporary Western institutions, legal and non-legal, has many uses even for those whose prime interest remains small-scale societies. Armed with careful specification of appropriate fields for comparison, anthropologists might more easily resist what Mary Douglas calls 'Bongo-Bongoism, the trap of all anthropological discussion. Hitherto when a generalization is tentatively advanced, it is rejected out of court by any fieldworkers who can say: "This is all very well, but it doesn't apply to the Bongo-Bongo". To enter this present discussion the Bongoist must precisely specify the cultural field within which his comparisons are drawn.'[82]

---

[81]'A New Instrument for the Interpretation of Law — Especially Primitive', *op.cit.*, p. 1238.

[82]*Natural Symbols* (Harmondsworth, 1973), pp. 15 – 16.

3

A sociologist's view

Klaus A. Ziegert

Presenting a sociologist's view of law raises the question which kind of sociology should be presented. My decision to present a macrosociological structural sociology may be resented by those who expect sociology to give answers to behavioural microsociological questions. But whatever criticisms one has of the macrosociological approach, it has at any rate the advantage that it can help to locate 'zones of societal malleability'[1] and thus show us where to direct further inquiry. It is thus possible to discuss not only law but also legal science and sociology of law. An obvious disadvantage of structural theory is its analytical design: on the one hand rather involved, and on the other hand very often wrongly taken for an attempt to describe social reality. This should be kept in mind in reading what follows. Its purpose is an analytical study of law, not a description of law.

I Society, law and control

The history of mankind is the history of the struggle for control: control over the dangers and threats from the human environments, control by particular societal groups over other social groups, control by individuals over other individuals within their social groups. Control is the instrumental essence of power. It stands at the same time for Prometheanism, for the message (found in the Bible and the Koran) that the world must be subjected to human will and for the eschatological promise of Marxism that the world belongs to the working class. Seen in a wide range of different historical settings and in the light of countless variations of the societal organization of human life, this struggle for control takes on the features of a 'natural law' and has, accordingly, stimulated the thinking of philosophers of all ages. Given this long-standing topicality of control in the long history of human thought, as something central to human nature, it comes as no surprise that *law* has been and still is at the very core of the discussion on control. Law is one of the oldest

---

[1]Cf. Edward W. Lehmann, 'Sociological Theory and Social Policy', *International Journal of Comparative Sociology* 19 (1978), pp. 7–23.

and one of the most obvious societal techniques for controlling human societies and their environments. Yet it is far from being the only one or even always the most effective one. This chapter on the sociologist's view of law seeks not to depict law in its astonishingly colourful course through the history of mankind, but rather to develop a perspective on the functions, and on the limits of the functions, which law offers in different societies. This is a soberly analytical task and it is important to clarify at the outset the different levels of this analysis and the various 'actors' to be found in our scenario.

In order not to blur the issue and not to complicate matters by theoretical and methodological considerations right from the start, it is sensible to make society itself our first focus of attention. This means that the first level of analysis will be a sketch of how societies organize control and what the position of law in this frame of reference is (section II). As such a sketch has to cover a wide range of societies over a long stretch of time it cannot but be very general and hypothetical.

A second level of analysis therefore has to take a closer look at the societal organization of the profession which dealt and deals with law, i.e. at the genesis and development of legal science and jurisprudence, its merits and its shortcomings (section III). This will lead inevitably, as the sociologist is inclined to assume, to the discussion of sociological perspectives of law developed in jurisprudence and their influence on legal science and jurisprudence (section IV).

It is not until this point that *sociology* comes into play as a third level of analysis, no longer viewing law as a professional problem of people with legal training, but as a societal problem, i.e. as a problem that goes beyond the mere technicality of the applications of normative propositions (rules and regulations). This is above all the realm of a special branch of sociological knowledge: the sociology of law (section V), which poses, however, also special problems of scientific organization.

Having examined the various ways in which sociological knowledge deals with law and its sources, we shall finally be in the position to take up the sociological analysis of law once again, but in more depth than where we left it before we started our *tour d'horizon* on how scientific knowledge on law comes about (section VI).

The rationale of this report of a sociologist's view of law is thus, in short, that the control which law exercises can be neither properly understood nor adequately applied in a socio-technical sense without a sufficient understanding of the organization of societies (macrosociological perspective) and the social behaviour of human beings (microsociological perspective). Both require an answer to the question how such scientific knowlege about law and society has been and still is organized by society. The 'actors' in our scenario are thus not only law, science and society, but above all social structure, social organization and social change.

II Societal devices for gaining control

Obviously 'control' is not a legal term, but a technical or — in our context — political one. As such it is much more linked to sociology or political science. Sociology, indeed, to a large extent, owes its genesis and existence to a scientific demand for a social parallel to the natural science and technology that gained prestige in the boom of discovery and invention in the early nineteenth century. Men sought a science and technology of human affairs, as the writings of Saint-Simon and especially those of Auguste Comte with their idea of a social physics, make clear. We shall return to these historical questions later (section III); the interesting point to note here is that though law (i.e. legal structure) very rarely gives any explicit thought to control, lawyers almost constantly and invariably do so. Law is a very basic technique of gaining and exercising control in society. How does it work?

This question becomes more operable if we try to give a more exact definition of what we actually mean by 'control' and of what our concept of law looks like. As our introductory remarks suggest, both the concept of control and that of law are linked to the observation of a social performance guided by social structures. This means that in this chapter 'control' is conceived of as (human) acts and/or structures with

   (a) the power of directing and/or restraining other acts and/or structures,
   (b) the right (i.e. legalized power) to the supervision of other acts and/or structures,
   (c) the means (i.e. factual political and economic power) of checking or verifying the results of other acts and/or structures.

The English language focuses predominantly on (a), which is a slightly modified version of the definition of the word 'control' given in the Oxford English Dictionary. The German '*Kontrolle*' and above all the French '*controle*' have rather the 'legalistic' connotation of supervision stressed in (b). It is clear in all three instances, however, that the basic feature of control, as discussed in this chapter, is that of a societal power of various and as of yet undefined social agents that amounts to a technique. 'Law' on the other hand is conceived of, so far as this chapter goes, as social acts and structures guided by a normative structure organized within society, which tends to become specialized and markedly differentiated as societies proceed in evolutionary development. As for the relation between law and control one could say that control is a societal technique which becomes refined and moulded by social agencies, among them legal ones, which make use of it. Law, on the other hand, is a basic and special structure in all societies which requires for its accomplishment certain societal techniques, among them control. In order to make the distinction clearer and to demonstrate the social relativity of the concept of control, we want to give three examples of the social organization of control before proceeding to a broader discussion of law (section III).

1 Social control

Whereas the meaning of 'control', even in a sociological perspective, is a very wide one, covering all fields of human[2] activity where action or organization of action brings about a certain command or structures of command over things or other people, the term 'social control' has generally a much narrower scope and even more so when applied by sociologists. Here the basic feature is meant to be not the power of a particular social agency or a special social group (though this, as we shall see later, can be modified),[3] but the normatively guiding influence of the social environment of individuals. As such, social control is an indispensable condition for any human behaviour and sociologists accordingly focused their attention on this phenomenon[4] at a very early stage. It is however remarkable that the emerging outline, after the massive scholarly interest taken by sociologists in the topic of social control in the early and mid-sixties, is that of a coercive mechanism to keep social *deviance* down and conformism in society up. Deviance is indeed the key-word for sociological research in this field. It marks the burning social and political questions of late industrial and post-industrial societies, where deviance in fact means both the pathological inability to cope with societal norms and rules and the deliberate non-compliance with established normative structures that often are oppressive in order to seek innovation. Deviance as being out of (social) control fascinated sociologists for its disruptive dynamics, which, not only as a social phenomenon but also as a sociological topic, stood very much in opposition to the academic discussion of behaviourism and early structural functionalism. Deviance as a sociological topic could bring in, on a microsociological level capable of being put to empirical test, theories of conflict and *anomie*, in this way cutting short 'speculative' macrosociological theories on social change. On the other hand, sociological studies and research very drastically falsified the inadequate picture of law which sociologists had and still have, which many mistake to be the sociology of law: if social control is a check on social deviance, what else can law be than a state check on social deviance, what else can law be than a state check on possible criminal behaviour? Without doubt, the vast majority of the lay public would equate law with criminal law in this way.

Given this, in our opinion, danger of relating social control too much to voluntaristic perceptions of our own societies, a more favourable starting

---

[2]Using the word 'human' whenever the word 'social' or 'societal' should be used is only a concession to non-sociologist readers. It is, however, the basic sociological notion, shared in this chapter, that whatever human (as against animal) relation, action or sentiment there is, is *social* in the sense of necessarily relating to actions or sentiments of other human beings.

[3]Cf. the rich sociological literature on social deviance. A good selection appears in Joachim Israel, editor, *Sociala Avvikelser och Social Kontroll* [*Social Deviance and Social Control*] (2.revid.uppl., Stockholm, 1968), pp. 437–49.

[4]Cf. Emile Durkheim, *De la division du travail social* (Paris, 1893; references are to 8e éd., 1967).

point for a sociological analysis of social control is the anthropologist's view. This will show, in our opinion at least, (but see chapter 2), that the basic feature of social control is 'cohesion' rather than oppression, though the latter is — relative to subjective consciousness — what individuals may feel. The objective, material side of social control, however, is what Emile Durkheim called 'the social bond which corresponds to a repressive law so much that its rupture constitutes a crime'.[5] The experience we have of little-differentiated societies, i.e. of those which are in their full wholeness the objective of social anthropological research, can help us to see that social control is the cornerstone of social organization and that our complex industrial and post-industrial societies only diversified social control beyond recognition without being able to replace it by 'social freedom'. In undifferentiated societies we find characteristically the smaller but closer knit networks of families in various, but stable, lineage and kinship-patterns. Mobility and fluctuation in these societies are low unless families and/or neighbourhoods move as a whole (e.g. while grazing cattle). The individual person born into this family network experiences social life from the start as a game with firm and reliable rules and the world beyond his family, neighbourhood and village as dangerous and threatening. He is learning to rely on social life as his secure base to operate from when dealing with the world outside (e.g. in hunting, fishing, clearing wood, trading etc.), by attaching his expectations, knowingly or unknowingly, to the stability of the rules he knows, as they tell him what others in his family, clan or neighbourhood expect him to do. Finally, he is also learning to differentiate time by getting to know what to expect as an immediate reward and what to expect in the more distant future.

The chance of disappointment, i.e. the failing of expectation, is rather small in this (ideal) stable small-scale society, but empirically there are always, even here, small areas of contingency, where the rule is not to expect too firmly, something or someone to do something, and — naturally — there are also, even here, rules that are broken and 'rightful' expectations that are not met. Finally, there are conflicts over rules, i.e. open questions as to which expectations were the right ones to have. Obviously, what we see here as expectations is just the subjective side of a network of norms, but it is also much more than that: it is the very base of social action and as such of societal organization.[6] Norms exercise their guiding functions not indepen-

---

[5]Durkheim, *op.cit.*, p. 408.

[6]Our approach is a rather simplified version of the foundations of Parsons's theory of action and his structural functionalism: cf. Talcott Parsons, *The Social System* (Glencoe, Ill., 1951). Parsons amalgamated in a most impressive way Durkheim's and Weber's macrosociological theories with American microsociological findings (among others) and thus represents a still unrivalled though not unchallenged comprehensive sociological theory. The further theoretical guideline in this chapter will nevertheless be the sociological systems theory of Niklas Luhmann, which in our opinion represents the modern type of general sociological theory — cf. Niklas Luhmann, *Funktionen und Folgen formaler Organisation* (Berlin, 1964) und Klaus A. Ziegert, *Zur Effektivität der Rechtssoziologie* (Stuttgart, 1975).

dently, but always and only in the context of the interdependence of social actions (= the social system). It is only the interlocking of social actions by norms which makes social systems work: without the chance of the disposition over 'proper' expectations human action is not feasible. This, however, does not mean that any individual action is guided by one or several norms. The very basic physiological needs in a human being, for instance, can spark off spontaneous actions. But it does necessarily mean that the functioning of social systems, as constituted by the reference of social actions to one another along the guidelines of normative structure, would come to a stand-still without the existence of norms. On the other hand social systems are obviously not sufficiently explained by guidance through normative structures[7] — the adaptive capacity of social systems is such as to allow for innovation, change, revolution. But even the dynamics of social systems, such as the fading away of old social structures and the genesis of new ones, seems to be in fact the adaptive and corrective thrust of society at its changing material, i.e. above all at the economic and technological environment, carried out with the organization of social systems and directed by normative structures.[8] To clarify therefore the importance of generating normative structures we have to return, once again, to the model of an undifferentiated society.

Continuity and *security* as to the way interactions are expected to take place are experienced as something desirable. This is in fact the subjective side of the objective necessity that interaction as a social system organizes devices of schematization which are indispensable for the continuation of interaction and further action with the help of differentiated interaction systems.[9] Loss of continuity and disjunction of actual behaviour from a normatively expected one is experienced as something threatening (which is only the subjective side of an objective loss of structure for further action). Small-scale societies therefore develop a very firmly set pattern of how to interact with one another. One function of the normative structure of this pattern is surely to shield expectations (of how certain others will interact in certain situations) from disappointment, i.e. from insecurity about the defined norms of interaction. However, one must not overlook that a further important, if not even more important, function of the normative pattern of interaction, especially in undifferentiated societies with high existential risks, is to ensure that there will be no loss of structure for interaction, that there will be continuity and security in interaction systems, that the mutually understood basis for interaction will be kept.

---

[7]But it is important to keep in mind that, in the concept of sociological systems theory, social systems are not just an accumulation of acting individuals but a body of meaningfully directed actions organized to achieve a certain aim (function) which can be specified.

[8]The interaction with the environment is, by the way, a further constitutive factor for social systems.

[9]Cf. Niklas Luhmann, 'Schematismen der Interaktion', *Kölner Zeitschrift für Soziologie und Sozialpsychologie* 31 (1979), pp. 237–55 at p. 248.

It is therefore functional (or subjectively: valuable) that societies differentiate, i.e. organize[10] special interaction systems which try to guard the keeping of norms and the securing of the continuity of expectations. This specialization of interaction systems is functional because meaningful social life would be jeopardized if every new situation demanded assessment by a new concept of mutually agreed-upon action which would have to be established on the spot — in fact this is absolutely unthinkable. It is here that we hit 'social control' again and that we leave the level of social-psychological reasoning. Social control is the special interaction system (i.e. system of interaction systems) which has as its main function the securing of a basis for social life in society by

   (a)   selecting a set of norms by which interactions in society are guided (= orientation),

   (b)   organizing special devices of schematization of interaction which make a return to used patterns of interaction possible if a norm of interaction has been broken or questioned (= security of orientation).

In the case of our undifferentiated society, this means that family and neighbourhood watch closely how every individual behaves, whether he is behaving according to the 'old sacred' rules or not. In the case of suspicion that a rule is being infringed upon or, at times, of an open clash with existing rules, family members or members of the public indicate by their reactions that they have been watching the misconduct and request through them that the 'wrong doer' explain his behaviour and — if need be — revoke and 'repent' it. This means that there must be a public acknowledgement by the 'delinquent', that there is a norm of behaviour and that this norm is also valid in the future for him and all the public, in spite of his actual trespass. This norm control is enacted in the first instance clearly not to oppress other members of society, but to keep the norm structure in good order and thus uphold the basis of common interaction and social life.

It is important to note that the consensus about valid norms in a society of this type is brought about by actual behaviour as anybody can be watched and 'checked', but that many areas of social life are exempted from normation and accordingly 'not watched' (aspects of juvenile behaviour) or 'taboo' (e.g. areas with religious or mystical connotations[11]). Actual, occuring, inter-

---

[10]Here and later in this chapter 'organized' is used in the broad theoretical meaning of specializing specified interaction systems in society for a particular purpose. E.g., society 'organizes' science by interlocking the interaction systems of 'observation', 'teaching', 'testing' etc. in a special way and developing this organization of structures further.

[11]It is significant for the effect of taboos on social life that they are not, as might be expected, effective because of their strong normative value but, on the contrary, are experienced as something frightful and gloomy by their 'norm vacuum', i.e. they 'drain out' all structures which could serve for interaction and are — on purpose — kept out of social control, thus furnishing a fine political tool in the power struggle of developing societies.

action selects norms of behaviour and assures them a place by norm-abiding repetition, accepted by all members of the public. The dialectic of norm selection and of norm assurance thus guarantee the integration and homogeneity of a small-scale society. But it is here that our ideal picture of undifferentiated societies has to be left behind: social control, even if basic, is only one of many interaction fields in society and as societies grow in complexity the device of social control is fragmented into many different societal concerns and superseded by other social systems organized with different functional aims.

2 Law

One of the results of the differentiating processes is a specialization of normative structures, i.e. a selection of a special set of norms and of a set of special interaction systems out of the many existing in society. In the language of systems theory the trick by which this works is easy to describe: intensification and improvement of the efficiency of social organization through the application of reflexive mechanisms, i.e. the turning of selection procedures back onto themselves, or, in the case of normative structures: a normation of norms. On the level of societal action this is obviously not so easily achievable. But it appears that at a certain historical point in the evolutionary development of every society the normative network of social control no longer manages to produce the normative guidelines of interactions in a given society and that, on the other hand, the overproduction of norms in all different spheres of interaction, now detached from an all-round public inspection, makes society establish a special norm set (= selection) in a special framework of interactions.[12] Law, at first sight, is very much involved with 'non-legal' norms (moral norms, religious norms, practical economic and political directives). Yet it is distinguishable by the outlines of the arrangements of special interaction systems: roles, procedures, values and norms. This means we now find a special apparatus in society to deal with 'the production of a secure base for social action' by generating norms and rules, by checking and re-establishing them in case of breach and by changing them with caution in case of insufficiency. 'Progress' — as compared with the mechanisms of social control — is achieved by introducing cognitive elements into the normative structure; situations are assessed by a scheme of dualism, either proceeding according to the norms or adapting the norms to the (new) situation by procedure.

The 'costs' of this advance, which historically or social-anthropologically might be called Ting, moot, iudex, kadi, chief, tribunal, or just court, are twofold. First, the legitimacy of a norm-producing and norm-defining agency of that sort can no longer rest on the actual consensus of all members

---

[12]Cf. a more comprehensive and thorough presentation of this concept of the genesis of law in Niklas Luhmann, *Rechtssoziologie* (2 Bde, Reinbek bei Hamburg, 1972), I.

of society. This means, law operates under a fictitious consensus and under the tacit agreement on all sides that legal norms are factual social norms. This fiction has, evidently, vast organizational advantages but it is at the same time risky, as actual consensus can be questioned at any time. As a safeguard against the problems of consensus, the legitimacy of law is kept up by special devices, as for instance by the *institutionalization* of legal norms, roles and procedures, thus making legal rules safer against temporal changes.[13] Secondly, related to its 'technicality', the impact law has with regard to the bringing about or abolishing of a certain behaviour is rather limited, and legal norms very often have to resort to religion, morals, politics and simple social control. This very often blurs the borderlines between law, customs and other normative structures, but it is a consequence of the course social evolution takes that law does not replace older forms of social order but is only a better response by society to its growing complexity. 'As is typical for complex orientations, complex personal systems, complex societies, the complex structure is not simply substituted for the more simple structure; the development is only carried so far that alongside with simple forms more complex ones can also be chosen.'[14]

It would be illuminating and entertaining to illustrate the rather sketchy and general outline of the general features of the emergence of law with examples from different times and different societies. This would show the wide variety of the possible forms the principle of the institutionalization of legal roles, procedures and norms can take, while still serving the same function of providing orientation and security for action. However, this always happens in relation to the level of social, economic and technical development in every society and so it may suffice, in the framework of this essay, to cut short the empirical evidence for the development of legal services in societies and only, finally, to refer to the tendencies this development has so far taken.[15]

A first important trend in the development of law is its movement from, as might be expected, a mixture with other norm structures in a very diffuse combination[16] to a highly specialized, well defined norm structure in the more differentiated societies (industrial and post-industrial societies). Another trend, however, is that the legal structure, while being more refined in its normative effectiveness, shifts its structural focus from a highly norm-

---

[13]*Institutionalization* is in fact the generalization of expectational norms in the social dimension: once everybody has agreed to the institution *as it acts* it is difficult to counteract the assumed consensus and get actual attention for 're-specialized' issues, cf. Ziegert, *op.cit.*, p. 18.

[14]Luhmann, 'Schematismen der Interaktion', p. 252.

[15]For a better illustration of this point, see Luhmann, *Rechtssoziologie*.

[16]To give one example, as late as in the fifteenth century the mystery play in England was a very important source of legal knowledge for the public but also of suggestions on legal policy and of critique of legal (mal-) practice, interwoven with norm-generating interpretations of biblical texts: cf. Lynn Squires, 'Law and Disorder in *Ludus Coventriae*, *Comparative Drama* 12 (1978), pp. 200–13.

repairing punitive law of the criminal law type in little-differentiated societies to a highly norm-creating instrumental law of the legal programme type
in more differentiated societies. Again, as has been said, the development of
new structural options does not mean the replacement of the older forms,
but only the addition of new forms and the shift of importance towards
them. Finally, a third tendency is the monopolization of legal forms by state
authority. In little-differentiated societies we find a great number of
differing local legal systems, with the law of the chief or the king as only one
among them, whereas the differentiation of societies is brought about
through a centralization and coordination of legal forms by state law.

Before turning to the effects which this evolution of the legal structure has
had on its current appearance and to a more thorough sociological look at
modern law, the fairly general picture of the societal construction of law we
have so far given has to be enriched with some more substantial lines, which
put this isolated look at law into perspective.

3 Political structure

The normative structures, especially in their specialized forms as law, have
not developed apart from other social action or in an absolute way but are —
as we have argued — interactions systems in themselves. It is only the differentiation of societies which segregates the special legal structures from other
forms of interactions. Specialization, and this means *functional* differentiation, implies a higher degree of dependence of the specialized sub-systems
upon each other. As long as the community in a small-scale society itself
decides about activities, politics and law are one. Development, triggered off
and kept going by economic adaptation to changing material environments,
very soon makes the political structures differentiate. Normative structures,
and above all legal ones as being the most effective ones so far as normative
effects in society go, are dependent on political power in so far as it creates
the frame within which actual interaction can take place. Political structures
are thus the reality of enacted norms and legal structure is not more than
interaction in society can realize. The specialization of political structures,
i.e. control of power by making it a technique, also brings about the use of
law as an instrument of power. In the various actual historical forms of
economic adaptation there are different sorts of combinations of political
and legal structure, but it is fairly obvious that there is no automatism that
the political will finds its way into legal structures, nor that law backs up
political power automatically. This is basically due to the structural difference in political and legal structures. Political structure is an interaction
system that serves the function of reaching goals, whereas legal structure
serves the function of orientating and securing interaction and exchange
relations. These structures, specialized in various forms in the course of
history, are not linked by necessity. Obviously the normative structures are
very much related to the feasibility of everyday interaction; they are formed

according to the social milieu where life and exchange actually take place. It is only when political structures are able to control social milieus that legal structures also follow the turn taken by actual social life, because interaction on a new level now has to be channelled by normative forms. Thus, the linking of law to political aims is only achieved when interaction 'ratifies' political aims, at least where the actual effects of legal norms are concerned and not ideological programmes in the form of law only. Specialization of political structures in the form of the 'state' brings about a new quality in legal structure, however. Law now not only reinforces individual action but also reinforces and legitimizes state action. One very important consequence for the legal structure is that the instrumental elements in law are dynamized: law is pushed towards its positive form, i.e. its technical form can be used to submit the legal structure itself to changes and thereby also the guidelines for interaction in society. However, the possibility of *social* change by law should not be overestimated. Being basically a normative structure, law is bound by the devices of 'producing' high durability and security of expèctation and it is rather limited in its instrumental capacity. The latter social change is the domain of political structure and its instrumental devices of allocating action and interaction for new goal orientation and motivation for change. Law is, as always, the second step to safeguard the territory gained and to guarantee 'business as usual'. The state as such is not necessarily a precondition that normative structures will be law, but it certainly makes legal structures a part of the political power struggle in society, in so far as state power also means legal power and state law means exclusive rights to use the special interaction systems of the legal structure for the implementation of political programmes. The analysis of political structures would reveal a much more subtle gradation of the relationships between states and their legal structures. Here it is above all important to point out that the functioning of law has to be seen in the context of political power and economic struggle.

III   Law as a pragmatic problem: the law makers

So far we have only looked at the societal mechanisms which lend themselves to forms for social interaction. Many people think that this approach is disappointing: it seems to tell very little about the human individuals who actually deal with law, either as legislators or as arbitrators, mediators, councillors and judges, i.e. in sociological terminology it tells little about legal roles. From our approach it should however be clear that in the evolutionary spectrum of the emergence of law, a certain legal structure already exists long before legal roles emerge in their specific shapes. The differentiation of special roles through social organization and the identification of them as such, indicate that the legal system is already at an advanced stage. It thus appears, in other words, that the societal conditions for dealing with one another and having exchange relations of any kind with one another determine the legal forms and therewith the legal roles within that society. That, not the individuals taking these roles, 'creates' the law. However, having once reached this level of differentiation in the course of the development of a society, we find a new element in the construction of law: the lawyers' law.

Legal roles in their beginnings are linked, above all, with the basic element of legal structure: the continuity which is implied by, in its essence, the temporal quality of norms.[17] Thus old people, who have a long-standing acquaintance with the customs, rules and habits in a society and who can recall a great variety of 'cases', are above all entrusted with the role of mediator, arbitrator or finally judge. Further, and this is constitutive for the emergence of a legal structure, it is not necessarily conflict or the need for conflict resolution which brings about legal roles (though inevitably the legal 'knowledge' of an old chief, head of the clan or elderman attracts the passing of sentence in — unavoidable — clashes of interest in a society). It is rather the ability to know and record a body of legal rules which are held to be binding in a social group. This is demonstrated, for example, by the social organization of the old Nordic law where a 'recorder' reported all the legal rules he knew by heart before every congregation of the eldermen (Ting), although it was not he but the congregation who decided on the cases brought before the 'court'. It is significant that the 'state law' of the kings, after their central power had risen with organized warfare, later found its way into this organization of law via the 'recorder', in the replacement of him with a state official. Again, at first this state official was just the secretary in the traditional procedure, but he soon acquired the status of judge.[18]

The special achievement of the activities of people taking legal roles is the preparation of procedural norms and interaction systems, which make applying legal norms a *technique* and the refinement of this technique a *profession*. Legal technique and the legal profession demonstrate a degree of societal development which requires a more flexible, and hence a more instrumental, normative structure in order to enable exchange processes to take place and to guide interaction by orientating and safeguarding it. This goes beyond installing or restoring social order through social control. The legal professional at this stage (in the sense of the person of professional skill and not of the man earning a living by a full-time job) is rather inflexible as to the material law norms, which cannot be changed so easily, but he learns to handle the legal procedure as an important instrument in the range of social technology. The law-maker of the time, therefore, is not a legislator but a judge who resides over the thesaurus of (material) behavioural norms piled

[17]Norms are here defined as a generalization of the time variable in expectations: without regard to any specific situation certain behaviour is expected to be found, time and time again. As for disappointment and institutional immunization against norm breaches, see above, section II. 2; for further implications of the time variable on the legal structure see section VI below.

[18]Cf. Klaus A. Ziegert, 'Rechtssoziologie in Skandinavien', *Informationsbrief für Rechtssoziologie* No. 14 (1978), pp. 27–72 at p. 31.

up by tradition and who measures actual behaviour against them with procedural skill.

Legislation, on the other hand, is another evolutionary twist in legal history. As long as the normative structures of a social group or even of a society are rather rigidly directed at maintaining tradition and stability (prototype: the agrarian or peasant society) the set of rules and regulations is, and in fact has to be, little changed in its structural composition so as to orientate interaction. Only ideological reasoning as to its origin is refined, with the effect of increasing the legitimating power of such law. Legal rules are at their beginning identified with an eternal order, without a beginning in the past and without an end in the future.[19] Cutting down the vague and frightful apprehension of an animated universe to the more amenable and above all, the more manageable, world of gods and then of one God, Allah, Buddha or the Tao, the orderly organization of religious belief systems reflects the increasing technical control social systems gain over their material and social environments; the eternal order of gods or God can be interpreted and it can finally, if procedural rules permit, be changed. But this means that there must be a political will and a *value orientation* which is strong enough to override old traditional and religious guidelines and to replace them, though very often taking their form, with new orientations. Obviously this is a very gradual process. The legal structure, especially in an early stage of a highly diffuse conglomeration of law with religious structures, is extremely resistant to overall changes for technical reasons: in a normative interaction system not everything can be changed or questioned, and not all at once, without risking the breakdown of the system. A change is a risky undertaking as it requires that the political structure be strong enough to take over the legitimacy of the old order (endogenous change), or to overthrow the old order altogether (exogenous change, e.g., by conquest). The implementation of a new order or pieces of a new order, by either fitting it in into existing normative structures or by leaving the existing norm structure totally aside,[20] is certainly not the work of lawyers, though they have their share in the task. It is the work of politicians: bishops, kings and warriors, and the society where all this is taking place is a society of strong central political powers competing with one another (prototype: war or warrior society) and trying to subjugate every diverging political opposition.

[19]Note again the time variable in normative expectations as the expression of the desirability of utmost reliability in a social 'order'.

[20]So far as we know, it is not possible to find nor is there a historical example of a legal structure, superimposed on an existing one, totally replacing the latter without absorbing elements of the former normative structure. At best it can push it aside and thus isolate older normative elements, as extremely militant or, for that matter, imperialistic movements have tried to do, though always only in an initial phase, when the political aim was conquest and not consolidation. Consider the fate of the Roman empire, the empire of Genghis Khan, the Islamic conquests, the destruction of the Aztec culture by the Spanish conquistadors and last but not least the Bolshevik revolution.

Once the political order is established it is again law and lawyers who make the web of interactions work by harmonizing old and new (political) values and forging them into one, common law.

Through the introduction of the legal roles of judge, legislator and lawyer, the basic elements of the legal structure, and legal change too, have entered upon the scene. In the further course of societal development we find the elements in various structural combinations in legal history. The comparison of the development of the English common law with the continental common laws and subsequent (codified) civil law offers a good example of the interplay of economic structures, political struggles and legal reciprocation of the societal conditions. England and later the United Kingdom was able to develop a stable commercial and then industrial activity comparatively sheltered from external influences (after the Norman Conquest) by virtue of its insular isolation, reflected in the evolution of a traditional but highly flexible legal structure which resorts to judge-made law and ancillary, and thus unsystematic, corrections by legislatory acts (a process which can be called incrementalistic).[21] The continental states were forced by their constant political unrest and wars and consequently less favourable economic conditions, to organize their law in a different way. Here it is not the lawyer and judge chosen from the lawyers' ranks who forge the legal structure, but the legislator and the judge as a semi-state official who adjudicate the law. Fitting in with the development of a legal structure strongly influenced by the dominance of the political and economic risks run by the state is the way in which the body of legal rules and norms was not handed on in a relatively loose accumulation of judicial decisions in respective cases (as in England) but was systematically drawn together in vast comprehensive codes, which to a certain degree 'programmed' the judges and lawyers to conform with state law.

This comparison, however, can also point to a new feature in the development of law which is not altogether new in legal history but which leaves its distinctive mark on European (continental) civil law: the reflection of law (as a societal normative structure) in the *production of knowledge* about mankind. This is certainly no mere accident: the impotence of European legal structures against strong internal and external state pressures accounts for the scholastic and dogmatic refinement of legal reasoning which tries to find a legitimacy of a higher order in the, falsely reproduced,[22] Roman ancient law.

[21]This is also a connotation to the time variable in social organization: incrementalist action is action in a process of 'heaping up' step after step with, by definition, a very short-term time perspective: law works from case to case. As we shall see this may or may not also be a functional organization of the legal structure with reference to social change, cf. section VI below.

[22]Cf. Leon Petrażycki's many critical remarks on the activities of the draftsmen of the *Bürgerliches Gesetzbuch* (BGB: The German civil law code) at the end of the nineteenth century in his *Die Lehre vom Einkommen* (2 Bde, Berlin, 1893–5). Petrażycki, like that other great father of the sociology of law, Eugen Ehrlich, was a Roman law specialist and held a chair of Roman law at the University of St Petersburg. Because he was of Polish noble descent he appears on books published in Germany as Leo v. Petrażycki.

But on the other hand the intensive scrutiny of the logical and linguistic configurations which make up legal rules paves the way to a jurisprudence and legal science which, with its many offshoots into legal philosophy, social philosophy, economics and economic philosophy, moral philosophy and theory, represents a substantial and basic 'preliminary sociology'.[23] It must be said, however, that the eminently pragmatic orientation of legal training and legal thinking on the whole prevents the legal scholars and lawyers — who are at the very heart of a social technology — from seeing the links between their practice and its societal preconditions. Law is for them, in general, still a natural order and not an expression of society itself.

IV Law as a scientific problem: the malleability of law

It took the impact of heretics to shake the self-sufficient legal scientists out of their dreams about a perfectly harmonious natural law. These heretics came not in the form of revolutionaries[24] but in the form of liberal lawyers. Their message was nonetheless radical. They maintained that legal science was no science at all, but only a practical business without a proper scientific foundation. Without this foundation, however, law (= legal science) could not live up to the technological demands modern industrial society inflicted on lawyers.

This critique was in the making throughout the nineteenth century and was spurred on by several structural changes in the organization of the societies of Europe and Northern America. First of all the bourgeois middle class came to demand a share in the political system to equal the economic power which it had acquired in the course of the technological improvement of the means of production. At the same time science and technology were organized in a more conscious and systematic way, which in turn heated up economic development. Under these circumstances human activity had also to come into the *scientific search-light, shrugging off all religious and other superstitious* inhibitions. The Glorious and the French Revolutions prepared the way for thinkers like Saint-Simon, Comte, Bentham and John S. Mill, who in cool and sober scientific analysis could postulate something like a 'social physics', an anti-metaphysical and positivist view of societies and their statics and dynamics. This brought into reach ideas of the malleability of societies through social and political technologies, while the rapid growth of a mass of uprooted industrial workers made these technologies sorely needed, as Marx tried to prove. But sociology (as the new science of

[23]Cf. Vilhelm Aubert and K. Coward, *Rättssociologi* (Stockholm, 1972: orig. publ. as *Rettssosiologi* in Oslo, 1966), p. 264.

[24]The content of actual theory in Marx's writing and in other radical thinkers was far too slight and unimportant to have a serious effect on the solid building of academic law training and law schools. This is no accident: law is not a revolutionary instrument but rather an object of identification with the established order.

the forms of social organization came to be called) was then, and as yet still is, far from being able to make straightforward practicable offers of malleable technologies.[25]

Here the legal professionals are in a better position, as their work is eminently practical and constitutes social policy. However, it lacks the guiding theoretical lines and the macrosociological mapping of the lever points where legal social policy could take its stand. In view of the atmosphere of positivistic thought and technological advance of the middle and late nineteenth century and especially of the turn of the century, it is a rather belated start that legal theorists have made on reflecting upon the role of law in the rapidly changing and changed societies. It is also a rather uncertain start, as can be seen from the different directions which this endeavour takes.

In direct answer to the positivist reasoning of the nineteenth-century lawyers but also in opposition to metaphysical conceptions in the philosophy of law, some names stand out in legal science. These were to become the bearers of a new perspective on law and of a new scientific method for the study of law. They are Eugen Ehrlich (1862–1922) in Austria, Leon Petrażycki (1867–1931) in Russia, Axel Hägerström (1861–1939) and Vilhelm A. Lundstedt (1882–1955) in Sweden, Oliver Wendell Holmes Jr (1841–1935) in the USA and Raymond Saleilles (1855–1912) and Edouard Lambert in France. These scholars of law (Ehrlich, Petrażycki, Saleilles and Lambert were law professors, Hägerström and Lundstedt were philosophers, Holmes was a legal practitioner and finally a supreme court judge but also a member of the famous 'metaphysical club' together with William James and John Dewey — among others — and thus one of the eminent figures of American pragmatist philosophy)[26] were by no means members of the same movement, nor are they the only ones who could be named in the context of a transformation of legal thought. On the contrary, they are part of quite different 'schools' in legal thought or fathers of those schools. But they have the one thing in common. They, with the introduction of their thoughts on legal science, mark a turning point in legal history. From that time onwards, dogmatic, legalistic and metaphysical thinking and teaching in law schools and law faculties was no longer accepted without criticism and from that time on the society behind the legal norms began to emerge. These were the beginnings of a sociological perspective on law.

Eugen Ehrlich, being the first to use the term 'sociology of law', is most

---

[25]In the sixties and seventies of the twentieth century a more concentrated and interdisciplinary scientific approach to this problem of practical social science has developed under the heading of 'social policy'; see, among many, Amitai Etzioni, *The Active Society: A Theory of Societal and Political Processes* (London and New York, 1968).

[26]Concerning the influence of pragmatist philosophy on American society and for biographies of members of the Metaphysical Club, see C. Wright Mills, *Sociology and Pragmatism: The Higher Learning in America* (New York, 1964).

widely respected as the 'inventor' of sociology of law, [27] but like others of his contemporaries named above, he is rather a critical lawyer who voices a protest against the insufficiencies of legal science in his time. By trying to lay open the societal foundations of law, legal norms and legal decisions, he aims at a more scientific assessment of law. His starting point in doing this is the good legal argument that lawyers under the system of the European civil law far too often make their decisions along formal and dogmatic lines, because they are forced to do so by the organization of legal thinking or because they are unable to see the factual social conditions behind legal rules. In the course of proving his point, Ehrlich develops a fully fledged sociology of law, which makes 'living law' its main finding.[28] Living law, according to Ehrlich, is the sum of all the different elements of legal structure which only in their interplay permit an adequate description of the functioning of law in society. Without a sufficient knowledge of this functioning, lawyers are ill-equipped to tackle the legal and above all social problems they are called to solve. In the concept of 'living law' we already find a remarkable analytical approach to the study of the legal structure in sociological but also in historical perspective: law is the evolution of organizational norms, which are engraved on society by the mere necessity to get things done, into a more complex normative structure which consists, apart from the very basic organizational norms which come close to 'folk-ways', of a procedural apparatus — the lawyers' law — to make legal decisions possible and, finally, the legislative apparatus — state law — to make the political will enter into the interactions in society. For Ehrlich these evolutional stages are connected with historical phases through which societies pass, but — as a lawyer — he does not want only to describe law but also to deduce some practical suggestions from his findings. Ehrlich's suggestions are that state law is actually a dead end in the development of law, as it is stifling and counteracting norms in society and that the lawyers' law, as performed in the old Roman and in — contemporary — English common law, is much better suited to connect law to social change. Quite obviously Ehrlich was guided in his analysis by a large amount of critical opposition to the legal system as it existed in the Austrian empire. His 'sociology', in fact, was instrumental to the aim of advocating a 'free law' movement, which meant not much more than taking over some features of the English jurisdiction into the 'closed system' of continental civil law. But because of their abhorrence of an

[27]Cf. his most famous book, *Grundlegung der Soziologie des Rechts*, (München, 1913, repr. 1929 and Berlin, 1967; English translation by Walter L. Moll, *Fundamental Principles of the Sociology of Law*, introduction by Roscoe Pound, Cambridge, Mass., 1936). This is only part of a major work planned on the theory of judicial decision-making which, because of unfavourable historical circumstances and Ehrlich's early death in 1922, was never completed. For a fuller account of Ehrlich's life and work see Klaus A. Ziegert, 'The Sociology behind Eugen Ehrlich's Sociology of Law', *International Journal for the Sociology of Law* 7 (1979), pp. 225–73.

[28]One of Ehrlich's most promising ideas was the creation of an Institute for Living Law at Czernowitz, which however aroused no official interest in far-away Vienna.

anarchically 'freely deciding judge', Ehrlich's suggestions were unacceptable to his fellow lawyers. So it is not surprising that we find no enthusiasm for Ehrlich's work on the continent; his major impact on the scientific community is through the writings of Roscoe Pound in the USA.

The fate of Leon Petrażycki's work is very similar. As a brilliant student and post graduate in civil and Roman law at St Petersburg University, Petrażycki was admitted to the seminar which the Russian lawyers held in Berlin. There he came into contact with the work on the codification of the German civil law (*Bürgerliches Gesetzbuch*) and did not conceal his contempt for the many blunders and mistakes in this work, which German lawyers had greeted with pride and great admiration.[29] For Petrażycki it was clear that any legal policy was not a matter of gapless and logically coherent dogmatic systems, but a question of accurate scientific description and explanation of the functioning and effect of law. Since such a scientific approach was nowhere to be seen in the legal science of the day, Petrażycki set to work himself and issued, after his return to St Petersburg, works on a theory of the functioning of law, based on his own studies in psychology, sociology and economics. As in Ehrlich's case, the legal faculties and law schools did not respond to this social science approach to legal studies and to legal policy. This was partly due, no doubt, to the unfortunate historical context of the appearance of Petrażycki's work (a theory of law was not the most important thing preoccupying Tsarist Russia in its years between revolutions and before a war), and partly due to the language barrier. But even when Petrażycki returned to his country of origin, Poland, after it had been restored in 1918, the impact he made on the unimpressed traditional legal science of the time was negligible. Depressed and worn out Petrażycki committed suicide in 1931.[30]

Less dramatic but also more successful were the reformist ideas of the Swedes Hägerström and Lundstedt. They could direct their ideas at a society which was much further on the way to becoming an industrial society than the ones Ehrlich and Petrażycki turned to. While the small Swedish society was organizing industrial relations on the political principles of democratic self-organization and through a disciplined labour movement, the vast multi-national states of imperial Austria and Tsarist

[29]Petrażycki, *op.cit.*

[30]His major publications were at first all in Russian and Polish; *Law and Morality*, a translation and abridgement of his earlier Russian book, by Hugh W. Babb (Cambridge, Mass., 1955), came rather late. But the complicated, egotistic, idealistic and unempirical character of Petrażycki's writings may be equally to blame, with the historical setting and language barrier, for their poor reception. The adherence of modern Polish sociologists of law, especially Adam Podgórecki, to the Petrażycki tradition shows how much sociological re-thinking is needed to identify Petrażycki with the foundations of social science in legal theory, cf. Adam Podgórecki, *Zarys socjologii prawa* (Warszawa 1971; English transl. *Law and Society*, London, 1974) and Klaus A. Ziegert, 'Adam Podgórecki's Sociology of Law — The Invisible Factors of the Functioning of Law Made Visible', *Law & Society Review* 12 (1978), pp. 151–80.

Russia were going through the agonies of the clashes caused by backward political structures trying to ward off the social changes induced by fundamental changes in the economic base. Whereas in Sweden a broad, well educated middle class could react rationally to the growing demands of the working class, the reactionary bureaucratic elites in Austria and Russia kept a tight feudalistic grip on an almost entirely peasant population, which was illiterate, uneducated and lethargic; the middle-class intelligentsia was small in number and confined itself to fruitless coffee-house discussions, the industrial working-class was still small and politically insignificant, despite the efforts of small groups of young middle-class revolutionaries. The preconditions for the spreading of ideas of legal reform were thus quite different in Sweden, Austria and Russia respectively. Accordingly it was enough for Hägerström and Lundstedt and their Uppsala School of legal theory to dismantle the metaphysical philosophy of law which prevailed at the law faculties in Sweden and replace it by a realistic, social-science orientated one in order to impel the development of legal thought into new directions — neither sociology nor psychology were needed to accomplish that.[31]

This effect was very similar to that of the work of Oliver Wendell Holmes in the United States, but for different reasons. Here the common law did not represent such an insurmountable obstacle for realistic perceptions of the social forces behind the law being capable of adapting more smoothly and to a certain degree empirically to social change, just as Eugen Ehrlich had claimed. A sound social-minded and pragmatic argument by a Supreme Court Judge easily found acclaim from American lawyers.[32] On this foundation of a basic understanding felt for a sociological interpretation of the functions of law, the sociological jurisprudence of a Roscoe Pound could subsequently count on wide acceptance.

A further modification of the way sociological reasoning was introduced into legal science can be seen, finally, in the work of Saleilles and Lambert in France. Analysing exactly the potential of legal structure they saw the major contribution of law to the solution of social progress in industrial societies to lie in legislation. Unlike Petrażycki's, their approach to scientific legal policy was not an idealistic, self-made theory of law, but the very empirical, rational 'législation comparée'. By collecting data on successful or unsuccessful legislation in several countries and relating these to the differing societal conditions in these countries, it should become feasible to extract an optimal scientific solution to various legal and societal problems. It is obvious that comparative law, at least in its theoretical concept if not always in its

---

[31]Cf. Hans-Heinrich Vogel, *Der skandinavische Rechtsrealismus* (Frankfurt a.M., 1972). It was only much later that a sociologist of law, Theodor Geiger, attacked the Swedish realists for not being radical enough and for retaining a lawyer's normative attitude in discussing the societal mechanisms of law: Theodor Geiger, *Debat med Uppsala om Moral op Ret [Discussion with Uppsala about Morality and Law] (Lund, 1946).*

[32]For a comprehensive study of the work of Holmes see (James) Willard Hurst, *Justice Holmes on Legal History* (New York and London, 1964).

methodical comprehensiveness, also traces legal structures back to their societal origins and thus shares the same perspective on law with sociology.

V Sociology of law

The examples given of sociological perspectives in legal thought, and they can only be examples, show that law had become visible as a societal organization and as such represented much more than just legal norms and legal decisions. They show at the same time, however, that lawyers, when crossing the border into sociological scientific territory, still did that with the practical purpose in mind of rendering legal action more meaningful or of making legal policy more efficient. In taking short cuts on sociological theory and sociological methodology, the representatives of sociological jurisprudence or legal realism generally fell short of their aim of offering exhaustive explanations of the functioning of law in society or a sociological theory of law (if they at all intended to do so). Since the legal structure *is* a product of societal organization it must be rather doubtful whether it is at all feasible to explain the law and its functioning merely by looking at the law and the state. It would seem to be much more fruitful, from a scientific explanatory point of view, to study law in the broader perspective of social interaction and social organization. But here one has to leave the realm of legal science and one has to turn to social science (if one accepts the traditional separation of different academic subjects and different scientific communities).

The question, then, has to be put as to what sociology has to offer to describe and explain the functioning of law adequately. A quick answer would be: both much and very little. This puzzling answer is related to the special way of producing knowledge on society and can be explained accordingly.

In contrast with legal science, which it would perhaps be more appropriate to call legal technology, sociology in general is a very basic science which is primarily analytical and not technical and thus gives very few *practical* answers to the lawyer. On the other hand sociology, like any science, actually strives for a predictive quality and in this sense can be used for technical reasons. It offers at the macrosociological level ways of locating levers for socio-technical action[33] (but also: of unmasking levers for manipulation) and at the microsociological level ways of predicting conditional chains of social interaction (if A is given, then B will follow). So it depends very much on putting the right questions to sociologists if lawyers want to get satisfying answers. Obviously many more of the lawyers' questions lie on the microsociological level and are not at all concerned with the sociology of law, but with the sociology of the family, the sociology of juveniles, the sociology of deviant behaviour, the sociology of industrial relations, the

[33]Cf. Lehmann, 'Sociological Theory', p. 13.

sociology of professions etc. But a very significant part of legal questions, namely where legislation is concerned, are properly directed at the macro-sociological level. These are questions about the impact of laws, about court structure, about special legal policies where the social areas at which they are to be directed are as yet unclear etc. It is here that sociology of law comes in — it is, in modern terms, an 'in-between discipline' of the policy science type.[34]

Sociology of law, then, is an interdisciplinary task, which cannot rely exclusively on the findings of one scientific branch. Interdisciplinary coopera-ation. is an asymmetrical-functional one, i.e. the contributions of the different sciences linked together are different according to the different levels of analytical and technical aspiration of each discipline. In the case of the sociology of law, this would mean that the analytical elements (i.e. theory and methodology) are brought in by sociology, social psychology, social anthropology and other analytical sciences, the technical elements (i.e. valuation, strategies, technical know-how etc.) are brought in by legal science, economic science and other normative sciences. Sociology of law as an 'in-between discipline' presupposes that there are sociologists, lawyers, economists, psychologists, etc. working together in the field across the tradi-tional disciplinary lines. In a strict sense, there is no such thing as a 'socio-logist of law' but only sociologists, lawyers, economists etc. working in the field of sociology of law. To contrast the first, almost amateurish attempts by lawyers in socio-legal fact finding with the very latest results in scientific organization of socio-legal research[35] is certainly unfair. It omits the fact that there was also a long way to go in sociology from the comprehensive sociology of law of Max Weber[36] and Emile Durkheim,[37] which is in fact general sociology that uses law as an example of social evolution, via the more specific sociologies of law of Georges Gurvitch,[38] N. Timasheff,[39]

---

[34]Cf. Amitai Etzioni, 'Policy Research', *American Sociologist* 6 (1971), supplementary issue on sociological research and public policy, pp. 8 – 12.

[35]It is a significant development that socio-legal research is predominantly conducted at specially set up research centres which stress interdisciplinary links, such as the Center for the Study of Law and Society of the University of California at Berkeley, the Institut for Rettssosiologi at Oslo University, the Rättssociologiska Seminariet at Lund University, the Centre for Socio-Legal Studies, Oxford, the Social Science Research Group at the Max-Planck-Institute for Foreign Private and Private International Law, Hamburg, West Germany, etc.

[36]Cf. Max Weber, *Wirtschaft und Gesellschaft* (5.rev. Ausg., Tübingen, 1972). Note that not chapter VII 'Rechtssoziologie' [sociology of law] alone but the work as a whole represents Weber's sociology of law.

[37]Cf. Durkheim, *op.cit.*

[38]Cf. Georges Gurvitch, *Sociology of Law* (New York, 1942).

[39]Cf. Nicholas S. Timasheff, *An Introduction to the Sociology of Law*, (Cambridge, Mass., 1939). Both Gurvitch and Timasheff were Russian emigrants after the October Revolution and propagated the work of L. Petrażycki in France and the United States respectively without having a lasting effect on western sociology of law.

Theodor Geiger[40] or the considerations given to law by general sociologists like Pitirim A. Sorokin[41] or Talcott Parsons,[42] to the more concentrated and methodologically refined sociology of law after 1960.[43] But in its latest form of scientific organization, sociology of law seems finally to be performing the role which lawyers, legislators and politicians expected and expect an 'exact' legal science to perform: to give answers to questions about the social malleability of law and the problems of legal service, though the answers given are not as clear cut or as practical as many practitioners would like. For the complexity of social systems evades simple socio-technical advice and the part which sociology plays in the interdisciplinary undertaking 'sociology of law' is still dominant and still 'destructively' analytical.

VI Law in the view of the sociologist

Having attempted to shed some light on the social organization of legal norms versus the norms of social control, on the organization of legal professions, and finally on the organization of legal science and sociological perspectives on law, we can now resume the task of a sociological analysis of legal structure. The main elements of legal structure — normative expectations (norms), legal roles and procedures, political values, legal programmes — have been presented. It remains to bring these elements into relation with one another as legal structure does when organized by society. As we said earlier, a historical course of development has to be taken into account. This development is not an independent fulfilment of 'nature' but shows legal structure to be very much a variable, dependent on the economic structure, i.e. on the way in which interaction commodities (goods and services) are exchanged.[44] Law as a specialized normative structure is organized by

[40]Cf. Theodor Geiger, *Vorstudien zu einer Soziologie des Rechts* (Aarhus, 1947; Neuwied, Berlin, 1964). Geiger was a German sociologist, forced to emigrate from Nazi Germany, who was influential in establishing radical analytical approaches to law.

[41]Cf. Pitirim A. Sorokin, *Society, Culture and Personality, Their Structure and Dynamics: A System of General Sociology* (New York, 1947). Sorokin was a Russian emigrant and disciple of Petrażycki's, under whose influence he became one of the few general sociologists to assign law a major place in their sociological theory.

[42]All Parsons's works deal more or less expressly with law, cf. Parsons, *The Social System* and T. Parsons and Edward Shils (eds.) *Toward a General Theory of Action* (Cambridge, Mass., 1957). Special reference to law is made in T. Parsons, 'Hurst's *Law and Social Process in US History*' [review article], *Journal of the History of Ideas* 23 (1962), pp. 558–64, and Parsons, 'The Law and Social Control', in William M. Evan (ed.) *Law and Sociology* (Glencoe, Ill., 1962), pp. 56–72.

[43]This modern interdisciplinary and cooperative sociology of law arose suddenly and simultaneously in many western countries and in Poland in the early 1960s. It has produced a massive quantity of studies and theoretical treatises impossible to survey here. For more recent reviews of the development of sociology of law see Podgórecki, *Law and Society*, and Ziegert, *Zur Effektivität der Rechtssoziologie*.

[44]See Richard Kinsey, 'Marxism and the Law: Preliminary Analyses', *British Journal of Law and Society* 5 (1978), pp. 202–27, as an example of how a more subtle sociological structural analysis can be employed in a Marxist approach if it wants to explain law as more than just a tool of the ruling class.

societies in order to serve a double function and accordingly we find two distinct structural lines in the development of law in relation to the development of each society:

1 the development of an expressive capacity of the normative structure which renders orientational guidelines for interaction secure, i.e. as far as possible 'immune' against norm-untrue action;

2 the development of an instrumental capacity of the normative structure which gives orientational guidelines for interaction (on the basis of the mechanism of fictitious 'consensus' = *qui tacet consentire videtur*).

It is very important to see that the categories of 'expressive' and 'instrumental' represent a structural differentiation of interactions systems in the time perspective (and are thus indicators of how much complexity social systems can deal with by their own complexity).[45] A structure organized on expressive lines is directed at the present time in any given moment and does not organize interaction into any length of future time;[46] a structure organized along instrumental lines is directed at future results of interaction and working out the preconditions for their possible success.

The evolutionary quality of law is given in any normative structure which realizes both these functions in the one structural device and at the same time. Historically this means that social control was more or less congruent with the normative disposition of expectations at a very early stage of evolution, whereas today in modern post-industrial societies it is only a minor, but nevertheless important, part of the legal structure and very close to what we understand today by penal law: the instrumental capacity of orientation is almost exclusively made up of the normative capacity of the structure; norms are very durable and 'secure' but rather inflexible and deep rooted in behaviour.

On a further step of legal evolution we find that the highly diffuse norm structure made up almost exclusively of normative dispositions — which empirically should be a rare case among societies over the course of time and which is very much what the final stage of communism promises to be when state and law have withered away — does not meet the structural needs of securing and orientating exchange in a more differentiated society as sheer size and complexity of interactional references grow. Accordingly the diffuse norm structure is specialized by the institutionalization of legal roles and procedures which make the legal structure more productive so as to mould, amend and change normative expectations without losing their security and orientation function. Empirically this is the case where the general public watches and judges interaction between parties or where

---

[45]Cf. Parsons, *The Social System*, pp. 137 ff.

[46]Correspondingly norms fill the gap of orientation for future action very well by suggesting that there ought to be no change in the prerequisites for action at all. In this sense norms are an auxiliary device when knowledge about the future is absent and yet one is bound to act.

actions or members of society are transformed into the role of a formalized 'third man', who takes over all the functions of mediator, arbitrator and judge, not necessarily vested in one person. By organizing the legal structure in this way the expressive capacity of a legal structure is decreased (a judge can decide quite contrary to normative expectations in his evaluation of a case), but the technical quality of the legal structure is increased. Norms can now — cognitively — be adapted to special situations in cases and to social change. In this way law begins to step out of the diffuseness of normative structures and begins to take on its special, technical form, while other normative structures 'specialize' in the expressive function: morality and religion organize structures for security and orientation on the basic level of undisturbed normative expectation.

In modern post-industrial societies the process of specializing legal roles and procedures is far advanced. The centrality in legal structure of differentiation and specialization of interaction systems calls for an ever increasingly specialized and highly technical legal treatment. One should not, however, overlook the fact that a legal structure, even if differentiated into norms and legal roles and procedures, is still fairly low in instrumentality, i.e. the legal decision structure makes orientation of interaction incremental, from case to case, rather than covering longer prospects in time. It is retrospective rather than prognostic. Legal structures which rely very heavily on legal roles and legal procedures, i.e. the legal process and judge-made law, like common law in England and the United States of America, concede much leeway to structures other than legal ones where complex planning for future issues is concerned. That means that either there is very little sympathy for the concept of comprehensive social planning or that there are forces in society ('the free market forces') which are quite happy not to be bound by instrumental legal structures and which are doing well in legal process from case to case. In fact, however, English and US legislation is also superseding the basic common law structure by a considerable number of instrumental legal structures, i.e. legal programmes of decisive instrumental value.

As mentioned earlier, political structures also differentiate and societies develop special political forms of organization, which give those societies the technicalization of power at the cost of stratification and class segregation. By their very special function, namely that of mediating power, political structures tend to instrumentalize law, too, by introducing political values into the legal structures and thus gaining normative support for political actions. It is obvious here that the instrumental capacity of a legal structure is increased as political values, introduced into it by state legislation, mobilize interaction for gains in the future. At the same time the level of the expressive capacity of the legal structure is kept rather high, so that the political system gains considerable normative support. Empirically, this type of law, where legal structure is differentiated into legal norms, legal roles and procedures and into distinct forms of political law and legislation, is extremely widespread and of a large scope. It coincides with the formation of rulers, kings, leaders and finally states and nations. It is then a matter of thorough analysis in any special case for a society to state which structural features law is taking and how many other, extra-legal structures are brought in to compensate the loss of expressive function or to complement its gaining instrumental function. In modern post-industrial societies the Soviet Union may be an example of a society which, in spite of a fully differentiated legal structure, has its structural centre of gravity in the legal arrangement of introducing a constant sequence of political programmes into the legal structure with a high normative appeal, while at the same time underrating (and underestimating) the technical quality of legal roles and legal procedures, which may here be referred to as 'legal culture'. This leads, under the impact of a highly industrialized, complex society to an overstressing of the 'fictitiousness of legal institutions'.[47] As a result the credibility gap as far as the instrumentality of law is concerned is rather wide and the reliability of legal service (protection of individual rights, due process) is rather poor. It seems, however, that in recent years the political leaders of the USSR have realized this 'over-drawing' of the normative potency of political programmes and plans in the form of legal structures, so that now the *technical* normativity of the legal structure in the form of contract and legal service is gaining importance in the factual organization of social interaction in the USSR. As law is in this way structurally incapacitated in the instrumental functions required by the actual level of social organization, other auxiliary structures are organized to be 'law-like' (for instance morality), or acquire official legal status (for instance party programmes and decisions of the CPSU), so as to meet instrumental ends in interaction systems (i.e. 'to produce more effectively and with higher quality').

There is a fourth and final step to be taken in the differentiation of legal structure which aims at increasing the instrumental capacity of a legal structure. That is the development of legal programmes. Here the technical quality of law is refined as the interaction system of legal roles and procedures is linked to a wider, long-term perspective of a legal programme which contains various conditional chains of action with regard to situations in the future. The incremental character of case to case decisions is overcome by a comprehensive scheme and the retrospective orientation of jurisdiction is exchanged for a policy-orientated decision-making. Empirically this is the step which industrial societies have taken in order to come to grips with their many structural problems, but there is a wide range of possible 'mixes' as to how far mere legislation is an instrumentally high or low legal programme and how far the other structural elements — normative expectations (cf. developing countries), legal roles and legal procedures (cf. common law countries) and political values (cf. Socialist countries) — dominate the entire legal structure. The example of a society with fully differentiated legal

[47]Cf. above, section II. 2

structure which has its main legal focus on legal programmes would be Sweden. Here all interaction systems are covered by comprehensive legal programmes which link the procedure of legal examination to societal (= state) measures after a strategic plan. Accompanying the preoccupation with organizing above all the legal structures of legal programmes, we also find a high level of implementation of these programmes and active legal roles together with the creation of new ones in order to safeguard the integrity of persons and individual rights versus societal action.[48] It seems that this type of legal structure at an instrumental intermediary technical policy-orientated level, abridging mere expressive normative structure, serves the needs of a post-industrial society for societal guidance by legal structure best. It leaves the way open to opt for political structures and legal programmes where social welfare and freedom of the society as a whole are concerned and to opt for political morality and legal procedure where individual integrity and dignity is at stake. In this sense law will continue to be emancipated from social control and still serve the same cause: to give form to social interaction.

[48]It is an interesting fact, and corresponds to the Swedish legal structure as interpreted here, that because of the relatively high number of judges the ratio of judges to 'Advocaten' (attorneys) in Sweden, as in West Germany, is 1:2, whereas in England it is 1:12 and in the USA (California) 1:219. Cf. Eberhard Blankenburg, 'Zur neueren Entwicklung der Justiz', *Deutsche Richterzeitung* 7 (1979), pp. 197–203 at p. 200.

4

Law and internal peace*

P.H. Partridge

In the remarks that follow I have in mind those Western parliamentary, highly industrialized countries which have a long tradition of democratic thought and institutions. I start especially from the political and social turbulence of the 1960s which, in many countries — the US, France, West Germany, Italy, the UK — caused many writers to claim that respect for law, for legal and political authority, is being eroded. It is often argued that these industrialized countries are becoming increasingly ungovernable; that the use of 'direct action', of force, violence, of passive and far from passive disobedience to enforce collective demands is becoming a more frequent occurrence in political and social life; that the consensus which supported the processes of elected parliamentary government had weakened. During the 1970s the level of turbulence in the countries I have in mind has, of course, much diminished and the situation in the 1960s was certainly not unprecedented: we need only think back to France of the early 1930s. Domestic peace is perhaps never fully achieved; it is very seldom all-embracing within a society; it is certainly not indivisible. Yet the rise and decline of states of turbulence make it interesting to consider what the conditions are that tend to preserve a state of domestic peace and what are the conditions that tend to fracture it. These, of course, are enormously complex questions: I want to make only a few points, and I do not imagine that it is the same set of conditions which tend to destroy domestic peace in all circumstances and at all times.

I suppose one should begin by indicating what one means by domestic peace: peace is not a simple condition to identify. Obviously, it is a relative thing: peace exists in various degrees. In the internal affairs of societies as well as in their external relations we often have the condition once described (with reference to the then international situation) as one of 'no peace no war'. For my purposes here I shall mean by internal peace that state of affairs

*Delivered in the Assembly Hall of the Faculty of Law, University of Sydney, on Wednesday, 17 August, 1977 as part of the Public Symposium 'Law and Internal Peace' of the 1977 World Congress of the International Association for Philosophy of Law and Social Philosophy (IVR).

in which social transactions are taking place, political and other decisions are being made, and political and social change is occurring without the employment of force or violence, without the use of power in one of its many forms directly to coerce some members of a community to make them conform to the wishes of other members. I have in mind the sense in which we talk about 'peaceful change' in contrast with change brought about (or prevented from coming about) by force or violence. Obviously this is itself rather slippery; it can provide endless discussion of ambiguous cases, raise endless questions of the 'where would you draw the line?' kind. You might properly argue, for example, that even when men are coerced into accepting something they do not want, they yield to the coercion but keep the peace: they don't fight back, they don't use force to resist. But it is notorious that all the terms we use in discussing social peace are subject to the same difficulties of specification. This is true, not only of 'peace' itself, but equally of 'power', 'force', 'violence', 'coercion', 'consent' and so on. There are many who now tell us that the state's use of its legal authority, exercised in accordance with the law, is in fact 'violence'. So, especially in so brief a discussion as this, you must not look too closely at the currency we are trading with.

With the exception of some sects of anarchists everyone will agree that law is one of the main mechanisms for the institution and maintenance of domestic peace. This may not be its explicit or deliberate function always, but much law at least has the effect of providing conditions for peaceful social living. In what ways? In extremely broad and elementary terms, I want to specify four main ways in which law may be said to set the conditions for peaceful social living.

First, by defining, delimiting, apportioning, distributing, a complex body of rights and duties. One of the main functions of law is the allocation and management of a system of legal rights and duties — not a static system, of course, but one continuously being modified. In this sense, law defines legitimate expectations; legitimate spheres of interest and activity. In so far as the law is conformed with, it obviates collisions and conflicts.

Secondly, by its management of this system of rights and duties, law provides the processes by means of which, within the existing system of rights, conflicting claims and interests can be negotiated or adjudicated, areas of uncertainty resolved, and adjustments made as circumstances change. The judicial system, of course, has a large part in this. No doubt, within an active society a very great deal of stress and strain, conflict, negotiation and accommodation, and sheer turning of a blind eye to the law, occurs outside the legal system. Perhaps social life could not continue unless that happened; perhaps it would be a very strangulated kind of society in which law was all-pervasive and too much reverenced. Nevertheless, law is one of the major alternatives to the definition of interests and relationships by force and self-employed coercion.

Third, it is through legal processes that government employs its usually superior power to enforce observance of the system of rights and of adjudications made at lower levels within the legal system. Internal peace does not imply the total absence of governmental force or coercion because to some extent internal peace has to be imposed or enforced; not many of us are by nature so peace-loving and so law-abiding (if we have the power to be otherwise) that enforcement or the 'threat of it can be dispensed with.

Fourth, law of the kind we broadly call constitutional law defines the location of final political authority and the mode in which it is to be exercised — by whom, in what ways, within what limits, sometimes for what ultimate purposes. The function of law at this level is to spell out authoritatively, to put beyond dispute, questions concerning the location of political authority, how authority is to be constituted, how and within what limits it is to be employed, and so on. In a very complex society it is impossible to see how such conflict-generating matters could be arranged except through the machinery of a highly sophisticated legal system. As we know all too well, the existence of law is by no means sufficient to prevent violence from breaking out over these terribly important questions; but it is certainly necessary.

All this is elementary text-book stuff. It indicates some of the necessary conditions for domestic peace which only law can provide. But law alone, of these different forms or levels, is obviously not sufficient to ensure peace. Law is clearly a very fragile instrument of social peace. Other conditions are necessary to make it tough. Many sociologists have tried to provide a general answer to this question in terms of consent and consensus: law can do its peace-preserving job to the extent that it is supported by a fairly widely shared consensus, a 'supportive consensus' as it is sometimes called. Edmund Burke tells us that 'power should seek to rest on consent so that its distribution and its exercise may be stable — stability being a prime value both as an end and as a means.' Burke also thought that 'a nation is not governed which is perpetually to be conquered.' This expresses a tradition of thought about law and peace which is still very powerful. The notion is that law will work to ensure peace only if it is based upon widespread agreement about such·things as the value of the stability that law-observance produces, about the values enshrined in the legal order itself, the particular distribution of rights and duties, privileges and opportunities, provided within the legal system, about the fairness or legitimacy of the arrangements for determining the location of power and authority. Law helps to fashion consensus, and consensus in turn gives to law its peace-preserving function.

I do not find theories which postulate a large measure of consent and consensus intellectually satisfying. The words 'consent' and 'consensus' lump together a multitude of diverse situations. Without doubt a very differentiated complex society with a high measure of political and social stability owes its stability in part to a considerable measure of agreement about the sorts of things I have just mentioned. But there are other ingredients of stability and social peace as well. There is the ignorance of many people, their apathy, their sheer unenterprising habituation to the order of things as it presently exists. For many people law defines the boundaries of the possible — law made by men easily comes to be confused with nature's laws. There are the feelings of powerlessness to change existing arrangements and fears that resistance to some aspects of the *status quo* may turn out to be too costly. Many such possible situations go to make up the stability and the peacefulness of a society. Some of them are consistent with the existence of quite a considerable amount of discontent, disaffection, latent opposition and conflict. To identify some of these commonly ocurring types of situation with consent or consensus is double-talk. But in so far as such latent dissatisfaction, disaffection and conflict exist, law and the power it is seen to have behind it are very important factors in the maintenance of domestic peace.

The capacity of law to fulfil its peace-ensuring mission will depend vitally on other structural characteristics of a society. By way of illustrating this general proposition I want to discuss some characteristics of late twentieth-century industrialized open societies. The sociologist and political philosopher Robert Nisbet has written a book about our present condition which he calls *Twilight of Authority*. Nisbet's title and theme express a preoccupation of many students of contemporary Western societies. Much is now written about the difficulty of governing these societies, about the precariousness of stability, the tendency of individuals and groups to invite confrontation with governments and the forces of law and order, and, it is said, an increasing tendency to question the authority of government and the law, to attempt to nullify the law by resisting it either passively or violently.

If we look at the very industrialized, open societies of the West, we not some features which we would expect to make it more difficult for the state and for governments to preserve implicit respect for their own authority and for the authority of the law with which the state is identified. I will refer very rapidly to a few such closely interconnected features of late twentieth-century industrialized open societies.

First, there is the omnipresence of the state (or government) in contemporary social affairs: the now very general acceptance of the belief that stable relationships within a society must be managed or engineered, and very frequently by government itself. Governments have become a central agency in maintaining some sort of balance amongst conflicting interests and activities by legislation or by other means. It may constitute a special vulnerability of modern governments that so much of their social direction and control is so specific, i.e., so much concerned with very specific interests and demands of particular groups. A great deal of contemporary law is different from what F. H. Hayek, discussing 'the rule of law', thought law should be: general rules applying in the same manner to all members of the community, not discriminating between individuals or classes of individuals. On the contrary, modern governments are very deeply into the retail trade so far as economic and social interests and arrangements are concerned. In one sense, we might say that the authority (as well as the power) of modern governments has expanded enormously, in that governments are now commonly expected to provide the solutions to economic and social dislocations, to be the main engineer of happiness, prosperity, peace and welfare. When Nisbet and others speak about the twilight of state and governmental authority we are at first surprised because there has perhaps never been a time when governments were assumed and expected to be able to do so much for so many.

But this introduces what I consider to be a central paradox of contemporary government. On the one side, governments are expected to be enormously competent so far as the effective management of a very complex society is concerned. On the other side, the increasing direct and detailed responsibilities attributed to governments and assumed by them in economic and, indeed, almost all spheres of social life, have made them all the more vulnerable, all the more constantly exposed to widespread irritable opposition, criticism and disaffection. In other words, social and economic hopes and resentments tend to be concentrated and focused upon government — partly because it is widely held that it is government's responsibility to remove or at least alleviate social and economic disabilities; and partly because so much governmental action is intervention on behalf of some interests and against others. Perhaps it is bound to be the case that with the infinite number of particular pressures converging upon government the substratum of self-adjusting relationships or mechanisms gets weakened: the market is the best known example. And is it not bound to be the case that as more and more social conflicts and discontents get taken up into the governmental system itself, governments will become less effective and authoritative, and also, perhaps, more authoritarian?

Let me link this with another structural feature — the very highly evolved pluralistic structure of contemporary industrial societies, the proliferating organization of a very large number of separate, often competing, interests and groups. You may say that organizations have always been part of the driving force of a developed political system; but I think that contemporary industrial society is unique with respect to the multiplicity of organizations, their organizational sophistication, the power many of them have in consequence, and most of all with respect to their particularity: the particularity of the interests they often exist to protect and advance. It is also worth mentioning the heightened knowledge and publicity concerning political and social affairs. Contemporary industrial societies (at least those of the 'open' type) are deluged by information, publicity, propaganda, discussion. One important aspect of this more hectic awareness of the whole social system is the knowledge individuals and groups have about their *relative* situation *vis-à-vis* other sections of the community and their obsession with it. Listening to the clamour of political and economic debate in Australia, for example, one is sometimes tempted to think that many Australians are more concerned about what are called their 'relativities' than about equality or other social ideals. They are more concerned, that is, about maintaining the same position in the long march towards social betterment or welfare relative to other identifiable sectors of the community. Open industrialized societies for many obvious reasons seem to manifest more constant and more jealous sensitivity concerning relative changes and movements throughout the broad spectrum of society than earlier societies did or could do; this is a source of incessant pressure on governments. Michael Oakeshott once wrote about the 'over-activity' of modern politics. Over-active or not, I think it unquestionable that late twentieth-century societies are infinitely *denser* societies than any nineteenth-century society was. We should therefore expect them to be less settled and stable societies for this as well as for other reasons; we should expect those parts of the social framework which are concerned with peace-maintenance to be under more constant strain.

The chief significance for our purposes of this highly organized and institutionalized pluralism can be expressed in this way: it has tended to make central a particular mode of political activity and of public management. The tendency is for these more or less powerful, tightly organized, interest groups to seek to act directly on the state and on one another, either by consultation and negotiation or sometimes by exerting pressure of one or another type. In the evolution of modern government and law, much machinery has been devised to facilitate interaction between government on the one side and the organizations which speak for particular economic or other interests. This dimension of political and governmental decision-making is now at least as important in the parliamentary democratic industrial societies as the older institutions of parliament, political parties, general elections and so on. Much has been written about the increased interconnectedness of the separate regions or aspects of social life: about the fact that modern industrial societies are more tightly cemented together than the looser social systems of the past. But, on the other hand, the greater centrality of organized specific interests may also have tended towards a certain Balkanization of society. This would help to attenuate the idea of community, and to strengthen the habit of thinking of a society as being no more than, or at least as being predominantly, a set or system of separate, particular, more or less organized interests, each with its own fairly specific objectives. Such a conception of political society would in turn undercut older notions of a common good and a common interest, of the importance of widespread discussion and the slow formation of broad currents of opinion, of government by the majority in the old-fashioned sense. This newer conception of what a modern political society is, is very clearly expressed in the writings of the American pluralists: for example, in Robert Dahl's argument that democracy is government by temporary alliances of minorities. And this may well be a fairly accurate account of what a contemporary industrial democratic society in fact is.

The point I am concerned to make is that the increased centrality of this form of political structure is bound to affect prevalent social attitudes concerning the authority of the state, government and the law. The more laws are seen, and rightly seen, as a registration of the pretty narrow and specific demands of particular identifiable groups and interests, often achieved by the open exercise of pressure or veto-power, the less likely are they to be endowed with that authority and legitimacy that many thinkers through the ages have wanted to associate with the very idea of law. They come to partake more of the character of treaties which are assented to only because of victory and defeat in war; they invite resistance and attrition.

I would not argue that this is a type of polity which the framework of the law has failed to accommodate until now; on the contrary, it has been active in adapting itself; with more success in some spheres than in others — thus, the notion of industrial relations as a 'new province of law and order' has not had a very happy history. All that I want to claim here is that the polity of powerful, highly organized pressure groups, the pursuit of specific group interests by often unilateral group action, does enormously accentuate the pressures within the legal order: does create a general disposition to look much more critically and sceptically at law in general. And, in so far as the peace preserving capacity of law does depend upon a pervasive respect for law, that capacity is called into question. It would be going too far, I think, to say that the development I have been describing has played a significant part in generating that attitude of mind which looks to confrontation, demonstration and civil disobedience as not only a legitimate but perhaps the most effective mode of political activity. But there may be some affiliation or continuity between the politics of unilateral pressure group action and the less peaceful forms of industrial and social struggle. As Alexander Bickel argued, civil disobedience is both contagious and habit-forming.

5

Violence and political obligation*

Shlomo Avineri

I

The theme of this chapter will not be the justification of political violence as presented by those who engage in it. Such justifications are numerous, and can be classified under several categories. There is the plain revolutionary justification, viewing violence as an immanent component of revolutionary action — 'without violence no revolution'. There is a deterministic justification, sometimes but not always connected with an interpretation of history calling itself Marxist, which views violence as the necessary mode of social transformation. There is the expressive justification, maintaining, as in the writings of Eldridge Cleaver, that violence is a message given by the oppressed to the oppressors, telling them that their day has come. There is the redemptive justification, as expressed by Sartre in his presentation of the writings of Frantz Fanon, viewing the act of violence itself as a liberating factor. There is the relativist justification, subsuming all forms of political power under the rubric of violence and thus presenting revolutionary violence as just one example of an all-pervasive structure of violence in society. According to this last variant, bureaucracies, schools, advertising, TV and social welfare services all engage in one form or another of coercion and violence, and hence revolutionary violence is not the exception to the way the world is run and therefore calling for a specific. justification. It is rather the universal rule of everything social. Thus Klaus Croissant can compare the present political structure of the Federal German Republic to the Third Reich and hail the Baader-Meinhof group as equivalents to the 20 July conspirators.

Though far from exhaustive, this list does suggest how wide a spectrum of philosophies and approaches can be utilized in justification of modern political violence. But it is not these various defences or justifications of terrorism which will be the subject of my discussion.

*Based on a paper delivered to the Public Symposium 'Law and Internal Peace' of the 1977 World Congress of the International Association for Philosophy of Law and Social Philosophy (IVR) on 17 August, 1977, in the Assembly Hall of the Faculty of Law, University of Sydney.

Beyond and above these various possible justifications supporting and approving political violence, there has recently arisen in democratic societies a different, much more complex phenomenon. People who do not themselves directly support terroristic activities, out of their own commitments to the values of liberal-democratic societies feel it possible to express understanding of, and find mitigating circumstances for, acts of terror which are in themselves abhorrent and repulsive to them. Our interest will not be with the outsiders, with the revolutionaries who try to overthrow the existing structures of liberal-democratic societies, but with those insiders who support what is vaguely called The System, but who feel that those engaged in terrorism are not completely in the wrong and have to be 'understood' in some sense or other. By understanding they do not mean an historical understanding in the sense that the roots of Nazism have, of course, to be understood, but understanding in a sense which implies not necessarily sympathy but at least a certain degree of empathy. This empathy then intervenes in the political process required to deal with the phenomenon of terrorism itself. Such attitudes can be found among political thinkers and journalists, as well as in extreme cases — such as the somewhat bizarre examples of victims of hijacking expressing feelings of understanding and concern for the people who captured them, threatened their lives and held them captive under sometimes brutal circumstances. A recent example of such evidence can be found in Dorothy Rabinowitz's account ('The Hostage Mentality', *Commentary*, June 1977): a number of the victims involved in the capture of public buildings in early 1977 in Washington, DC, by the Hanafi sect expressed marked empathy for their captors, their motives and their actions when de-briefed and sometimes during subsequent psychological treatment. As the study shows, a mere psychological inversion of the victim/executioner syndrome would fail to explain the extent of the behaviour in this case and there are others, less well researched cases involving air-hijack victims. We have no parallel evidence of Nazi camp inmates or Soviet prison survivors identifying with their tormentors. The Washington, DC, victims only echo widespread ideas prevalent in the general culture of liberal democracy. Such ideas are not to be confused with sympathy for freedom fighters under dictatorial regimes and the blurring of the issues needs some clarification.

Traditional sympathy and support for 'classical' freedom fighters draws its justification from the argument that the regime or government against which they are fighting is not based on popular or democratic consensus. Thus even if one has some doubts about the use of terrorism or murder against an oppressive or tyrannical regime, this can at least be justified (as in the slightly vulgar end/means dichotomy) by the contention that a regime not based on popular consent or majority decision, or directly involved in outright repression, puts itself outside the pale of a consensus prohibiting the use of violence. It is at least arguable, and indeed it has been argued, that a government based on violence which cannot be brought down by peaceful means may not claim immunity from the very means which it applies for its own illegitimate preservation. In the cases under discussion here, however, the violence is directed against duly elected, legitimately established governments, basically abiding by the rule of law, with a free press and with universal access to an independent judiciary, open to all citizens, dissidents and non-conformists included. Whatever imperfections one may find in the political systems of any Western democracy, Locke's traditional invocation of 'crying to Heaven' as the only outlet is obviously inapplicable here.

Traditional acts of violence against oppressive regimes usually have been aimed at the oppressors themselves or at individuals symbolizing the oppressive system. If innocent bystanders were sometimes hurt, care was usually taken to avoid this; if there were such victims, it was considered a regrettable occasion. Hijacking and the taking of hostages strike immediately and directly at totally innocent victims, completely uninvolved in the grievances concerning the captors. If assassinating the Chief of Police in Czarist Russia can at least be presented as a strike at the roots of evil, how can one link Catholic pilgrims to Jerusalem killed at Ben Gurion airport by PLO-connected Japanese members of the 'Red Army' to the Palestinian grievances, or municipal workers in Washington, DC, to the claims of the Hanafi sect? The objects of hijacking or similar acts of terrorism are indeed viewed as *objects*, totally denuded of their humanity and degraded to mere instruments, to a 'thingness' wholly divorced from their human attributes.

The voices that call for understanding of such acts are raised in a climate of opinion which paradoxically abhors acts of violence carried out by the state. Certainly one of the most impressive achievements of the post-1945 era in the West has been an almost universal tendency to attempt to minimize the sphere and scope of 'official' violence. Involvement of the state in acts of war is considered most negatively in most Western societies. One of the present constraints on Western democracies in engaging in acts of war is fairly widespread resentment against such activities (consider French public opinion about Algeria and US public opinion regarding Vietnam). The abolition or severe curtailment of capital punishment has been almost totally accepted as a norm in Western democratic countries. Much more stringent regulations controlling police violence have been almost universally enacted. Serious and far-reaching reforms aimed at humanizing prison conditions have been introduced, albeit with varying degrees of success, in many countries. An unprecedented commitment to the concept of human rights has been incorporated into the belief systems and public credos of Western societies. Yet alongside this universal tendency attempting to minimize the use of force, coercion and violence on the part of the *state*, even against individuals and groups deviating from accepted norms, one discerns a parallel and contradictory tendency of condoning, understanding and explaining — if not outrightly justifying — acts of violence perpetrated by *individuals* or *groups* so long as these groups are not state agencies and use their own feelings — rather than a legally accepted code — as a yardstick for their motivation. The same person who would violently condemn (and rightly so, I would hastily like to add) the hanging of a murderer/rapist or a political dissident, will explain that Hanafis or Palestinians involved in hijackings in which innocent people are killed have to be understood, pardoned, guaranteed safe-conduct and even occasionally praised. What is considered unjustifiable under any conditions if perpetrated by the state — the taking of a human being's life — is considered justifiable, or worse, trivialized, as a means of at least 'drawing attention to injustice'. While such a quasi-utilitarian calculus is found repugnant in arguments calling for capital punishment as a means of deterring future rapists or murderers, its analogue is used when the reference is not to state violence but to violence carried out by individuals or groups with feelings of injustice, discrimination or neglect. A worse example of a double standard could hardly be found.

II

We are faced, then, with a novel phenomenon and with a new dilemma possibly involving a need for the explication of the acceptance of a double standard. One of the consequences of the syndrome delineated here results in a certain ambivalent attitude in democratic societies towards political terrorism — an attitude which in more than one case made it difficult to prevent acts of terrorism aimed at groups or individuals or to apprehend the terrorists after the act.[1] This ambivalence about the limits to the permissible reaction of democratic societies to terroristic threats, I shall argue, is deeply embedded in some of the common beliefs sustaining the liberal credo as practised today in the West. Such ambivalence cannot be explained merely in psychological terms as 'faint-heartedness', softness, and the like — terms sometimes used by right-wing polemicists. I would like rather to draw a distinction between what I call the *instrumental* and the *immanent* legitimizations of political authority and to argue that a merely instrumental legitimization of authority is open to the kind of criticism which ultimately makes it rather ambivalent towards political terrorism. An immanent legitimization of authority, on the other hand, may be the key to the emergence of a mode of political behaviour which could try to confront the issues raised by political terrorism in democratic societies.

As my text for instrumental legitimization I will not have recourse to the classical sources of modern liberalism: any student of Hobbes or Locke must be more than familiar with the *loci classici* of this view. I would like to suggest that we consider two talmudic texts. If this appears a slightly

[1]The West German position, in which there exists a widespread sub-culture which positively supports political terrorism (see the Buback and Schleyer cases) is perhaps an extreme case of this attitude. Given the memories of Nazism, an oversensitivity to authority in Germany may be fed more by the specificity of the German situation than by general ideas, and should be treated more carefully.

outlandish and far-fetched source for our context, I will try to show that these texts may turn out to be more helpful than the more traditional and celebrated references usually quoted in similar discussions.

The texts are:

1 Rabbi Hanina, the Deputy Priest, said: 'Pray for the welfare of the powers that be; for were people not afraid of them, they would have devoured each other alive' (*Pirkei Avot*, 3:2).

2 Rabban Gamaliel, the son of Rabbi Judah the Ethnarch, said: 'Beware of the authorities, for they do not favour a person unless it be for their own sake; they appear favouring you when it is in their own interest, but they do not help or sustain you when you are in need' (*ibid.*, 2:3).

On the strength of his remark, Rabbi Hanina may perhaps be called the first Hobbesian: his invocation to pray for the welfare and well-being of the powers that be is not based on any immanent concept of intrinsic value represented by the authorities. It is purely utilitarian and instrumental, aimed at self-preservation and bluntly suggesting the bleak alternative to the existence of political power — a life that would be cruel, nasty, brutish and short. To avoid this Hobbesian nightmare, Rabbi Hanina the Deputy Priest appeals to rational self-preservation as the supreme command.

The rational corollary — and reverse side — of this wholly instrumental view of government is to be found in the second quotation, attributed to Rabban Gamaliel. Here the tables are turned. If people view their links to authority as purely instrumental, then they should not be surprised if the authorities repay them in the same coin and view *their* relationship to their subjects as purely instrumental as well. Just as the subject relates to the powers that be on the basis of the cold-blooded calculus of rational self-preservation and regards the state as a mere instrument towards his own individual ends, so the authorities view their subjects as mere instruments, to be pampered or rejected at will, without any immanent obligation towards them. Thus the relationship between the government and the governed is nothing else than a constant tug of war, a war of wits, a Leninist equation of 'Who — Whom?'. The utter cynicism of the Hobbesian subject *vis-à-vis* his government, which ultimately leads him to discard his sovereign if he does not deliver (if the sovereign cannot defend him and his property any more), necessarily leads to completely Machiavellian cynicism on the part of the government. One cannot expect the government to be imbued with qualities and values that are much different from those of the governed if the motivation and causes of political obligation are determined by purely instrumental calculations.

My focusing on these two talmudic sayings is not motivated by merely antiquarian curiosity or a wish to suggest that Hobbes has been preceded by an obscure sage or to attribute to the rabbis of old a worldly, cynical wisdom reminiscent of that of Thrasymachus. This would be of merely bibliographical interest. Because these two talmudic sayings, in their complementary nature, expressed a well-rounded instrumental view of political obligation on both sides — the government and the governed — it might be illuminating to our *theoretical* interest to try and understand the historical context in which these precepts have been formulated.

Both Rabbi Hanina and Rabban Gamaliel were not uttering eternal verities about political obligations. In their historical situation, they were addressing themselves to a concrete problem facing the Jewish people after the destruction of the Temple in the year 70 AD, which meant the disappearance of the vestiges of Jewish independence and autonomy and the emergence of Exile as the mode of life of Jews under the Romans. Their dilemma was to find an answer to the question how the Jews should relate not to their *own* government (about this the Bible says plenty), but how they should relate, in Exile and under foreign yoke, to a *foreign government* imposed on them after the suppression of the Jewish revolt against the Roman Empire. Against the radical view of the Zealots of opposing and not obeying *any* form of Gentile and alien government — a view which would have led and did lead to numerous massacres and continuous tumult — the more accommodating rabbis advocated the prudential view of passive obedience, of a purely external and instrumental attitude to the foreign ruler.

It is from this historical context in which the two sayings of Rabbi Hanina and Rabban Gamaliel are embedded that I would like to draw a theoretical conclusion. If it is true that the precepts suggested by these talmudic texts do indeed reflect and resemble current liberal conventional wisdom as expressed in instrumental notions about political obligation, then we may be up against a surprising discovery: what talmudic rabbis saw as a mode of survival for Jews in *exile* and under *foreign* subjugation, modern instrumentalist liberalism views as *normative* behaviour under *legitimate* democratically-elected and constitutionally-controlled governments. What the rabbis saw as a survival kit, becomes a philosophical basis for political obligation and allegiance; the ways and by-ways of exile are elevated to universal norms of legitimate behaviour. In other words: the instrumental view of political obligation is really premised on alienation, externality, mere manipulation of exterior hostile forces. If modern liberalism is really based on principles analogous to those determining the behaviour of people in Exile, under foreign domination, then there is no immanent justification for obedience and the attitudes towards the body politic will be determined by concepts of mere rational self-interest, by opinions and subjective feelings which are totally at the discretion, if not the whim, of the individual. That individual in such a universe is considered a self-sufficient monad, relating to other human beings, i.e. to a community, for purely utilitarian reasons.

It is this external, instrumental attitude to political obligation which Hegel had in mind when he warned, in his *Philosophy of Right*, against regarding the state as a 'mere' contract, a compact entered at will and broken at will, nothing but an instrument for self-preservation in the market place.

Such an attitude, according to Hegel, is the legitimate norm of *civil society*, but he contrasts it with the immanent bond of the *political* realm. Similarly, the Marxian view of a communist society in which the development of each is the condition for the development of all and vice versa expresses a similar criticism of the purely instrumentalist and manipulative attitude regulating human behaviour in capitalist society under conditions of alienation.

But what, then, is the distinction between an instrumental and an immanent mode of political obligation? We have already seen that the instrumental mode relates to the commonwealth and to political authority externally, and leaves it to the individual's judgement and inclination to decide about the scope and depth of his political obedience, just as it leaves it to him to decide whether and how to invest in the stock market, change his banker and choose his business partner. In both cases there are obvious constraints — John Doe may have to do business with a certain bank rather than with another. Yet the rationale behind the activity is instrumental and there is no intrinsic obligation, outside the perceived self-interest, regulating this kind of activity itself.

The vulnerability of such a bond against external coercion is obvious. First, you do not stick your neck out; second, not having any immanent bond to the commonwealth means that when the commonwealth is being attacked or subverted, it is not you who feels directly threatened. Just as the bond has never been really internalized, so the threat remains external. The individual may either accommodate externally to the brute force applied just as he has accommodated in the past to political authority, or he may discuss, quite passionately, the claims and threats against the political structure as so many market fluctuations impairing his investments. In both cases the threats are conceived as external, as not aimed at him at all. Thus, as in the Washington, DC, siege, the feelings of empathy towards the black Hanafis may appear to be much stronger than the feelings of identification with the policemen sent to rescue the victim himself from the hands of the kidnappers. In the instrumental view of political institutionalization the policeman does not figure as an extension of your own political will.

What I would like to describe as the immanent attitude to political obligation assumes that the political bond is not external to man but immanent in him in the same sense as being a son or a father is not a man's external attribute but an intrinsic part of his persona; it assumes that man is a *zoon politikon*, a *Gemeinwesen*, and that the political nexus is not an appendix to the personality but one of its fundamental components. Law — not a particular law, which may of course be unjust or tyrannical, but the legal obligation itself — is ingrained in the person; it is not a mere calculus of self-interest, since many laws cannot be legitimized at all in such terms. Political obligation and obedience to the law in a society in which the law is not a coercive imposition but draws its mediated legitimacy from representative institutions and a free flow of ideas in public, are then obedience to oneself, not to an external force. The readiness to pay taxes or risk one's life in war is thus an expression of this immanence of the political relationship, and Hegel viewed this as a criterion for the existence or non-existence of a commonwealth. For Marx, who discerned in contemporary societies only the power of the market, the lack of such immanent relationship similarly serves as a critical yardstick by which to measure existing societies and find them wanting. The immanent relationship is then transposed by Marx to the future, projected into socialist society, where the dichotomies of individualism *versus* collectivism will be overcome by the dialectical communal unity of society, transcending self-oriented individualism as well as external collectivities imposed upon such alienated individuals.

The distinction between the instrumental and the immanent modes of political obligation, between attitudes founded on civil society on the one hand and the commonwealth (*Gemeinwesen*) on the other, can also be expressed in another way: the point of departure of the instrumental view is grounded — since Locke — in concepts of *rights*; that of the immanent view is founded on *relationships*.

A view based on rights necessarily starts with the individual. Moreover, it assumes that an individual exists as such prior to the existence of his rights or his claims to them. A relational view, on the other hand, does not suppose that individuals exist as self-subsisting entities prior to their relationships to others. Individuals are, in this view, bundles of relationships, not possessors of rights, and the richness of an individual is not dependent on the multitude of rights which he can claim but upon the variety, scope and abundance of the relationships in which he is involved.

Further, rights necessarily have to be expressed in relation to objects, even if they are injunctions to individuals. In a system conceptually based on rights, relationships to other human beings tend to be mediated through relationships to objects and beclouded by such an intrusion of objects into the inter-subjective bond ('reified' in Marxian parlance). A system based on relationships has human beings at its core at both ends, and objects appear only as objects, not as a mediation determining the relationship itself. If one takes political obligation to be immanent to the person and not merely instrumental, it is very difficult to conceive of those ambivalent attitudes towards political violence which can easily be squared with instrumental views. Any attempt to disrupt the political order not through the rules of the game is immediately conceived by the citizen as aimed at himself and not just at an 'external' political authority which is measured by each individual according to his own calculation of enlightened self-interest. The structure of the polity itself is part of the political self, not an imposed externality.

As Hegel pointed out, the parallel with the family may be instructive: family obligations are not based on rights, but on the immanence of the relationship itself; a father may not have any rights *vis-à-vis* his children, but they have obligations towards him. Only when a family breaks up, as in the case of a divorce, do these obligations based on the relationship itself become transformed into legally enforceable rights, as members of the (now dissolving) family begin to relate to each other merely as members of civil society. A system of political legitimacy based on rights has difficulties in translating these rights into obligations. John Stuart Mill's theoretical problems in attempting to transcend the language of the Benthamite utilitarian calculus have not been wholly overcome by such modern writers as John Rawls. Nor is there ultimately a coherent and valid reason universally applicable within such a system to urge against minority groups that see themselves as victimized by the majority and entitled to react violently under such circumstances.

III

One recent ambiguity inherent in some liberal positions regarding violence can be found in Ted Honderich's collection of essays entitled *Political Violence* (Ithaca, NY, 1976). This is not a book by an advocate of revolutionary violence. Yet, starting from the traditional liberal assumptions about political obligation, it arrives, after considerations which always regard the political realm as instrumental, to such conclusions as 'the ends which are thought to be served by the rules of democracy are at least sometimes served by the breaking of the rules' (p. 108). On this view the law and the political institutions of liberal democracy are merely a procedural device, not of any intrinsic value to the human being as a political animal. The aims of human existence are presented as lying beyond the realm of the political, which is construed as a mere system of means. Honderich goes on to give a number of examples in which violence serves the same end as the democratic process, and since these examples are neither exhaustive nor clearly defined, what remains is a situation where it is left very much to the judgement of each individual — i.e. to the subjective understanding of each person and each group — when and where they are entitled to use what he calls 'democratic violence'.

'Democratic violence' is that kind of violence, according to Honderich, which 'serves the end of freedom, or equality, or both'. Freedom and equality are thus defined as goals *outside* the political system, reached *through* the political system, but basically external to it.

If one accepts the individual's prerogative of justifying to himself under what conditions violence is morally permissible in democratic society, one views obedience to the law and breaking of the law as on the same moral level, both being related to ends beyond the political realm itself. Consequently, one may also judge independently whether one thinks that violence carried out by another individual or group is justified or not. Obedience to the law, and the authority of legally instituted bodies, are thus open not to universally accepted procedures, but to individually decided opinions. Obedience is optional, just as investment in the stock exchange is optional. The criteria justifying political obligation cease to be objective and universal (or at least universalizable), but are left to subjective opinion, with no possibility of judging the ultimate legitimacy of an opinion in a case of clash of opinions or loyalties. Opinions, good intentions and the good — or bad — faith of each and every individual are all degraded to the same level. If decisions duly accepted by majorities under clearly defined conditions and procedures are not immune from the violence of those individuals or groups who feel themselves victimized by these decisions for some reason or other, then no criteria for legitimacy are left except a will totally free of any institutionalized yardstick. Abiding by the law or breaking it become indifferent actions, matters relegated to a relativized calculus whose criterion is the individual judgement of each person, each searching in the darkness according to his own light:

> I have said that it seems to me that at least some violence has a moral justification. . . . It will be clear, that I do not suppose that the proposition that some violence has a justification can be derived from the fact alone that it is in the given sense democratic. To think violence can be justified this way is as mistaken as taking as a justification of a policy the fact by itself that the policy issues from the democratic practice. *If some bombs are like votes, they also kill and maim.* The deprivation and degradation that call up violence should never be absent from thought and feeling, and not so present in them as to obscure the other terrible realities (Honderich, p. 116; my italics).

In the concrete context in which Honderich is writing, this may be a call for moderation. It reveals, however, the utter limbo in which such political thought ultimately finds itself. Everything is relativized, no visible criterion is offered, and while a formalistic adherence to majority rule obviously does not give one an overall answer to the question of political obligation, it does at least suggest some universal frame of reference. This frame of reference can then be related to other value systems that are part of the democratic credo: but this can be done only if obligation itself is considered, as the body politic itself, in immanent terms. Otherwise one is left with the gentle reminder that bombs 'also' kill and maim, and the distinction between the hijacker and the rescuer is hopelessly blurred.

Part Two

Law 'for' Society

6

'Transforming' the law, 'steering' society

Eugene Kamenka and Alice Erh-Soon Tay

I

In the first chapter of this volume, we presented our conception of *Gemeinschaft, Gesellschaft* and bureaucratic-administrative paradigms of legal ideologies and legal arrangements. We were anxious to warn that these paradigms were paradigms or ideal types. They did not represent *prima facie* descriptions of any actual society or legal system in all its details but were a shorthand for three sets of divergent trends, each of them historically more important at some periods of time and in some societies than at or in others. The material — the mixture of arrangements, presuppositions and beliefs — making up each paradigm was interconnected through relations of mutual reinforcement, common presuppositions, implications and attitudes, often logically related and capable of development into a coherent system. The 'elements' that go to make up each paradigm are at least logically, and on occasion empirically, separable. This is the point of the Parsonian analysis of the *Gemeinschaft-Gesellschaft* dichotomy into pattern variables. It has helped anthropologists and sociologists to show that not all the important characteristics of a *Gemeinschaft* go together in all societies or situations with the inevitability of logical implication. Similarly, much modern criticism of Weber's conception of bureaucracy emphasizes that in particular bureaucracies, and especially in more generally changed social and work conditions produced by the computer, factors he took to belong together as part of bureaucratic rationality may come apart.

Nevertheless, Tönnies's concepts and the concept of the bureaucratic-administrative are not simply collections of accidental unrelated factors artificially held together by a theorist imposing his own pattern on reality. In that sense they are not mental constructs. Their 'subjectivity', their connection with the theorist or observer, is only the subjectivity of all science: the selection, by description and naming, of some features, characteristics and relations out of the infinite number of characteristics and relations that we find in any given situation. It is not true that models or ideal types are anything but shorthand for a set of propositions and it is not true that such sets of propositions are only useful or useless, but not true or false. What is true is that words, as signifying real characteristics and relations, never-theless serve complex functions, convey more than one truth. In any partic-ular theory or theoretical construction, some of these truths will be impor-tant and others not and distinctions that can be neglected for one purpose or in one context become crucial for another. *Gemeinschaft* attitudes and arrangements, *Gesellschaft* attitudes and arrangements and bureaucratic-administrative attitudes and arrangements do represent real, though not pervasive, features in the historical development of sophisticated, complex societies. They are systems and ideologies by which men or at least some men have lived or pretended to live and for which they have fought and died. Much of modern history and especially the reactions to *laissez-faire* capital-ism and the liberal view of the world, as well as the internal changes in modern capitalism, cannot be understood without these categories. That in itself would be enough to make them important for thinking lawyers. But they are even more important because they help to bring out that legal arrangements, while far from coherent and certainly not breathing a single spirit in any complex society, carry with them ideological attitudes, a conception of society, of the nature and function of law and the proper relationship between individuals and whatever the sovereign claims to represent. Law is neither passive — a colourless instrument to be used as one wishes — nor value-free. The distinction between *Gemeinschaft, Gesellschaft* and bureau-cratic-administrative law is, among other things, an attempt to bring out the implicit clash of values and attitudes between three major traditions of legal and social theory and practice, which to some extent coexist in all societies.

Talk about social and legal traditions, and especially the treatment of law as serving a social function, as representing a social will or social needs and solving a social problem, is often taken as evidence that the speaker holds a solidarist view of society or minimally believes in consensus as opposed to conflict 'models' of social behaviour. Conflict and cooperation, we have often argued in a variety of contexts, are equally part of human behaviour and social life: there is both division and consensus. The Marxist tradition, which has performed an important service in emphasizing the extent of con-flict and class struggle in human history, has also performed an important disservice in simplifying and vulgarizing that conflict into a conflict of atomic elements within a total whole. There is not a society but an infinite set of societies in any given country or region at any given time, held in complex relations of cooperation and division with each other, sharing some presuppositions while conflicting bitterly on others, displaying internal as well as external tensions. Not only groups of persons but individual persons themselves are complex economies or societies of motives, feelings and attitudes, forming sub-systems within the single mind, standing in relation of conflict and cooperation that cannot be reduced to a fixed and finite pattern. One of the functions of the *Gemeinschaft, Gesellschaft* and bureau-cratic-administrative paradigms as we use them is to bring out the com-plexity of any given social tradition or province, the fact that it does not breathe a single spirit, serve a single function, elevate one purpose or presupposition. We have also striven to show that the paradigms or elements we have singled out are in turn themselves complex, internally and externally in their relations with the other paradigms. To attempt to resolve these difficult issues into a choice between conflict or consensus models of law or society seems to us crude and uninteresting.

In Western democratic societies, but not only there, the tension between *Gemeinschaft*, *Gesellschaft* and bureaucratic-administrative conceptions of law is today especially acute. This leads, among other things, to uncertainty and confusion about the role of law in society, about the definition of law or its specific characteristics and about the value and character of the Western legal traditions. The specific value of the *Gesellschaft* tradition, we have argued, lies in the fact that it has a much more developed and coherent conception of law as a specific institution, carrying its own ideology, linked through its emphasis on the rights and powers of the individual with a tradition of freedom and through its connection with commutative justice with the theory and practice of equality. Of course, law involves coercion, though — as Professor Honoré has argued[1] — it stands intermediate between violence and what one might call education. It functions like an arch, it applies pressure but distributes it and protects the individual against arbitrary and unpredictable pressure. That function at the formal and ideological level is served far better and more consistently by *Gesellschaft* law than by any of our other types. And it might well be argued that the current concern with equality, with social justice and freedom as concrete, pervasive and not purely formal concepts is an extension of *Gesellschaft* ideals that could not have gained the strength they have without the *Gesellschaft*. They will not long survive in a society in which *Gesellschaft* procedures, laws and freedoms have become weak or in which the language people use is no longer the carrier of *Gesellschaft* conceptions and ideals. For those values in the *Gesellschaft* are built into the conception of law itself; in our other paradigms, they stand outside it, as the alleged content and concern of custom, morality, politics or policies which change much more readily than a legal system.

The limitations of *Gesellschaft* law are well known and they rest primarily on its inbuilt abstraction, its achievement of generality and rule-bound decision by distinguishing what is legally relevant from what is not. Not only in modern society does an inflexible and unintelligent adherence to *Gesellschaft* principles at all costs lead to suffering or the refusal to alleviate it, inequality and injustice. That, after all, is how the English law of Equity arose and how countless bureaucratic-administrative arrangements came to be made. At the very heart of the more modern Western legal tradition stand two great legal systems — that of the Common Law and that of the Civil Law

[1]Tony Honoré, 'Societies, laws and the future' in A.E.-S. Tay and Eugene Kamenka (eds.), *Law-Making in Australia* (Melbourne, 1980), pp. 3–10, at pp. 3–4.

of continental Europe. The former, as we have often argued, is a *Gesellschaft* system with strong *Gemeinschaft* features built into it in a controlled systematic fashion — through open-ended concepts, morally-loaded concepts and such central legal terms as 'fairness', 'reasonable care' and the 'reasonable man'. The latter is a *Gesellschaft* system with very strong bureaucratic-administrative features reflected in the role of the procuracy, the investigative nature of the courts, the state-dependence of judges, the weakness of an independent legal profession and of its role in the judicial system, the view of law as primarily deduction from legislation and analysis into clear and simple concepts or 'rational' principles, the much greater elevation of the state interest and of the interests of a solidarist society. Some of the perceived limitations of *Gesellschaft* law in practice are examined by Professor MacDonagh below and are there shown to emerge at the very beginning of the heyday of liberalism and freedom of contract. Today, those limitations of *Gesellschaft* law, as we have argued, are especially evident and demands for their supplementation or replacement by *Gemeinschaft* and bureaucratic-administrative procedures are to be heard on all sides.

The factors creating and furthering these demands have been referred to at many points in this volume. On the *Gemeinschaft* side, the spread of education and egalitarianism as an ideology, the increasing public visibility of all sections of society furthered by the mass media, have led to the consistent attack on or discounting of social distance, distinction and specialization, of all those things that made the individual more than an abstract atom without features or content. Accessibility, direct responsiveness, participation are among the important demands of the day and their effect has been to strengthen at least some *Gemeinschaft* traditions and ways of doing things, in law as much as in other social institutions. The new trends, it is true, do reject the *Gemeinschaft* elevation of status, common ideology and tradition, at least in principle — though it has already become evident that the elevation of *Gemeinschaft* values, even in this amended form, leads quickly to an acceptance of moral indoctrination, social pressure and assaults on freedom of conscience that were quite unacceptable in the classical liberal *Gesellschaft* tradition. Instead of law, we want schools to inculcate 'social responsibility' and moral values. And we speak readily, as Stalin did, of using the young to educate the old. For the young are indeed more malleable.

The very unstructuredness of *Gemeinschaft* demands as they are today, when they are shorn of status and tradition, in practice furthers bureaucratic-administrative values and arrangements — for the necessary structure, the resources and control in a world of atomic individuals not shaped in and by coherent institutions can only be provided by the State. We demand that the State create the community, fund it, safeguard it, give it 'recognition'. But other factors have led and continue to lead even more directly to the constant extension of the bureaucratic-administrative. The bureaucratic-administrative systems of the past — in Egypt, China, Mesopotamia — arose under the impact of great populations and large-scale economic activity, creating administrative imperatives that are even stronger in mass societies today. Even in law, the problem of scale and numbers — the ever-increasing pressure of time on the courts — leads directly to the constant extension of administrative bureaucratic justice, whether through registrars and masters or through special administrative provisions. The ideology of 'social science' — the rationality which Max Weber and Joseph Schumpeter saw as the inevitable ground of the bureaucratization or socialization of capitalism from within — has indeed had an equally strong impact. Roscoe Pound, in his large and great *Jurisprudence* noted that sociological jurists seek to enable and to compel law making, whether legislative, judicial or administrative, and also the development, interpretation and application of legal precepts, to take more complete and intelligent account of the 'social facts upon which law must proceed and to which it is to be applied'.[2] They thus insist on study of the actual social effects of legal institutions, legal precepts and legal doctrines, on sociological and not merely comparative legal study in preparation for law-making, on study of the means of making legal precepts effective in action, on psychological study of the judicial, administrative, legislative and juristic processes and philosophical criticism of their ideals and on recognition of the importance of individualized application, of reasonable and just solution of individual cases. They emphasize the need for a sociological legal history and they elevate in Common Law countries the bureaucratic-administrative concept of a ministry of justice which will be more than a government or public legal adviser, but will oversee the working and planning of the whole legal order. The very titles of one recent series of volumes show both the direction of the ever-increasing interest in law as a form of social control, as something to be understood sociologically and seen administratively, and the contrast with other conceptions. They include *Negotiated Justice, The Social Control of Drugs, Decisions in the Penal Process, Law and State, Magistrates' Justice, Deviant Interpretations, Inequality and the Law, Pollution, Social Interest and the Law, Durkheim and The Law, The Politics of Abolition, Social Needs and Legal Action, The Search for Pure Food, Crime and Conflict, Knowledge and Opinion about Law, Deviance, Crime and Socio-Legal Control.*

All these trends are being made manifest in an ever-increasing body of legal reforms, change of judicial attitudes, restructuring of courts, creation of tribunals and enactment of legislative provisions. Our personal belief — still shared by many — in the importance and centrality of the *Gesellschaft* legal tradition does not imply a belief that it is suitable for all purposes, that it should be elevated rigidly and unthinkingly at all times without supplementation and amendment in the light of *Gemeinschaft* and bureaucratic-administrative realities and concerns or that the increase in knowledge given by macro- and microsociology of law is not in principle both practically and theoretically valuable.

[2] Roscoe Pound, *Jurisprudence*, 5 vols. (St Paul, Minn., 1959), vol. 1, p. 350.

Very recent years, indeed, have seen as something of a countervailing trend a marked revitalization of the *Gesellschaft* tradition through the elevation, municipally and internationally, of the language and propaganda of human rights. At the theoretical level no doubt, many of the Unesco discussion papers and declarations do or seek to weaken the concern with civil liberties by focusing attention on social and economic rights as somehow more fundamental or important. This creates an aura of justification surrounding curtailment or reinterpretation of the classical doctrine of human rights as rights above all maintained and maintainable against the state. It is welcomed by many communists and Third World countries for that reason. Nevertheless, in Western democratic societies especially, the extension of the doctrine of human rights to social or economic rights has had the effect of judicializing new social areas and new aspects of social life. It has brought or is bringing tribunals and agencies concerned with the allocation of what used to be seen as benefits or services more and more under *Gesellschaft* law by proclaiming such benefits or services to be rights. On the other hand, in both Western democratic and authoritarian and centralized societies, the concern with social and economic rights has for its main thrust the further elevation of the state as the provider, guarantor and protector of rights and the consequent constant extension of bureaucratic-administrative arrangements, values and attitudes.

II

Let us take some examples. The legal reforms that began with the plea in mitigation and ended with the concept of diminished responsibility seem to us far more sensible and just — even though they raise further and difficult problems — than the McNaghten Rules. But it is one thing to provide for exceptions to or mitigations of the *Gesellschaft* legal presumption that individuals are responsible adults; it is another to insist that all deviance is an illness to be cured, or all crime a social danger to be dealt with 'objectively' until it has been eliminated. Similarly, it is one thing — though a matter on which there can be argument — to make courts less overwhelming and judges less remote. It is another to convert courts into popular assemblies or to elevate palm-tree justice over a system of visible adherence to legal principles and procedures. In fact, we are moving in practice toward what is quite properly and openly a mixed system in which the centrality and presumption in favour of *Gesellschaft* law has not been abandoned in Western democratic societies. Communist though not all Third World societies at least pay lip-service to most of the central principles of *Gesellschaft* law. The problem of determining the optimal mix — not only externally, for different areas, but internally in the one area, e.g. family law — is not as simple as the proponents of change often assumed. In Australia, the emphasis in the Family Law Act 1975 on informality of procedure has already led one judge of that court, to the outrage of one of the parties appearing before him, to take the view that he was not conducting a judicial hearing but something 'more in the nature of an inquiry and an inquisition, followed by an arbitration'. The High Court of Australia had no hesitation in rejecting the learned judge's construction of the Act and conception of his function.[3] The complainant, of course, recognized perfectly well the extent to which such a mixture of *Gemeinschaft* and bureaucratic-administrative procedures as extolled by the judge of first instance put the parties totally in the hands of the court and failed to protect specific rights — in this case property rights — in what he would think of as the proper legal fashion. The point is not only taken by men of property — even much feminist agitation today, while wanting easy access to the courts, wants those courts to determine and vindicate rights rather than elevate harmony, accommodation and other *Gemeinschaft* virtues. Further, while there are obvious merits in restricting publication of family proceedings, the turning of family courts into closed courts has in fact had very bad effects on some aspects of the work of the court and the type of justice it dispenses in particular cases. The Australian Family Law Act, partly as a sop to anti-divorce sentiment, but with strong bureaucratic-administrative implications, provided that an Institute should be established that would conduct research into and monitor the operation of the Act and the new Family Court on the basis of the emerging statistics. The Institute has now been established and a director just appointed. In a system wedded to the centrality of *Gesellschaft* law, the findings and recommendations of such an Institute would influence the court only indirectly, being addressed to politicians and legal reformers, though they might well have more direct effect on the staff of social workers, marriage counsellors etc., that the Australian Act associates with the work of the Court. In a fully bureaucratic-administrative system, matters would be different, as they were in the Soviet Union where the number of divorces granted, the time taken to fix dates for hearing and even the capacity of the parties to lodge the required newspaper advertisement of intention to divorce were directly determined, until recently, by government policy. It is striking indeed that at the same time as there is much enthusiasm for *Gemeinschaft* and bureaucratic-administrative conceptions, there is constant extension, as we have said, of the demand that courts and legislatures protect specific individual rights — to employment, to absence of discrimination, women's rights, children's rights, employees' rights, the rights of minorities and of recipients of State benefits. Only 50 years ago, the informal and closed character of Children's Courts was widely hailed as progressive. Today more and more studies show that juveniles before such courts regard the procedure as demeaning, discriminatory, as an unacceptable form of parental law, and prefer to be dealt with as though they were adults. It is out of such sentiments, of course, that *Gesellschaft* ideology was born. But now there are new concerns and in each of the chapters that follows in this second

---

[3] *R. v. Watson, ex parte Armstrong*, (1976) 9 A.L.R. 551.

part of our volume, the contributor takes up not the problems of individuals but the problem of administering an area, a social province, or of remedying by a combination of legislative and administrative action a particular social ill.

The bodies established in recent years to hear complaints of unfair dismissal or of racial and other discrimination may have been established, as courts originally were, by legislative-administrative action and they may have been denied the title and status of courts. Nevertheless, in the English-speaking world, these panels, commissions, tribunals, dealing with complaints that an individual has been dealt with unjustly, are not simply or always bureaucratic-administrative bodies: they do consciously apply and seek to apply principles of *Gesellschaft* law oriented toward protecting the rights of the individual before them. They are in this sense quite different from the commissions or tribunals which regulate an activity, license those who wish to take part in it, lay down rules designed to protect the public at large, or to further the welfare of the industry. Of course, Common lawyers as *Gesellschaft* lawyers can and do also, in the process of determining an individual case, take such matters into account but they do so in a subsidiary way, as part of the determination of rights and the requirements of justice, not as the *raison-d'être* of their own being and as a superior concern to which the interests of the parties are in principle and *ab initio* subordinate.

The fact that the *Gemeinschaft, Gesellschaft* and bureaucratic-administrative paradigms are not classificatory boxes or Procrustean beds into which any particular legal body can be thrust should be sufficiently indicated by the extent to which many of our panels, commissions and tribunals today are mixed bodies, in which *Gemeinschaft, Gesellschaft* and bureaucratic-administrative procedures and aims stand in often deliberately incorporated tension. This, too, has always been so. Much state action — such as the Poor Laws over a number of centuries — serves a variety of purposes, giving rise to quite fundamental tensions of aims reflected in resultant conflict of values and procedures. This is true in many quasi-judicial bodies today and the principal value of the paradigms we suggest lies, in these areas, in helping to reveal the ground and nature of the tensions and the likely results of each distinct strain if it gains supremacy.

On the other hand, as we have also warned in our opening chapter, the *Gemeinschaft, Gesellschaft* and bureaucratic-administrative analysis is not useful for all purposes. Many lawyers and political theorists are extremely conscious of the strength of the judicial model — of one aspect of *Gesellschaft* court procedure — in public and political life in the Common Law world, with its royal commissions, its public hearings, its readiness to use lawyers and the court style for gathering and assessing evidence. The result is that many bodies that are purely bureaucratic-administrative in terms of their function — such as tariff boards, electoral boundaries commissions and even parliamentary committees of inquiry — operate in quasi-judicial ways in gathering, hearing and assessing evidence.[4] It is often argued, indeed, that this way of doing things in these areas is not the best; that such bodies would do better work if staffed by economists, demographers *etc.* doing research in an organized way rather than 'hearing' divergent views from interested 'parties'. But it should be noted that the introduction of one aspect of *Gesellschaft* legal procedure does carry with it others — a concern with individual or particular interests, with balancing the claims of people, with paying attention to individuals as people, which is not built into the ideology of research and development or the very structure of the bureaucratic file and the computer.

III

The outstanding thing in the practice of Western democratic societies, then, is the mix of current approaches, the extent of the tensions that arise in the course of such mixing, the fickleness of fashions and ideological demands and the complexity and frequent unpredictability of the results — the constant production of unintended effects, new dissatisfactions, unexpected inequities. There is no doubt, however, that in law even more than in many other areas, bureaucratic-administrative arrangements are growing stronger and stronger. The simple reason for this, of course, is that the state is doing more and more. It is expected to do more and more — despite a libertarian backlash in recent years — by more and more people in society. They belong to all classes and walks of life, but especially prominent among them, perhaps, are those who in particular practice or in general principle seek to turn the state into the agent of the redistribution of wealth and who see law as an instrument to that end. The state does this more and more directly, and it is increasingly expected to act in the light of 'social science' — that is, systematically collected and evaluated knowledge of social conditions, social demands and social effects including the complex calculation of consequences and prognostication of future trends. Much of this bureaucratic-administrative trend is carried forward by sensible proposals for information gathering, attempts to 'rationalize' the work of the courts, especially of the lower courts, the revision and systematization of legislation along 'rational' lines that would take account of change and also of the present needs and likely future development of whole areas of social activity, bringing them in line with social or government policy and with what are seen as objective requirements, desirable policies and social realities. It is in the process of seeking to generalize such proposals that there is a temptation to go far beyond proposals linked with particular problems and particular areas. Many now seek or promote a general redefinition of law and legislative activity meant to exclude or drastically weaken the concern with

---

[4]See Colin A. Hughes, 'Government action and the judicial model' in Tay and Kamenka (eds.), *Law-Making in Australia, op.cit.*, pp. 263–89.

individual responsibility and the vindication of individual rights — now often regarded as involving unfair accountability and power over others and as a barrier to progress. There is the insistence, explicit or implicit, that law is not for the individual but for society, that it is a form of social control, a means — as the 'socialist' states now frankly put it — of steering society, and that individuals are themselves blameless social 'progressive' products.

The tradition in English-speaking countries, at least, is still fundamentally Benthamite. If it does not share Bentham's concern to protect property it does agree with him in seeing rights as conferred by society and having no independent claim against it. It uses the concept of utility — now welfare — as the frank or unstated basis of a science of legislation that merges all specialized traditions, institutions and concerns into a general administrative machinery. That is indeed still the main trend in our own societies, though Benthamite individualism and Benthamite empiricism result in a continued, if decreasing, respect for people's actual, empirical attitudes, wants and desires. But where the utilitarian calculus was fundamentally static — based on existing and individual desires, treated with respect — the conception of law as steering society is fundamentally dynamic, geared to major social change and to depreciating existing institutions, values and demands as not being 'suitable to the future' or representing the 'real' interests and potentialities of man. The formulation of goals and policies, the resolution of disputes, the handing down of decisions, come to be seen as a political, moral or administrative matter, rather than as a legal one and the concreteness of formal legal or commutative justice comes easily to be left out of account. It is striking that the central legal concept in the communist states is not that of justice but of socialist legality — i.e. strict adherence to the rules laid down by the state. While there is lip-service, as we have said, to the principles and procedures of *Gesellschaft* law these are made subordinate to a pervasive bureaucratic-administrative structure and ideology and are themselves interpreted in a bureaucratic-administrative manner. The protection of rights, the new Soviet and Chinese state constitutions proclaim, is dependent upon the citizen's exercise of his duties and his support for the socialist system and on the rights themselves not being used for 'anti-social' purposes. The hopes created by Khrushchev's alternate toying with, or limited licensing of, *Gemeinschaft* and *Gesellschaft* demands on the Soviet legal system have disappeared with the patent elevation of bureaucratic-administrative values by his successors. That elevation has created, no doubt, an increased legal professionalism in the Soviet Union and a sophisticated recognition of socialist societies' need for complex and detailed laws. But the laws are seen as a system of regulation for steering society. It is not unimportant that even in a country like Poland, with a much richer legal tradition than the Soviet Union, the teaching of Roman Law as Roman Law has now been abandoned. It is now taught — most implausibly — as part of the law of slave-owning societies, as of purely historical interest. (Our own earlier abandonment of Roman law, less vulgarly justified, still carried some of these social implications, making the modern law school, in its unintelligent professionalism, an easy target for facile radicalism.) In the area of social and legal philosophy, of course, official communist theorists are still totally debarred from recognizing fundamental conflicts or irreconcilable tensions in socialist societies, or from criticizing such concepts as 'the will of the people' or 'the needs of society' in the way they are encouraged to criticize 'bourgeois' consensus theory or Duguit's solidarism.

The movement toward more and more bureaucratic-administrative interpretations of law in the Western world is less authoritarian and more complex, having to cope with the inconsistent and contradictory demands of a pluralistic society and a pluralistic culture. Certain widespread sentiments in the West — demands for participation, accessibility of courts and the constant elevation of new demands into 'rights' — in fact militate against straight and simple bureaucratic-administrative solutions. But perhaps one of the main carriers of bureaucratic-administrative values and incentives towards new bureaucratic-administrative arrangements is the concept of social cost. The economic analysis of law, centred on the University of Chicago Law School and closely linked with the Chicago School in economics, is seen by many of its critics as profoundly individualist, putting law in the service of economic man. But its central message is that law is a form of social control, a way of achieving social effects rather than proclaiming a morality and that the achieving of social effects should be subjected to cost-benefit analysis. Social insurance may simply be cheaper than a system of litigation to determine fault; frustration in contract should be looked at in terms of business assumption of risk; the task of law is simply to spread loss in the most acceptable way or to create economic disincentives in the pursuit of market rationality. Law, in short, is a form of economic management, allegedly superior in this refurbished form to the traditional principles just as aversion therapy is allegedly superior to sermonizing or costly forms of imprisonment.

Strident demands for quick, pervasive or fundamental change are normally enemies of the recognition of complexity. Revolutions have simple programmes; the complicated codes and structures come only *after* the revolutionaries have assumed control. One of the main results of popularization, democratization and the growing importance of the media as vehicle of popular emotions has been the transfering of much discussion of great but complex social questions from professional circles to mass-oriented institutions, politics, the media, the street. The transfer has brought to light underground histories, sentiments and demands, made visible inequities not noticed by those who were previously heard. But it has also produced a mass of self-seeking exhibitionism, intellectual dishonesty and emotional nonsense. These threaten, in varying degrees, the very rationality of decision-making and discussion, and many of the valuable ideals and legacies in important though necessarily limited social institutions. Paradoxically, they make the bureaucratic and time-serving theorists of the Soviet legal system sound as though they had a better appreciation of the strength and importance of legal traditions, of the complexity of social arrangement and administration and of the value of predictable rule-bound behaviour and the stable life and expectations it makes possible. But they, of course, have known the opposite.

7

Pre-transformations: Victorian Britain*

Oliver MacDonagh

A historian talking law at a lawyers' conference is of course a child. But it was a child who asked about the emperor's clothes. Not that I suggest that you are not, in every sense, metaphorical and otherwise, richly caparisoned. But it is possible that other eyes may notice rents and shreds, unperceived from high, which nonetheless need attention. In plain words, because his angle of vision, interests and patterns of thought are different, the historian may be able to question usefully assumptions made so naturally by lawyers as to be passed about by them unscrutinized. For the historian's coinage is time; his grammar change; his absorption the interplay of intention and circumstance. John Plamenatz explains this last well:

> Because it is true that society is nothing except men and their habits and laws . . . it does not follow that men make societies. For to make is to contrive for a purpose, and implies a conscious end and a knowledge of means. It is only because we use words that suggest purposes to describe nearly all the consequences of human activities that it comes natural to us to describe social and political institutions as if they were made by men. . . . Men are always trying to adapt their institutions to their desires, and to some extent they succeed. But all this makes it no less true that these institutions are not the realizations of human purposes, and that they affect these purposes just as much (and perhaps much more) than they are affected by them.

The historian's training and cast of mind, then, incline him against using 'transformation' in too purposive or deliberate a sense.

The present paper employs, not this word, but the convenient if unpleasant neologism, 'pre-transformations'. The purpose of the change of terminology is to indicate, firstly, that the phenomenon which we are discussing has precedents; secondly, that it is a multiple and complex rather than a single and simple concept; thirdly, that the process which it describes

---

*Originally presented to the Canberra Seminar 'A Revolution in Our Age: The Transformation of Law, Justice and Morals' in August, 1975, this paper was written to be read aloud, and has been left in its original form.
[1]J. Plamenatz, *The English Utilitarians* second edition, (Oxford, 1958), p. 151.

may be confused and contradictory, without clear beginning, trend or culmination, the agitation of a tideless sea; and finally that we are to some extent the prisoners of our nineteenth century inheritance — or at least still wandering in the same maze. Perhaps this is overloading even a compound neologism. At any rate, these are the general considerations which I wish to place before you.

R.C.K. Ensor once observed that Victorian Britain was unique amongst modern, industrialized societies in being a 'people of a book':[2] he meant, of course, the Bible. By extension, it was unusual if not unique in being a people of the Law. The two were of course related. In particular, the Old Testament must have engendered, or at least reinforced, the feelings of awe and numinosity with which the early Victorian public approached their own rabbinical system. But there was much more to all this than reverent passivity before the inscrutable decree and its arcane priesthood. Early Victorian society was also drawn towards law because of its histrionic and spectacular elements, and because of the widespread sense, especially before 1848, that the social floor separating order and chaos was both thin and insecure. In a period without mass-circulation newspapers or organized field sports, law provided a significant form of entertainment and vicarious contest. It was a staple of literature, discourse and argument to a degree incomprehensible to the present century. This awful eminence and this general currency of law render the variety of meanings which we can attach to the concept of legal and juridical transformation in the middle quarters of the nineteenth century all the more arresting.

In the first place, there are the obvious organizational and conceptual transformations (or transformations *manqués*) which lie scattered about the surface for us to pick up at will. The legal reforms of 1825 – 75, rightly associated more with Brougham than any other single individual, changed in sum the English judicial structure quite significantly. Apart from specific innovations such as the bankruptcy court or the Judicial Committee of the Privy Council, the county court system both rearranged and minutely subdivided the legal map of England and reordered the idea of gradation in offences. Moreover, because the new county court districts of 1846 were made to coincide exactly with the new poor law unions of 1834, the Justices of the Peace, the traditional dispensers of law and obligations in the localities, suffered a double reduction in standing — a profound social and economic as well as legal change. Similarly, the contemporary measures to substitute salaries for fees for various classes of legal officers had implications well beyond the mechanics of the legal system. Behind such operational changes lay changes in general attitudes and assumptions. Utility, efficiency, economy and quantitative evaluation were all challenging the prescriptive, reverential and hereditary views of law and its institutions. This

---

[2] R. C. K. Ensor, *England 1870–1914* (Oxford, 1936), p. 137.

was one great line of battle, one apparent thrust towards transformation.

But if the angle of vision is changed, the whole matter may be inverted — or more exactly perhaps, we can see the obverse side of this coin. If opinion — 'progressive' opinion — was attempting to make or remake law, the opposite process was simultaneously at work. For, as Dicey once wisely observed, 'Laws foster or create law-making opinion'.[3] An obvious and critically important example within the period is Sir Henry Maine's re-casting of earlier legal development as a progression from status to contract, and his use of such a measure to gauge advance or progress in particular societies. Maine was summarizing in a phrase, and giving a local habitation and a name, to something which his generation of Englishmen sensed cloudily and inarticulately about their immediate past.[4] In particular, he gave meaning and definition to their impression of the trend of statute law and appellate decisions over the previous two centuries and a half. Maine's concept was based upon lines of cases stretching back well into the seventeenth century, which, under the pressure of rising commercialism, had grounded themselves on the essentially contractual and atomistic nature of civil society. It was also built upon mounds of Georgian Enclosure Acts (so many spearheads of capitalistic farming); upon the chain of land legislation designed to render ownership an absolute condition and landlord-tenant relationship fully contractual; and upon the repeal of the Laws of Settlement and the latter-day Statutes of Artificers, the amendment of master and servant legislation and the modification of the Combination Acts — all of them tending towards the establishment of unfettered bargaining between capital and labour. The jurist, looking back, seemed to see one grand tendency in law, a majestic movement bearing all before it in field after field as it progressed to higher social forms; and its epitome was contract. Had this conference been a mid-Victorian one, were it that Birmingham conference of 1862 on the contemporary transformation of law imagined by Trollope in *Orley Farm*, at which the great German jurist, von Bauhr, and the great ornament of the English judiciary, Staveley, read papers and the great English silks of the day, the Furnivals and the Chaffanbrasses, were bored to tears — had the present conference been then and there, the advance of contract, utility and the rule of law would doubtless have been the British theme.

Now, how do these contemporary impressions of what was happening

---

[3]A. V. Dicey, *Law and Public Opinion in England During the Nineteenth Century*, second edition (London, 1914), p. 41.

[4]It is interesting to note, however, that although his adoption of the 'historical method' led Maine to (in Butterfield's phrase) 'a whig interpretation' of the development of social organization, it did not lead him to a similar interpretation of the development of political organization. As Barker noted, 'History does not furnish Maine, as it furnished Acton, with any guiding thread of growing freedom; and the process towards contract does not appear in the issue to be a process towards liberty', E. Barker, *Political Thought in England 1848 to 1914*, second edition (London, 1928), p. 167.

match what was actually taking place? Professors Kamenka and Tay informed me when issuing their invitation that they would like papers to begin with the general and move on to particularity: and I shall be obedient. The main body of the paper will be concerned with measuring the mid-Victorian concept of legal transformation — the burgeoning of contract and of simplification and certitude in procedure — against three actual cases of nineteenth century change. The first of these cases, the ocean passage contract, is obscure; the second, the Irish landlord-tenant relationship, is moderately well known; the third, the employer-employee relationship, will be very familiar. Together they will, I hope, indicate clearly both the very limited degree to which contemporaries comprehended and evaluated correctly what was happening about them, and the degree to which the mid-Victorian issues were the same as those with which we are concerned today.

From 1803 onwards, every passenger upon a trans-Atlantic vessel sailing from the United Kingdom was guaranteed by law certain quantities of food, water and medicine, and certain superficial and other areas of space on deck and in the sleeping quarters.[5] There were additional requirements which need not concern us now; nor need the motives behind this first piece of protective legislation in the field. We should note, however, that even at the time of its passage, it was objected that this represented an unwarranted curtailment of the rights of the respective parties, the passenger and the ship's master or broker, to contract with one another for the ocean journey. After the end of the Napoleonic wars, with high unemployment and seeming overpopulation now the spectres, a gale of agitation against the restrictive statute suddenly sprang up; and over the next decade amending acts gradually reduced the ship-master's obligations. By the mid-1820s the protest of British shipowners that their trade was being handed over to the Americans and would soon halt all emigration to the British colonies was being accompanied by campaigns in the *Edinburgh Review*[6] and other journals for the removal of all restraints upon free contract.

The upshot was a select committee of 1826:[7] which eventually recommended the total repeal of all passenger legislation, partly to cheapen and enlarge emigration, and partly on an *a priori* condemnation of restraints on trade. The recommendation was adopted by both houses of parliament early in 1827, and the Atlantic passage was completely 'unfettered' (to use the word of one of the enthusiasts of the committee) for the remainder of the year. Reports of unprecedented miseries at sea, including actual starvation, soon crowded in; and, in particular, the 'free contract' was reviled. As one Emigrant Society reported, 'many of the poor emigrants were deluded from their homes by the false but specious statements of brokers and ship-masters

[5] O. MacDonagh, *A pattern of Government Growth 1800–60: the Passenger Acts and their enforcement* (London, 1961), pp. 58–9.

[6] *Edinburgh Review*, vol. xxxix, pp. 315–46.

[7] *Report of Select Committee on Emigration, 1826*, H. C. 1826 (404), iv.

. . . as the passage money is paid in advance, it is of little consequence to them in a pecuniary point of view whether the helpless victims of their cupidity perish on the voyage . . . .'[8]

In consequence, restrictive legislation was re-imposed in the next session; and in the course of its passage, the principle of curtailing contractual 'rights' was debated for the first (and indeed also for the last) time. The radical individualists and free traders, led by Hume, Poullett Thomson and Warburton, argued that 'every arrangement by legislation' was injurious, and that the comparisons frequently made with the slave trade were misleading because the passengers were free agents in contracting, whereas the slaves were compelled to undertake the voyage. None of the Bill's supporters challenged the general assumptions of its assailants. Instead, they urged that only the 'barest minimum' of regulation was being attempted, and that the case, being quite exceptional, in no way invalidated the general rule. But, Huskisson said, when passengers starved to death, when their water was foul, when a naval officer of vast experience in the preventive service proclaimed their vessels worse than the vilest slavers he had ever seen, it must be the state's duty 'to put an end to these enormities . . . even in the teeth of science and philosophy'. E.G. Stanley (later to be three times prime minister) argued that a trade in the hands of greedy and unscrupulous adventurers constituted a special case; that whereas one of the parties was permanently employed in the business the other, totally inexperienced, was engaged in it but once; and that if regulations were required for even stage coach passengers, how much more imperative was it to guard unlettered emigrants? Wilmot Horton observed that members should be ashamed to raise a cry of 'free trade' when it was a matter of ensuring enough food and water for life to those necessarily ignorant of what was required.[9]

Now the critical argument appears to have been that, the consequences of their application being demonstrably 'intolerable', the principles of free contract and free trade would have to give ground in this particular instance. Time was to show that the doctrinaires' fears that principle would be swiftly eaten into by 'exceptions' and 'peculiar cases' were amply justified. But it is also true that their concepts were empty abstractions, even in the 1820s. Only if they were quite blind to ordinary life about them could they have believed that society existed, or ever might exist, upon the basis of private contractual relationships, or that such relationships were necessarily free in anything beyond the most formal sense. There were a hundred 'contractual' activities in contemporary society in which the assumption that the parties were equal or nearly equal in knowledge and bargaining power was absurd. The 1828 Act[10] and its advocates were groping towards the counter-notion

---

[8]H. I. Cowan, *British Emigration to British North America, 1783–1837* (Toronto, 1928), pp. 207–8.
[9]*Hansard*, 2nd, xviii, pp. 962–6, 1208–20.
[10]9 Geo. IV, c. 21.

that passengers should be protected persons, and the 'liberty' of contract correspondingly reduced.

Over the next fourteen years pressure mounted to modify the passage contract further. Primarily, this was because an executive corps to enforce the protective legislation had meanwhile been appointed; and they had discovered, in a litter of failed prosecutions, the unenforceability of almost all such contracts against masters and brokers. The colonial under-secretary, James Stephen, who had practised long and successfully at the bar, took this philosophically: 'These Irishmen are not the first, nor will they be the last, to make the discovery that a man may starve and yet have the best right of action a special pleader could wish for.'[11] But the executive corps, all half-pay naval officers, simply insisted that the abuses were 'intolerable'. An amending act of 1835 proved insufficient; but another, seven years later, produced really radical change.[12] Firstly, it laid down that every passage contract involved the supply by the ship of certain minutely prescribed quantities and qualities of food, water and other necessities; the passenger was no longer allowed to opt out of being furnished with provisions by the vessels. Secondly, passengers had henceforth to be supplied (or appropriately compensated) from the appointed sailing date, no matter what the wind or weather and no matter what bargain to the contrary might have been made: once more the passenger could no longer opt out of the arrangement. Thirdly, because contracts had 'commonly not been fixed with sufficient exactness to meet the objects of the law or to be a matter of legal evidence', a prescribed printed and written form of contract (set out in the act) was made obligatory for all agreements concerning passages. This form attempted to cover all the numerous areas in which dispute might occur. Finally, to meet the problem caused by Liverpool principals or principals in other major embarkation ports repudiating the contracts entered by their country agents — this almost invariably happened when an action was threatened — all passenger brokers and agents had to be licensed annually, and their licences might be withdrawn at any time for proved misconduct. This clause, like that concerning the prescribed contractual form, involved several technical legal difficulties, and was carefully and laboriously framed.[13]

On this occasion, 'principle' did not raise its voice in opposition. In fact, the former Poullett Thomson, now Lord Sydenham, who had in 1828 insisted on the absolute liberty of passengers to make what contracts they saw fit, was a leading advocate of the new measure. The only resistance came from the self-interested shippers. Yet freedom of contract was being absolutely abandoned. No contract was valid except in the specified form; in fact, it was now an offence to attempt to make an agreement concerning an

---

[11]C. O. 384/35, 27 September, 1834, Stephen's endorsement.
[12]This was 5 & 6 Vic., c. 107.
[13]For further discussion of the 1842 passenger act and its implications, see MacDonagh, *op. cit.*, pp. 144–61.

ocean passage otherwise; and in two areas at least the parties were specifically incapacitated from varying the contract terms. Moreover, the critical
matter of agency bulked large, not merely in the 1842 Act, but also in the
immediate efforts to enforce it. To take but one instance, the emigration
commissioners fought a case against a Glasgow shipping broker, who had
acted as a sub-agent without written authority, at heavy expense and over a
period of two years right up to the Scottish Court of Sessions.[14] In brief,
ocean passengers had become a special category of protected persons. It is
interesting to note that in the same year, 1842, another body of adults in
another field, women engaged underground in the coal mining industry,
were similarly 'deprived' of many of their 'rights' to enter labour contracts
— and on essentially the same practical-humanitarian line of reasoning.

I shall pass over the succession of amending statutes which over the next
thirteen years modified more and more nicely the passage contract, and
ground again at the Consolidation Act of 1855,[15] passed six years before the
publication of Maine's *Ancient Law*. This act marked the climax of the process whereby 'free contract' had lost ground steadily since 1828, and (in one
sense of the word at least) status was elevated. Let me give three from
amongst several examples of the change as manifested in 1855. Firstly, in
the case of shipwrecked passengers resuming their journey, brokers had
hitherto been liable only to the extent of the fare stipulated in the original
contract; and as late as 1853 the emigration commissioners had said that this
was only equitable because brokers could neither control the further expense
nor insure against it, as 'an unlimited risk'.[16] Now, however, in the light of
proven passenger needs, the liability was increased to double the contract
fare, while the liability for daily sustenance money was increased to treble
the amount contracted for. Secondly, brokers might employ agents only if
they were authorized to act as such by a positive recommendation of the local
chief constable or emigration officer. Thirdly, as to procedure, all monies
involved in passage contracts were recoverable before two Justices of the
Peace; two JPs might try a case in the absence of the defendant if a summons
were not answered; one JP might issue a warrant without any preliminary
summons, if he believed that the party concerned were likely to abscond. If
the monies or costs were not immediately forthcoming, two JPs might
directly commit the defendant to gaol for three months; no objection was to
be allowed or conviction quashed 'for Want of Form'; and no action might
be taken against an emigration officer without ten days' clear notice, or after
three months had elapsed, and in any such action the officer might 'plead
General Issue and give the act and any Special Matter in evidence'. More-

---

[14]*Fifth General Report of Colonial Land and Emigration Commissioners*, 13 (617), H. C. 1845,
xxvii.

[15]18 & 19 Vic., c. 119.

[16]*Fourteenth General Report of Colonial Land Emigration Commissioners*, 33 (1833), 1854,
H. C. xxviii.

over, the number of prescribed schedules was increased to twelve, and included forms of summons, conviction and order of adjudication for the benefit of JPs, although, as has been indicated above, the JP's decision would not fail if he did not use, or used incorrectly, such a form.[17]

Let us now look more rapidly at the other cases. The Act of Union between Great Britain and Ireland in 1801 at first subjected Irish land — and all other Irish affairs — directly to a parliament where English (I do not even say, British) concepts and presuppositions predominated. For the first forty years of the nineteenth century, educated English opinion generally assumed that ownership should be untrammelled legally by social obligations or other objects. The good landlord would instinctively shoulder some responsibility for those in his territorial sphere. But defining this responsibility in statute and making it enforceable in law were no more to be thought of than, say, compelling business corporations to set up educational foundations would be today. The philosophy that ownership was, in law, an absolute condition did in fact issue in a stream of Irish land legislation between 1801 and 1840. But these acts — the Sub-letting Act of 1823[18] is a prime example — were designed to secure the landlord's position by cheapening and facilitating ejectments, evictions and the consolidation of holdings, and by attempting to render these courses physically safer through stamping out peasant counteraction.

In the 1840s, partly because of the endemic agrarian conflict in the Irish countryside, the emphasis gradually changed. Increasingly, the failure of Irish landlordism was attributed to the absence of a system of fully and genuinely contractual relationships in the Irish agricultural economy. The Devon Commission's report of 1845 was the first official acknowledgement that the problem of Irish land was a peasant's as well as a proprietor's problem; and during the great famine of 1845 – 49 Irish landlordism became discredited among the British public who believed that they were being saddled with relief expense which the proprietors should have borne. In consequence, legislation in 1847 – 49 attempted to redress the supposed injustice and to facilitate the transference of Irish land from financially embarrassed Irish landlords to more solvent owners. The Encumbered Estates Act of 1848,[19] which embodied this last objective, has been aptly described by Professor W. L. Burn as an attempt to establish free trade in Irish land.[20] Like all other Irish land legislation between 1845 and 1865, the Act was 'reformist' in the sense that it aimed at making landlord-tenant relationships wholly a matter of 'free contract' (as against status and custom); at

[17]For a further discussion of the Passenger Act of 1855, see MacDonagh, *op. cit.*, pp. 290 – 303. See also O. MacDonagh, 'Delegated legislation and administrative discretions in the 1850's: a particular study', (1958 – 9) Vol. ii, No. 1, *Victorian Studies*, pp. 29 – 44.

[18]4 Geo. IV, c. 36.

[19]11 & 12 Vic., c. 48.

[20]W. L. Burn 'Free trade in land: an aspect of the Irish question', *Trans. Royal Historical Society*, 4th series, xxxi, p. 68.

eliminating entail and primogeniture and similar clogs upon the purchase and sale of land; and at enabling open competition and the unfettered pressure of supply and demand to establish the level of rents and the terms of tenancy agreements. The basic principle was clearly expressed in clause 3 of Deasy's Act of 1860:[21] 'The Relation of Landlord and Tenant shall be deemed to be founded on the express or implied Contract of the Parties, and not upon Tenure or Service'; and this Act, together with Cardwell's Act of the same year,[22] proceeded to set out the covenants implied, unless specifically repudiated, in such contracts and to establish mechanisms for determining the contractual obligations of the parties, when in dispute.

For a whole generation, however, all Irish writers of significance upon the question had abandoned the traditional concepts of proprietorial right and contract as hopelessly inappropriate to the Irish situation and argued within a new framework of dual interest and co-ownership;[23] and on 16 March 1868 this radical reappraisal reached the foreground of British politics in the famous clash between Robert Lowe and J. S. Mill on an Irish land bill, with Mill announcing his conversion with, 'I am sure that no one is at all capable of determining what is the right political economy for any country until he knows its circumstances'.[24] This was the overture for Gladstone's first Irish Land Act, that of 1870.[25] In legislative, as distinct from intellectual, terms, the turning point had been reached. Perhaps we should say the half-turning point. The measure was presented as quite orthodox — that is, as fully respecting proprietorial and contractual rights — and that it was accepted as such is testified to by the lack of serious opposition in either house. Its leading principles, as lengthily elaborated and 'elucidated' by Gladstone, seemed comparatively innocuous. They were, to render statutory the 'Ulster custom' (the outgoing tenant's right to sell his 'interest') where that usage existed; elsewhere, to compensate the tenant for disturbance according to a fixed scale of damages, unless the cause of disturbance was non-payment of rent; and to compensate the tenant for improvements in the property even if the cause of eviction was non-payment of rent. The complacency with which this was received was not immediately disturbed because the Act was practically inoperative; and, if further comfort were needed, it might be said that it gave the tenants little which they really wanted, and perhaps still less of what they really needed.

Nonetheless, the half-turning had been made. The right to compensation for improvements made even in opposition to the landlord's wishes, the limitation upon his powers to evict, and the statutory recognition that a tenant might own a saleable interest in the proprietor's land, all denied the

[21] 23 & 24 Vic., c. 154. 'An Act to consolidate and amend the Law of Landlord and Tenant in Ireland'.

[22] 23 & 24 Vic., c. 153. 'The Landed Property Improvement (Ireland) Act, 1860'.

[23] O. MacDonagh, *Ireland* (Englewood Cliffs, 1968), pp. 35 – 8.

[24] *Hansard*, 3rd, cxc, 1525 – 6.

[25] 33 & 34 Vic., c. 46.

landlord unbridled control over his own property. The corollary, of course, was that this property was no longer wholly 'private'. The tenant now possessed legal rights, calculable in money terms, in the same soil; and whatever his contract said, the landlord could not deal with it freely as he wished.

This dialectical though empty triumph of 1870 was translated into substantial achievement for the tenants under the pressure of the agricultural distress of 1877 – 82 when farm prices and incomes fell catastrophically, and the levels of evictions and tenant counter-militancy rose to new heights. The familiar Irish pattern of coercion-cum-concession was to be repeated over and over again. The most critical concession was Gladstone's second Land Act, passed in 1881.[26] This met the original — though not the current — tenant demand. It provided security of tenure, no matter what the nature of the original agreement; it empowered the tenant freely to sell whatever interests he might have acquired in the property; and 'fair rents' were to replace the current rentals. Special land courts were to determine 'fairness' in this matter. The land act of 1881 was thus an undisguised acceptance of co-ownership. 'Free contract' was wholly abandoned, largely to be replaced by status. The state was to be permanently involved in the conflict between the wrangling partners through the institution of the land courts, enjoined to fix 'judicial rents'.

As we should expect, co-ownership proved to be an unstable condition. For example, what was to be the response to the massive accumulated arrears of rent under the new circumstances? The answer (as again perhaps we should expect, though it came as a thunderbolt to Victorians) was that the state should meet the bill. The Arrears Act of 1882[27] cleared tens of thousands of holdings of debt by paying £2m.[28] of public monies to the landlords. Moreover, the land courts, although presided over by judges, were far from judicial, as the word was then understood, in their determinations. Well before the first sat, the tenants were told by the Land League that the level of rents set would depend on their level of agitation and the extent of the civil commotion which they created. So it proved. 'Judicial rents' were essentially 'political rents', and the judges essentially ministerial conciliators and public appeasers. Inevitably, as this war of pressures began to seem endless, and the intervals between the fixing of rents diminished, the state moved towards the elimination of landlordism altogether. A succession of land purchase acts in the later 1880s and the 1890s[29] culminated in Wyndham's Land Act of 1903[30] by which the government managed the acquisition and reallocation of estates, with lavish cash bribes to the proprietors and the bribe of low interest rates and lengthy repayment periods to the tenants. A once-ruling class was thereby dispossessed, even if most tenderly

[26]44 & 45 Vic., c. 49.
[27]45 & 46 Vic., c. 47.
[28]*Annual Register*, 1882, p. 80.
[29]The first of these statutes was Ashbourne's Act of 1885, 48 & 49 Vic., c. 73.
[30]3 Edw., VII, c. 37.

and on favourable terms. 'Dispossession' is not too strong a term, for the alternative of compulsory purchase of estates had long been waiting in the wings and would certainly have taken the stage in 1903 if the main body of proprietors had proved intransigent.[31] It was still less than half a century since parliament had enacted clause 3 of Deasy's measure.

In our third area of concern, the most familiar, we may enter the story conveniently in 1824. As with the ocean passage contract, the labour wage contract was subject to various limitations in the early nineteenth century — amongst them, prohibitions on artisan emigration, master and servant laws, the Factory Acts of 1802 and 1819 and, the focus of our attention now, the virtual outlawry of trade unionism by means of the Combination Acts of 1799 – 1800. These acts rendered it illegal for workmen to organize for purposes of raising wages or shortening hours of labour, and declared that all such organizations fell within the common law category of conspiracy. In effect, this made a strike a crime, a trade union an unlawful organization and workmen involved in either liable to transportation or life imprisonment. Again like the ocean passage contract, the labour wage contract was suddenly 'freed', and almost immediately re-restricted during the 1820s. In 1824, the Combination Acts were totally repealed; trade unions at once proliferated and industrial conflict developed upon a mammoth scale; the pressure to reimpose the Acts mounted rapidly; and it was only by the exercise of consummate political skill that the promoters of the repeal, Francis Place and Joseph Hume, were able in 1825 to rescue any of the gains of the preceding year. The Trade Unions Act of 1825[32] permitted the formation of unions for two, and only two, purposes, the regulation of wages and of hours of work.

It is important to emphasize that Place and Hume neither desired nor anticipated collective bargaining in industry. Both were radical individualists, committed to the principle of the 'free contract' and personal liberty of choice and action. Place, whose experience of craft unionism was wide, wrote to his fellow radical, Burdett, 'Combinations will soon cease to exist. Men have been knit together for long periods only by the oppression of the [combination] laws; these being repealed, combinations will lose the matter which cements them into masses, and they will fall to pieces. All will be as orderly as even a Quaker could desire'.[33] This points directly, of course, to the liberal dilemma of the next half-century. The individual's right to enter into his own wage contract was practically in conflict with his right to associate with others for the same purpose. The 1825 Act and the trends of educated opinion and judicial decision alike did not hesitate to prefer the first. The act rendered 'intimidation', 'molestation', 'obstruction' and the

[31]MacDonagh, *Ireland, op. cit.*, pp. 41 – 2.
[32]6 Geo. IV, c. 129.
[33]J. F. Rees, *Social and Industrial History of England* (London, 1923), third edition, pp. 44 – 5.

attempt to enforce a closed shop illegal; and this was so interpreted by the courts, over time, as to make even peaceful picketing and therefore most strikes also, in effect, illegal — in fact, criminal offences punishable by hard labour. Moreover, because of its potential interference with 'freedom' of labour contracts, the trade union was from the start likely to be regarded as an association in restraint of trade; and this had grave implications indeed for the 'new .model' unionism which developed in the 1850s.[34] If a trade union, as an association in restraint of trade, were denied the normal legal protections, its funds (and new unionism was built upon the accumulation and maintenance of considerable capital) might be embezzled or sequestered with virtual immunity. This danger became clearly apparent in 1855 when in *Hilton* v. *Eckersley*[35] the Queen's Bench held that an employers' combination was one in restraint of trade; and on appeal the Court of Exchequer confirmed the decision in the following year: 'th[e] bond . . . is framed to enforce . . . a contract by which the obligors agree to carry on their trade, not freely . . . but in conformity to the will of others; and this . . . is contrary to the public policy'.[36] A decade later the disastrous condition of trade unions in this regard was finally confirmed in *Hornby* v. *Close*[37] when it was argued successfully that a trade union was not a friendly society within the meaning of 18 & 19 Vic. c. 43 but in fact an illegal body, 'in restraint of trade, and depriving the workman of the free exercise of his own will'.[38] Thus, at one level at least it seemed as if atomistic contractualism was in the ascendent in the forty years which followed the 1825 Act.

Against this must first be set the flood of factory and similar and tangential legislation, especially concentrated in the seventeen years, 1833 – 50. In effect, this set new parameters to the wage contracts first of children, then of women and finally of men, and first in textile manufactures, then in mining and finally in a plethora of like industries. State controls also spread laterally into the regulation of such matters as truck, on the one hand, and the safeguarding of machinery and cleansing of the workplace, upon the other. But still more interesting, from our present standpoint, was the actual course of industrial disputes begun in the 1850s, and in particular of two of them, the Preston lock-out of 1853 – 4 and the London building trades lock-outs of 1859 – 61. The essential characteristic of the early industrial disputes of the new model unions was the leadership's conception of them as essentially struggles over opinion. In the very first of the series, the engineering lock-out of 1852, Allen and Newton, the leaders of the new Amalgamated Society of Engineers deliberately sought publicity for their case, stressed the workmen's moderation, respectability, reasonableness and eagerness to negotiate

---

[34]For the subject of 'new model' unionism generally, see R. A. Buchanan, 'Trade unions and public opinion 1850 – 1875' (unpublished Ph.D. dissertation University of Cambridge).
[35](1855) 119 E. R. 781.
[36]*Hilton v. Eckersley*, (1855) 119 E. R 789, at pp. 792 – 3.
[37](1866 – 67) 2 Q. B. 153, at p. 155.
[38]*Hornby v. Close*, (1866 – 67) 2 Q. B. 153.

on all occasions and attempted systematically to 'educate' opinion. Immediately, the ASE lost the contest wholly; the men eventually returned to work upon the employers' terms. But the leadership considered the battle well lost for the war's sake. As Newton observed, 'Out of evil comes good. . . . We have gained greatly in public opinion by showing that we are capable of moderation. . . . That advantage we must not lose.'[39]

The lock-out of the Preston cotton operatives followed essentially the same course, although more lengthily, as that of the engineers in 1852. It ended in total defeat for the workers upon the issue of the hour; but during the six months of the conflict opinion had completely veered about. At first, general sympathy lay with the employers, the original mass action of the operatives to enforce a simultaneous increase in wages and reduction of working hours for all being anathematized as tyrannical. But the silence and cruelty of the millowners, contrasting with the union's sedulous attention to public relations, worked the change. What really signified in the Preston dispute, however, was the union's proposal, half-way through, that the government should act as arbitrator: the Home Office, in fact was designated. The notion gained ground rapidly among the public; it was with increasing difficulty that the cabinet fended it away.[40] It seems scarcely too much to see this as a climacteric, as one of those fugitive moments at which one orthodoxy begins to slip away in favour of another. For implicit in the swift advance of the secondary campaign was the replacement, as the norm of conduct, of the idea of the 'free contract', individually ordered, by the idea of coercive social arrangement of such things. This tendency was confirmed in the London building trades dispute which opened five years later, occasioned by a 'nine-hours-day' movement. Once again, initial sympathy lay largely with the employers, who were presented as resisting a collective use of force to alter labour contracts. Once again, however, the conduct and tactics of the respective combatants (and the artisans' campaign was directed by George Potter, chairman of the London Trades Council and possibly the deftest public relations man of his day) led to a complete turnabout in opinion, over time, and to rapidly growing pressure upon the government to intervene. At last, arbitration was forced upon the employers; and one of the law lords, St Leonards, was appointed to conduct the inquiry, which issued eventually in a compromise accepted by both parties.[41] In certain respects, this development anticipated the Irish 'land court' and the assumptions underlying the concept of 'fair rent'. It was also an ironic accompaniment to *Hilton* v. *Eckersley*[42] and *Hornby* v. *Close*.[43]

The dualism now manifest in this area of social relationships demanded resolution; and the 1867 Royal Commission on Labour, appointed for quite

[39]*Operative*, 13 March, 1852, quoted in Buchanan, *op. cit.*, p. 40.
[40]Buchanan, *op. cit.*, pp. 16–40.
[41]*Ibid.*, pp. 64–85.
[42](1855) 119 E. R. 781.
[43](1866–67) Q. B. 153.

other reasons, happened to provide the opening for such a determination. Yet again the employers' interest proved tactically inept. It was clear from the beginning that the unions' Achilles' heel was their collective 'coercion' of others, and in particular the threat which they presented to the individual's freedom to contract and to work. The employers concentrated, however, upon corruption, violence and conspiracy as marks of the trade union movement. The new model unions had no difficulty in demonstrating the absurdity of these charges, and scarcely exaggerated in parading self-help, mutuality and respectability as the true characteristics of the contemporary movement. The majority report of the commission endorsed the unionists' self-portrait, with warm approbation of the 'worthiness' of such men. The commission, however, also included two Christian socialists, Thomas Hughes and Frederic Harrison, and a tractarian labourite, Lord Lichfield, and in their minority report these three went over to the offensive. They proposed three interrelated principles as the basis of future legislation: that no act committed by a workman be illegal unless it would be illegal if committed by another person; that no act committed by a combination of workmen be illegal unless it would be illegal if committed by a single individual; and that trade union funds be afforded the special statutory protection given to friendly societies, but without the degree of minute supervision and regulation imposed upon the latter.[44]

The minority report was instantly seized on by the labour movement as a precise legislative programme, and its advice to use political pressure to achieve the necessary statute followed in the general election of 1868, the first to be held after the concession of household suffrage in the boroughs. The initial parliamentary response, in 1871, was in effect to formalize the dualism. The Trade Union Act of that year[45] incorporated the substance of the recommendations of the minority report. It was specifically declared that 'the purpose of any trade union shall not by reason merely that they are in restraint of trade be deemed to be unlawful'; unions might register on even more favourable terms than friendly societies; and they could not be sued for damages. On the other hand, the concurrently enacted Criminal Law Amendment Act[46] rendered any act of violence or molestation, or threats uttered, in the course of an industrial dispute an offence. In effect, the Criminal Law Amendment Act meant that even peaceful picketing, and the other normal accompaniments of strikes, were illegal, for clause I gave 'molestation' an extremely wide range of meanings. Thus while the trade union was granted extraordinary security and immunities as an association *per se*, on the one hand, the renewed defence of the 'free contract', and of individual liberty of negotiation and work, practically emasculated unionism in action, on the other. Another turn of the screw in labour's

[44]*Reports of Commissioners (on) Trade Unions and Other Associations*, 1867, xxxii, 1867-8, xxxix, 1868-9, xxxi.
[45]34 & 35 Vic., c. 31.
[46]34 & 35 Vic., c. 32.

political organization, and another general election in 1874 with a set 'test' for candidates, were sufficient to break contractualism at last. The Conspiracy and Protection of Property Act of 1875[47] not only confirmed the disentanglement of the trade unions from the meshes of conspiracy in common law, but it also specifically legalized peaceful picketing and the usual concomitants of the industrial strike. In other words, the Criminal Law Amendment Act of 1871 was undone; in fact, it was specifically repealed. To all appearances, then, 'freedom of contract' would no longer stand where it conflicted with collective bargaining or mass power; and the trade union now rested safely upon the peculiarity — in fact, uniqueness — of its status in law. Such at least was the parliamentary intention and the general expectation of 1875. As we know, the 'revolution' of 1875 met its counter-revolution, to be succeeded by counter-counters and their counters in turn. But more than twenty years were to pass before *J. Lyons & Sons* v. *Wilkins*[48] and *Quinn* v. *Leathem*[49] set off premonitory shocks in one direction, and Taff Vale (*Taff Vale Railway Coy.* v. *Amalgamated Society of Railway Servants*)[50] detonated an eruption in another. In the interval few could have believed that the classic radical-individualist body of concepts would ever dominate this field again.

At the outset of this paper, I said that I hoped to show that the phenomenon which we are called on to discuss had precedents, and that one at least of these was complex and multiple in form, dialectical and convoluted in development and, to a degree, involved in the same issues as we are today. I have made a more or less random boring of the intricately-layered and veined soil of nineteenth-century Britain in an attempt to test the dominant mid-Victorian conception of the current 'transformation' in law, justice and morals against three actualities of the day. It would be too much to conclude that the two, the painting and the painted, were altogether unrelated. In each of our three cases, there was a phase, however brief, in which complete anarchic liberation and the supersession of status by contract (using the words in a very loose and general sense) were attempted. There are also some rough correspondences between the three cases to be discerned. But overall what strikes one most is the gross misreading of past and current trends, and the failure to allow for complexity, contradiction or reversal, in the mid-Victorian self-analysis. Moreover, although I have been dealing almost exclusively with movements in expressed or underlying ideas, the same judgement would hold good for the institutional and structural elements in the story.

By 1855, the Passenger Acts had been, to a large degree, removed from the ordinary domains of law. The executive officers had received absolute

[47]38 & 39 Vic., c. 86.
[48](1899) 1 Ch. 255.
[49](1901) A. C. 495.
[50](1901) A. C. 426.

discretions over a host of affairs, ranging from the setting of azimuth compasses to the stowage of pig-iron: in the designated areas no appeal from their decisions was allowed. Meanwhile, the commissioners had been awarded extraordinary powers of delegated legislation.[51] Many of the schedules and penalties set out in the statutes could be varied by them at will, and, for all practical purposes, without accountability. Novel summary jurisdictions were being devised almost annually to meet the exigencies of the particular problem. Conversely, the arbitration systems developed for both labour and Irish landlord-tenant relationships had created extra- (and perhaps also pseudo-) judicial roles for the judiciary. Their new work was, at bottom, both theatrical and political. In its exercise, they were subject to incessant organized pressure, for the tenant disturbances, designed to force down 'fair rents', had as their mirror-image the ostentatious abstention from violent agitation by the new model unionists, designed to force up 'fair wages'. In a sense, the Victorian arbitration systems might even be regarded as Star Chamber *redivivus*, with public policy being advertised and particularized rather than decided by legal instrumentalities — except that the driving force was now mass rather than royal power.

In saying all this, I do not in the least mean either to patronize the mid-Victorian grand speculators, or to suggest that the mid-Victorian situation may be on all fours with ours. History not only had to have, it should also glory in having had, its Macaulay, and the equivalent is true of law and Maine; and we today possess not only hindsight and perches on innumerable new shoulders, but also modes and frames of scholarship not afforded to our great-grandfathers. Nonetheless, I return again to the cautions with which I began. 'Transformation' is an immense and ramifying word. It implies (to me, at least) singularity, homogeneity, simplicity, departure point, direction and completion. I have tried to convey something of the historian's unease at — to put it at its mildest — too exuberant and unreserved an embrace of so bold and bountiful a term. But, it is hoped, a longer view may cut off, or at least cut short, some follies.

[51]MacDonagh, *Patterns of Government, op. cit.*, pp. 294–5.

8

Restrictive trade practices and unfair competition

J. D. Heydon

The economic struggle has often made heavy demands of those who have to take part in it. These demands could have been met by traders using forceful or dishonest methods — murdering rivals, stealing their stock in trade, damaging their machinery. Alternatively, they could have been met only by 'fair' means — those within the courtesies of a social code observed by gentlemen. The first response has long been forbidden by the general criminal law: any direct destruction of a rival's person or physical property is proscribed by the law of murder, assault, trespass and conversion. The second response has commonly been found inadequate to the needs of the struggle. There is a third response lying between the first two. This involves the use of many practices which traders have found useful but which the larger public has over the generations found odious in different degrees. Today we sometimes call them 'restrictive trade practices' and 'unfair competition'. Lord Bramwell once asked in this context: 'What is unfair that is neither forcible nor fraudulent?'[1] The modern judges and modern Parliaments have given his cynical question a different answer from that which he expected. But their answer is not wholly coherent or satisfactory.

Restrictive trade practices fall into three main groups: agreements between rivals — between buyers or between sellers; certain agreements between a seller and a buyer; and substantially unilateral conduct injurious to rivals.

Agreements between rivals — 'horizontal' agreements — are usually regarded as the most pernicious. They include cartel agreements to fix prices, limit or regulate production, share markets, pool profits or restrict competition on quality and service. They include collective boycotts — agreements to deny rivals certain facilities, or agreements by sellers to drive a particular buyer out of business. But they also include such practices as the creation of single new large firms by the merger of smaller ones which may be beneficial, in that the greater scale of the merged entities permits economies of production not available to any of the original parties.

The second kind of restrictive trade practice arises by agreement, coerced

---

[1]*Mogul Steamship Co. Ltd.* v. *McGregor, Gow & Co.* [1892] A.C. 25, at p. 47.

or not, between buyers and sellers. In modish jargon, this is 'vertical integration by contract'. A supplier agrees to supply on condition that the purchaser will not re-supply to certain persons or in certain areas; or on condition that he will not obtain any of his requirements of the thing supplied other than from the supplier. Similarly, a supplier may agree to supply all his output to a purchaser or may agree to supply no other purchaser in a certain area. These agreements may sometimes have beneficial consequences: the supplier obtains an assured outlet, the purchaser may obtain an assured source of supply, perhaps at stable prices, and both may plan their future activities with more assurance. Another kind of vertical agreement is the 'tie-in'. A supplier agrees to supply product X on condition that the purchaser also buys some of product Y; or a supplier agrees to supply product X on condition that the purchaser also buys product Y from another supplier. These agreements are usually thought less likely to produce benefits; a monopoly in product X is used to restrict competition so far as product Y is concerned. There is also 'vertical integration by merger' — as where a steel manufacturer, instead of contracting to take iron ore from a mining firm, takes over ownership of the mining firm itself.

The third kind of restrictive trade practice typically involves unilateral conduct. A supplier discriminates among purchasers as to the price at which he sells, because of pressure from a large purchaser to offer discounts not offered generally. A trader may 'monopolize' his section of trade. He can do this in several ways. He may buy out rivals. He may offer so many services that new rivals find it difficult to enter that line of business. He may buy up many patents and refuse to license them, and he may harass rivals with litigation alleging patent infringement. He may cut prices to unprofitable levels in order to force competitors out of business, relying on his strength to survive. This strength may not be based on efficiency, but on adventitious factors, such as capacity to advertise more, to get finance on easier terms, to force suppliers to lower prices by making bulk purchases. The monopolizer intends, once rivals are driven out, to raise prices to gain a monopoly profit in the future.

Most of these restrictive trade practices are intended to reduce competition between rivals, either by agreement or by elimination of the rival from business. On the other hand, the practices termed 'unfair competition' do increase the level of competitive activity, but in an impermissible way. The struggle becomes more intense, just as the struggle becomes more intense between examination rivals who cheat or steal each other's books, or between jockeys who strike each other with their whips. Unfair competition may arise when one trader interferes with the performance by third parties of a second's contracts. One trader may deprive a second of profits he anticipated by intimidation of the second's customers, employers, employees or suppliers. One trader may lie about the qualities of his own goods, or of a rival's goods; or he may claim that his goods are in fact the rival's, or share some desirable quality with them. One trader may steal trade secrets or other valuable confidential information from his rival.

Why should the law object to this behaviour? When it objects, how is the behaviour legally regulated? It is convenient, historically appropriate and to some extent logically sound to consider first the common law approach and then Parliamentary supplementation of the common law.

The common law regulated restrictive trade practices and unfair competition by two main bodies of law. Restrictive trade practices were to a limited extent controlled by the ancient 'restraint of trade doctrine' and related monopoly doctrines;[2] unfair competition more recently by the 'economic torts'. The restraint of trade doctrine has been classically stated by Lord Macnaghten. 'All interference with individual liberty of action in trading, and all restraints of trade of themselves, if there is nothing more, are contrary to public policy, and therefore void [unless] . . . the restriction is reasonable — reasonable, that is, in reference to the interests of the parties concerned and reasonable in reference to the interests of the public'.[3] In England this general statement meant less than on its face it suggested. The doctrine prevented an ex-employee being restrained from competing with his employer, it prevented the seller of a business being restrained from competing with the buyer, and it prevented agreements restricting partners from competing, unless, in each case, the restrained party had learned some trade secret in the business or had gained some special connection with its customers such that it was just for him to be prevented from using this advantage unfairly. Beyond that, the doctrine in England had some shadowy application to monopolies, and to price fixing, market sharing and production limitation agreements; it has recently been applied to some vertical exclusive supply and requirements contracts. In America the doctrine received a somewhat more forceful application in all these areas, but even here it did not prove a fully effective method of vindicating the public interest.

Why did this come about? The phenomenon requires explanation, for at the end of the medieval period there were signs that the restraint of trade doctrine would develop a very wide scope. In the *Ipswich Tailors' Case*[4] it was said: 'at the common law, no man could be prohibited from working in any lawful trade, for the law abhors idleness, the mother of all evil . . . and especially in young men, who ought in their youth (which is their seed time) to learn lawful sciences and trades, which are profitable to the commonwealth, and whereof they might reap the fruit in their old age, for idle in

---

[2]One may leave aside the old common law and statutory offences, repealed in 1844, relating to middlemen who bought goods, mainly food, before they came on the general market. The hatred of the entrepreneur and the specialist distributor revealed by making badgering, forestalling, regrating and engrossing unlawful is quite alien to our modern, quasi-capitalist system.

[3]*Nordenfelt* v. *Maxim Nordenfelt Guns and Ammunition Co., Ltd.* [1894] A.C. 535, at p. 565.

[4](1614) 11 Co. Rep. 53a, at p. 53b.

youth, poor in age; and therefore the common law abhors all monopolies, which prohibit any from working in any lawful trade'. This view at first sight seems revolutionary — quite opposed to the detailed regulation of medieval economic life by guild and manorial custom, and by such statutes controlling the conduct and remuneration of labour as the Ordinance of Labourers, 1349. But the opposition to monopoly and to exclusion from trade was in .fact intensely medieval, and indeed was not fundamentally inconsistent with a much-restricted economy. The medieval view was that though a man ought not to despise or reject the degree in which he found himself, and though he ought not to practise more than one trade, he ought to practise one trade fully, and ought not be prevented from doing so.[5] It was a crime against God not to work, for the duty to work was as basic as the duty to worship.[6] It was a crime against the commonwealth to render oneself a charge on it, and to fail to make oneself a useful member of it. It was a crime against one's family not to support them. Therefore it was wrong for guilds or private parties to prevent men working. Guilds could prevent the entry of strangers, but they could not prevent those properly seeking to carry on a trade from doing so; — for example, they could not extend periods of apprenticeship unduly.

But the generality of the common law ban on agreements restraining trade broke down in the early seventeenth century. The guild system began declining, and the monopolistic power of the guilds over entry was attacked by the Court of King's Bench in the *Ipswich Tailors' Case*.[7] In *Davenant v. Hurdis (The Merchant Tailors' Case)*[8] the King's Bench had also held void a by-law of a market-sharing kind made by the Merchant Tailors' guild directed against the Clothworkers' Guild; it required members who put out cloth to be finished by non-members to have an equal amount finished by other members. The ground of invalidity was that the by-law tended to a monopoly: 'a rule of such nature as to bring all trade or traffic into the hands of one company, or one person, and to exclude all others, is illegal'.[9] It thus became easier for the courts to uphold restrictive agreements, for it would be easier than formerly for the party restrained to practise some trade other than that from which he was restrained. It came to be the law that a restraint which was 'general' — over the whole kingdom — was bad; but a 'special' restraint — limited in time and area — could be valid.

The early seventeenth century, which saw the attack on the monopolistic nature of the guilds, was an age profoundly concerned by monopolies of all

---

[5]See generally A.W.B. Simpson, *A History of the Common Law of Contract: The Rise of the Action of Assumpsit*, Vol. I (Oxford, 1975), pp. 519–21.

[6]In *Claygate v. Batchelor* (1602) Owen 143 a covenant not to work as a haberdasher for four years in two towns was struck down, and Anderson J. remarked that the covenantor 'might as well bind himself, that he would not go to Church'.

[7](1614) 11 Co. Rep. 53a.

[8](1598) Moore K.B. 576.

[9]*Ibid.*, p. 591.

kinds, but particularly those created by royal grant and used as a means of extra-Parliamentary finance. In *Darcey* v. *Allen, The Case of Monopolies*[10] a grant of the sole right of making playing cards was held void at common law for several reasons. It injured would-be manufacturers. The price would rise. The quality would fall, for it gave an unskilled courtier the right to manufacture at the expense of those who had 'the art and skill'.[11] This decision was one of several milestones towards the ending of royal monopoly grants after the Glorious Revolution at the end of the century. But the decision was not pregnant with general doctrines of monopoly control. It was directed only against royal monopolies. Nor was it available for use by individuals, for just as *Davenant* v. *Hurdis* involved a conflict between guilds rather than between an individual and guild, so *Darcey* v. *Allen* was essentially a conflict between the Crown and London Corporation, which supported the defendant infringer of the monopoly. The law on monopolies became part of constitutional law, not the law of contract or of economic regulation.

By the end of the nineteenth century the distinction between general and special restraints was rejected; suitable general — or even world-wide — restraints could be upheld, as was rational enough in an age of fast communications in which the effects of competition could be felt much more widely. The paramount concern of the law was with the individual interests of contracting parties, despite Parker CJ's account in the great case of *Mitchel* v. *Reynolds*[12] of the damage unreasonable restraints did to the public interest. This occurred for several reasons. Restraints can be grouped as 'direct' and 'ancillary'.[13] Ancillary restraints are those which are ancillary to the lawful main purpose of a contract, e.g. restrictions ancillary to a contract of employment, partnership or sale of business accepted by an ex-employee, or partner, or seller who agrees not to compete with his employer, partner or buyer. Here the public interest need not be argued as a separate issue; the party seeking to escape his obligations is more likely to succeed by pointing to his own immediate hardships rather than vaguer general public disadvantages. Indeed, the public may not be injured. The ex-employee or vendor cannot trade in a certain area; but the employer or purchaser is likely to remain in business serving public needs, and if he does not, nothing in the contract prevents any one else in the world entering the field. But 'direct' restraints, not linked to any principal transaction, raise different problems. Cartels injure the public; but the parties are unlikely to complain, for '[i]n combine cases the parties may be on velvet while the public is looted'.[14]

---

[10](1602) 11 Co. Rep. 84b.

[11]*Ibid.*, at p. 87a.

[12](1711) 1 P. Wms. 181.

[13]The clearest exposition is Taft J.'s celebrated judgment in *U.S.* v. *Addyston Pipe and Steel Co.* 85 F. 271, at pp. 282–3 (1898).

[14]F.D. Simpson, 'How Far Does the Law of England Forbid Monopoly?', (1925) 41 L.Q.R. 393, at p. 394.

There may have been a doctrine that conspiracies to fix or raise wages or prices were criminal; but in 1825 statute declared that combining to raise or lower wages was not criminal and any wider common law doctrine died during the nineteenth century. There was authority holding some such agreements in unreasonable restraint of trade, but others were often held justifiable. Until recently no third party right of action against the contracting parties was recognized, and in the absence of a state official to intervene, the unreasonableness of cartels could not be proved. In any event, most judges were inclined to give the public interest a small role. There was a reluctance to strike down contracts on public policy grounds. The principle of freedom of contract was felt to be more important; 'contracts when entered into freely and voluntarily shall be held sacred'.[15] The plea of illegality sat badly in the defendant's mouth. The state — including the judiciary — should, it was felt, intervene as little as possible in the economy. Did not the great Holmes J. himself say: 'the most enlightened judicial policy is to let people manage their own business in their own way, unless the ground for interference is very clear'?[16] The courts, lacking evidence and expertise as to economic consequences, distrusted having to decide such matters; so far as they were confident about their expertise, they usually regarded cartels as useful methods of avoiding the wastes of competition; so far as they saw risks in cartels, they preferred to rely on the safeguard of competition from third parties.[17]

But the American courts were less cautious in these matters than the Anglo-Australian. They tended to give public policy a wider role; they were less sanguine about the competition of third parties; they were sceptical of the benefits of cartels; they feared that in the long run those benefits would vanish and new monopolies arise. 'Experience shows that it is not wise to trust human cupidity when it has the opportunity to aggrandize itself at the expense of others.'[18] The American courts began to speak of evils they saw in language of a vehemence unheard since the time of Coke. As we have seen, the signs of a wide and powerful restraint of trade doctrine appearing about 1600 proved false; a highly developed but relatively narrow set of rules was created as the theological and political fires which produced the signs of something wider died down from the late seventeenth century on. But the crises of modern capitalism in America at the end of the nineteenth century witnessed, and helped to cause, the revival of wide doctrine. The political element was a centralist response to populism and progressivism — to unrest among farmers and labour. The theological element depended on the funda-

---

. [15]*Printing and Numerical Registering Co.* v. *Sampson* (1875) L.R. 19 Eq. 462, at p. 465, *per* Jessel M.R.

[16]*Dr Miles Medical Co.* v. *John D. Park & Sons Co.* 220 U.S. 373, at p. 411 (1911).

[17]See generally *Mogul Steamship Co. Ltd.* v. *MacGregor, Gow & Co.* [1892] A.C. 25; *A.-G. of Commonwealth of Australia* v. *Adelaide Steamship Co., Ltd.* [1913] A.C. 781; *North Western Salt Co., Ltd.* v. *Electrolytic Alkali Co., Ltd.* [1914] A.C. 461.

[18]*State* v. *Standard Oil Co.* 30 N.E. 279, at p. 290 (1892).

mentalist language of such politicians as William Jennings Bryan.[19] The Sherman Act of 1890 was the embodiment of this, and both in America and in the many countries which imitated it, it has proved one of the more enduring triumphs of progressivism. The Sherman Act has in America often been thought to descend directly from the common law. There is certainly strong evidence for this in judicial language just before the Act, and evidence in the same place for the constitutionalist-fundamentalist attitude of the age. We may take one example: 'Monopoly in trade or in any kind of business in this country is odious to our form of government. It is sometimes permitted to aid the government in carrying on a great public enterprise, or public work under governmental control, in the interest of the public. Its tendency is, however, destructive of free institutions, and repugnant to the interests of a free people, and contrary to the whole scope and spirit of the federal constitution.'[20]

How would an economist, or at least a statesman to some extent familiar with an economist's way of thought, put the justification for restrictive practices legislation? 'Monopolies', a term which for present purposes may include both single firms and cartels, have the capacity to behave without serious checks by rivals — in short, to restrict production and charge a higher price without fear of loss of business to rivals who are underselling. The existence of monopolies thus interferes with the production of goods and services which would be achieved in more competitive conditions: the price becomes higher, or quality lower, or service less, or range of choice less, or supplies less reliable. The higher monopoly rent achieved makes the monopoly company unduly rich at the expense of the remainder of the community; that is, it enriches its shareholders and its employees, who can force higher wage settlements without risk of bankrupting the employer. Admittedly the maldistribution of wealth that results can be corrected to some extent by progressive taxation policies, subsidies, and social security payments of various kinds, but the capacity to charge a higher monopoly rent may also cause cost laziness, the ill effects of which cannot easily be remedied by government policies. 'The greatest monopoly profit is a quiet life' says the aphorism; the monopoly profit may be low in terms of money because the monopolist takes it in indolence, inefficiency, lack of vigour, the failure to replace obsolescent plant, a swollen labour force, out-of-date techniques, the failure to innovate or to be aware of the basic facts of its situation. The higher monopoly price also ensures that less is sold; hence some buyers must buy less desired and harder to produce substitutes for the monopoly

[19]In 1899 he said: 'I do not divide monopolies in private hands into good monopolies and bad monopolies. There is no good monopoly in private hands. There can be no good monopoly in private hands until the Almighty sends us angels to preside over the monopoly. There may be a despot who is better than another despot, but there is no good despotism.' (quoted by R. Hofstadter, 'What Happened to the Antitrust Movement?', in E.F. Cheit (ed.) *The Business Establishment* (New York, 1964), pp. 126 – 7).

[20]*Richardson v. Buhl* 43 N.W. 1102, at p. 1110 (1889), *per* Sherwood C.J.

goods. That is, there is a 'misallocation of resources'; the men and resources that should have been employed efficiently by the monopolist in satisfying the wants of the economy are employed less efficiently elsewhere in providing less desired products. The economy is rendered incapable of efficiently meeting consumer preferences. And the greater the size of the firm, the weaker the profit motive. A small businessman will gain profits directly related to his own efforts; the larger the firm, the less is this likely to be so.

There are, however, traditional arguments in favour of monopolies and cartels. A monopoly may be the only efficient way, in certain states, of producing a particular kind of goods, because only firms of a large size, operating plants of a large size, can achieve economies of scale. A more specialized argument was vividly put by Schumpeter in 1942.[21] Modern industrial progress depends on new technological development, on the 'gale of creative destruction' which blows away outworn methods. This development will be impossible unless undertaken by monopolies, who can invest the vast capital sums required for research, development and new plant knowing they will be free of competition, and who can confidently build the excess plant capacity necessary to take account of the increased demand produced by the new development. Neither argument applies universally to monopolies, for new ideas are very often produced and developed by small firms. Certainly neither argument applies very convincingly to cartels, for there economies of scale are not realized, and joint research and development programmes do not usually justify the other aspects of the cartel agreement — if the research programme is advantageous it can be carried on without other restrictions. There are two principal arguments more convincingly used for cartels. One only has weight in depressed conditions, and applies to 'crisis cartels'. If there is declining demand, and much excess capacity, firms will be tempted to cut prices below cost simply in order to generate some income. This may deprive other firms of business and drive them out; when the depression ends and demand revives, the industry will be too small to satisfy it and prices will rise sharply. A price fixing or business sharing agreement will preserve capacity, prevent unemployment, and in the long run preserve the consumer's interest in low prices.

The second argument also has a limited application. A cartel agreement to exchange certain kinds of information (though it may be a cloak for price fixing) may facilitate the planned expansion of an industry and establish some relationship between expected demand and planned capacity. Both these arguments have their detractors, and their limited scope is no bar to a general policy against cartels with limited exceptions. The arguments for monopoly, however, have more force, and statutes against mergers and against the mere existence of monopolies are, at least outside America, normally more permissive than cartel laws. Statutes normally control the

---

[21]J.A. Schumpeter, *Capitalism, Socialism and Democracy* (London, 1954), Chs. 7 and 8.

behaviour of monopolies rather than their mere existence; for some monopolies do not arise by accident, but by practices designed to create and maintain a monopoly position — non-licensing of patents, heavy advertising, lengthy supply and distribution contracts, predatory pricing, and the creation of other barriers to new entry into the industry by potential rivals.

These relatively sophisticated arguments were not the real motives of those who enacted the Sherman Act, 1890. As a matter of short-term politics, some Congressmen were responding to agrarian discontent with the prices of consumer and manufactured goods, supposedly kept high by monopolies and cartels — the 'trusts'. They were concerned at the political power of trusts. While the lack of free silver was thought to press down upon the brow of labour a crown of thorns, and to crucify mankind upon a cross of gold, the trusts helped. The magnates who opposed free silver were those who ran the trusts. At a more general level some of the legislators accepted a group of arguments, or visceral feelings, usually associated with the names of Jefferson and Woodrow Wilson, and, among judges, Brandeis and Douglas JJ. In Theodore Roosevelt's caricature, and to some extent in truth, these arguments amount to a 'sincere rural Toryism'. They turn on the merits of competition in avoiding tyranny and in improving human character. It was felt better to have a large number of small producers who are independent and about of equal strength. (After all, for much of its history, America had been like this, a nation of small farmers and shop-keepers, at least in comparison with Europe.) Just as the constitution decentralizes the power of government both geographically and as between executive, legislative and judiciary, so economic power must be spread. Just as some forms of civil liberty are guaranteed in Magna Carta, the Declaration of Independence and the Bill of Rights clauses in the Constitution, so the Sherman Act was to be a 'charter of economic liberty'.[22] Small men who are permitted to enter trade and compete freely have the energy and rivalry that releases inventiveness, disciplines character, heightens morale, encourages thrift and care for family, produces progress and diminishes the risk of a small group of large firms dominating the economy and overbearing even the elected government — particularly the very small and partly corrupt governments and bureaucracies of those days. Judges of a later time have recognized the force of these background notions. Learned Hand J. said:[23] 'It is possible, because of its indirect social and moral effect, to prefer

---

[22]*Northern Pacific Railway Co.* v. *U.S* .356 U.S. 1, at p. 4 (1958). '[A]s a charter of freedom, [the statute] has a generality and adaptability comparable to that to be found desirable in constitutional provisions': *Appalachian Coals, Inc.* v. *U.S.* 288 U.S. 344, at pp. 359 – 60 (1933). Jefferson indeed protested to Madison about the absence from the constitution of a guarantee of restriction of monopolies: letter of 20 December, 1787, quoted by Eugene V. Rostow, 'Monopoly under the Sherman Act: Power or Purpose?', in Sylvester E. Berki (ed.) *Antitrust Policy* (Boston, 1966). p. 55.

[23]*U.S.* v. *Aluminum Co. of America* 148 F. 2d 416, at p. 427 (1945).

a system of small producers, each dependent for his success upon his own skill and character, to one in which the great mass of those engaged must accept the direction of the few.' Douglas J. said:[24] 'Industrial power should be decentralized. It should be scattered into many hands so that the fortunes of the people will not be dependent on the whim or caprice, the political prejudices, the emotional stability of a few self-appointed men.' These were the themes of Louis D. Brandeis's *Other People's Money* and *The Curse of Bigness* and of some of Woodrow Wilson's famous speeches in the campaign of 1912 which were the harbinger of an important successor to the Sherman Act, namely the Clayton Act, 1914.[25]

The Sherman Act and its successors, as applied in the American courts, have, crudely speaking, proscribed the following restrictive practices. Some conduct is an 'offence *per se*' under the Sherman Act — that is, without consideration of any actual effects on competition — for example, price fixing, market sharing, product limitation, and collective boycotts. To some conduct under the Sherman Act a rule of reason applies; consideration must be given to whether competition has been unduly or significantly or 'unreasonably' affected. Examples include some forms of exclusive dealing and perhaps information agreements. The Sherman Act also forbids monopolization. Conduct proscribed by the Clayton Act — exclusive dealing, price discrimination, and mergers — is illegal 'where the effect may be to substantially lessen competition or tend to create a monopoly'. All or part of this model has been followed elsewhere. In some jurisdictions there is a power to justify on the ground that a practice which is prima facie illegal confers a substantial public benefit (e.g. the United Kingdom and Australia). More important in practice are certain exemptions common to most systems. We shall return to them below. One concerns size as such — monopoly without malpractice. A second is the behaviour of nationalized industries, public utilities, and other government agencies. A third is the activity of trade unions not undertaken in concert with capitalists. A fourth concerns restrictive practices affecting exports: overseas markets may be damaged where the domestic one may not, for few oppose exploiting the foreigner. A fifth concerns monopolies like patents, designs and trademarks. Finally, cooperative organizations of agricultural producers are usually exempt because it is felt something must be done to regulate seasonal scarcity and gluts.

Let us turn from 'restrictive trade practices', where competition is reduced too much, to 'unfair competition', which, though strong, is of the wrong kind. Here, in contrast with the common law relating to restrictive

[24]*U.S.* v. *Columbia Steel Co.* 334 U.S. 495, at p. 536 (1948). See also *Brown Shoe Co.* v. *U.S.* 370 U.S. 294, at p. 344 (1962).

[25]A related trend has arisen. The courts have gone beyond striking down sole supply agreements between supplier and distributor which prevent competitors of the supplier from gaining outlets, to destroying them because they are 'unfair' to individual distributors bound.

trade practices, the common law is quite highly developed and there has not been much statutory intervention in favour of injured competitors, though there has been in favour of injured consumers and to protect trade union interests. It is possible to deal quite briefly with one trader's untrue statements about goods or services, or his theft of another's secrets. If a trader lies about his own goods, a purchaser may sue him in the tort of deceit, though a competitor may not. If a trader passes off the competitor's goods as his, the competitor may obtain an injunction and damages for the tort of passing off. If a trader lies about the qualities of a rival's goods, the rival may recover damages for the tort of injurious falsehood. Passing off has been extended to some instances where the trader falsely claims his goods possess the same geographical origin or other quality as a rival's. The equitable doctrines protecting confidential information permit the grant of injunctions against disclosure of trade secrets, and contracts against such disclosure are not bad — i.e. impugnable — for restraint of trade. Both passing off and the law of confidential information may be extended to misappropriation of such intangibles as another trader's reputation, whether he is a rival or not. The leading authority is the US Supreme Court decision in *International News Service* v. *Associated Press*,[26] where the copying by one news agency of the news collected by another was held unlawful. The soundest basis in the majority reasoning seems to be that misappropriation of the fruits of another's efforts should be enjoined (i.e. prohibited by judicial order) if the public interest demands some degree of protection for the plaintiff. But this common law creation of new legal monopolies alongside the deliberately circumscribed statutory systems of patents, registered designs, registered trademarks and copyrights has not proved popular in our legal system, nor even in America.[27] The legislature is better equipped than the courts to determine what should be protected and how; or to appoint specialist bodies who can make such determinations. The merits of some practices are not well handled in adventitious disputes between two individuals, but depend on evidence relevant to the whole economy and on consistent government enforcement. On the other hand, the common law protection does fill gaps and overcome difficulties in the statutory systems.

The main statutory contributions in the area of lies in trade are criminal or quasi-criminal false advertising statutes enforced by state officials, and the insertion of non-excludable implied terms into agreements.[28] These are principally for the benefit of consumers, though they also assist fair traders; they pose no paradox of the kind posed by the more extreme common law developments.

Another area of the economic torts regulates such practices as collective

[26]248 U.S. 215 (1918).

[27]*Victoria Park Racing Co.* v. *Taylor* (1937) 58 C.L.R. 479; *Sears, Roebuck & Co.* v. *Stiffel Co.* 376 U.S. 225 (1964); *Compco Corp.* v. *Day-Brite Lighting Inc.* 376 U.S. 234 (1964).

[28]e.g. Consumer Protection Act, 1969 (N.S.W.); Supply of Goods (Implied Terms) Act 1973 (U.K.); Trade Practices Act 1974 (Com.), Part IV.

boycotts, threats to customers or employees, and interference with existing contractual relations. A conspiracy between two parties to injure is tortious if unlawful means are used, or if (which is rare) the predominant motive of the parties can be shown to be malice or spite rather than self-interest. Persuasion of one party to break a contract with another makes the persuader liable for inducing the breach; and various more complex forms of interference are unlawful. And intimidation is unlawful, i.e., where A causes injury to B by threatening an illegal act against C.

In practice this group of economic torts has had potentially its widest field of activity against trade unions. Trade union strikes may involve some illegality which make them based on conspiracy by unlawful means; more commonly they involve threats of illegalities, or interferences with existing contracts between the employer affected and other traders, and while the employer, for the sake of future peace, may not sue, the injured third party may. For these reasons Parliaments have tended progressively to grant trade unions immunity from these torts; but the statutory protection does not always completely exclude common law liability, and it is sometimes difficult to determine the boundary between common law liability and statutory exemption.

We find, then, that trade behaviour is regulated as follows. The behaviour of private traders restrictive of competition may be unlawful; not so that of 'passive monopolies', nor trade unions, nor that of government instrumentalities. On the other hand, very active competition which takes the form of theft of another's ideas or schemes may be unlawful even though the idea or scheme could not be patented or registered as a design or trade mark. Conspiracy to advance one's material interests is lawful at common law (though it may fall within restrictive practices legislation as some form of price fixing or exclusionary boycott); but if inducement of breach of contract, or intimidation, or other illegality, is caused, it is unlawful, unless the statutory exception for trade unions prevails.

Our law then has not committed itself wholeheartedly to any single coherent policy, or to any coordinated group of such policies. Certain forms of anti-competitive abuse of power by capitalists are controlled — but not those of our twentieth century overmighty subjects, trade unions and government. Certain forms of ungentlemanly behaviour such as lies in trade are controlled, often very strictly, but not the threats or other coercive conduct of unions. Certain forms of immoral behaviour — misappropriation — are interdicted so as to create common law monopolies in ideas to the extent of making anomalous the much less extensive statutory monopolies. In America there have been recent attempts to remove one inconsistency and to attack large firms as such,[29] though these efforts have not yet received Congressional approval, and are likely to be vetoed by the President. If they

[29]The principal step was a Senate Bill introduced by Senator Hart.

became law they would probably cause economic ruin, at least in the short term.

The relationship between the law on restrictive trade practices, the economic torts and the promotion and regulation of competition is therefore confused. This is partly because in the nature of our system there is rarely an opportunity for a radical review and overhaul to remove anomalies. It is partly because our system has thrived on divergences between the common law and statute, and the fact that they often continue a long time; part of the glory of our system is its capacity to change over time, and out of its occasional chaos ideas are born and choices can be made. It is partly because our political system is pluralist, and exceptions to general principles are made in the special interests of particular groups. But fundamentally it is because Western economies are dominated as never before by three major groups who are increasingly immune to political and legal regulation. As we foreshadowed above, the first group is private monopolies which cannot be touched because of the high standard of living they buttress, or appear to buttress: the law can only regulate, or be allowed to regulate, such monopolies where misbehaviour is patent and gross. The second group is government instrumentalities, who apart from their immense influence on the conduct of private firms, are themselves very often in trade in the market under a more benevolent regime than their rivals. Their inefficiences are not checked in the same way as a private firm's. They can carry out predatory or exclusionary practices from which private firms are forbidden. The third group is trade unions, who do, after all, control much of the labour force, and often appear to do so almost as restrictively and wilfully as any Rockefeller, Harriman, Gould, or other robber-baron controlled capital in pre-Sherman Act America. Restrictive practices legislation prevents firms agreeing on their conduct on an industry-wide basis. But unions organized across industries, or even more widely, can have precisely the effects which firms are not permitted to cause. Unions may control how firms automate, what equipment is renewed and what methods of production may be employed. They may control hours of work and influence prices. They can therefore control levels of cost and output. They may seek to injure firms whose competitive success will destroy less efficient firms employing unionists. Unions which are engaged in business themselves can obviously use their control over competitors' labour restrictively. Normally, admittedly, the legislative exemption applies only to unions acting in defence of employees' interests in hours and quality of work and wage increases. Unions are not supposed to agree with one employer to drive another out of business, but in the fuzzy world of facts weak enforcement agencies and cautious courts tend to give unions the benefit of the doubt. Originally labour unions fell within the Sherman Act,[30] and in the conditions of the

---

[30]The Clayton Act, 1914, s. 6, and the Norris-La Guardia Act, 1932, created the present exemption.

time this was doubtless against the public interest. But the conditions of our time may be thought radically different.

Either antitrust legislation is successful or unsuccessful — worthwhile or not. If it is successful and worthwhile, it should be extended at least to government agencies and unions. If the law of economic torts (and its legislative extensions) is worthwhile, it should be extended to the malpractices of trade unions, and the statutory monopolies in ideas and designs should be overhauled to fit smoothly with it. But if these bodies of law are not successful, they should be abolished or severely modified. It is, of course, in the nature of our imperfect capacities highly unlikely that these bodies of law are completely successful or unsuccessful, or if successful, suitable for application *in toto* to all the areas they do not cover. Some of the traditional arguments for them may not have force now. But these questions as to the contradictions in the legal regulation of disputes and abuses arising in the economic struggle do not seem to be much considered by those who ought to be considering them.

9

The future of law in industrial relations

Robert Simpson

I

The role of the law in industrial relations has become the subject of almost continuous debate in Britain over the last two decades. Uncertainty as to the functions which the law can effectively discharge has not been confined to Britain, for the process of questioning the effects and desirability of perceived alternative roles for the law is widespread. Although it is unlikely to lead to a pattern of uniform or even broadly similar development in different countries it may be possible to formulate some general observations concerning the future of law in industrial relations.

Problems of definition

Any discussion of industrial relations and the law involves problems of definition. One of the weaknesses of many such discussions is a failure to appreciate the full extent of the subject matter of industrial relations. An outline of some of the principal views on the problem of defining industrial relations is therefore useful to establish a frame of reference for this paper.

J.T. Dunlop analysed industrial relations in terms of 'systems' involving 'three groups of actors: (1) workers and their organizations, (2) managers and their organizations, and (3) governmental agencies concerned with the workplace and work community', and creating 'a complex of rules to govern the workplace and work community. These rules may take a variety of forms in different systems — agreement, statutes, orders, decrees, regulations, awards, policies, and practices and customs.'[1] A. Flanders agreed with Dunlop's analysis of the subject in terms of a system, and concluded that the study of industrial relations could be described as a study of the institutions of job regulation.[2]

The widespread acceptance of this theory is acknowledged by H. A. Clegg in his most recent study of British industrial relations where he also includes

[1]J. T. Dunlop, *Industrial Relations Systems* (New York, 1958), pp. viii–ix.
[2]A. Flanders, *Industrial Relations: What is Wrong with the System?* (London, 1965), p. 10.

'the study of trade unions, management, employers' associations and the public bodies concerned with the regulation of employment' and 'the study of industrial conflict, and the use of industrial action' within the ambit of the subject.[3] In his article with G. S. Bain on a strategy for industrial relations research, Clegg joined in a more critical appraisal of the Dunlop/Flanders systems approach.[4] He and Bain suggested extending the systems approach to include behavioural as well as structural variables and unstructured as well as structured relationships. The subject of industrial relations could then be defined as 'the study of all aspects of job regulation — the making and administering of the rules which regulate employment relationships — regardless of whether these are seen as being formal or informal, structured or unstructured.'[5]

For the purposes of this paper it is not necessary to adopt or disagree with any of these theories of industrial relations. It is sufficient to state that industrial relations embrace a complex of relationships between workers, employers and government basically concerned with the determination of the terms and conditions of employment of the working population. It is, however, particularly important for the lawyer seeking to elucidate and evaluate the role of the law in these relationships to demonstrate that he understands the full extent of the subject of industrial relations. Because of the tendency for some lawyers — and others — to assume that industrial relations can be equated with the legal structure of employment relationships, it is necessary to emphasize that this is not so. Bain and Clegg's definition is most valuable to this end, especially in their emphasis on the distinction between industrial relations and the subjects on which it draws.[6] Whether or not labour law or industrial law is broader than industrial relations in any respect, there is no doubt that industrial relations embraces aspects of job regulation which do not concern the law.

The problem of generality

A further caveat is necessary concerning the extent to which it is possible to discuss the future of law in industrial relations with a generality which transcends national boundaries. In his first book on British industrial relations Clegg made the assumption 'that an understanding of industrial relations in this country requires an appreciation of a system of industrial relations peculiar to Britain, with its own sub-systems in each industry and each plant and with trade unions, employers' associations, methods of collective bargaining and labour law all differing in many respects from those

---

[3]H. A. Clegg, *The Changing System of Industrial Relations in Great Britain* (Oxford, 1979), p. 1.

[4]G. S. Bain and H. A. Clegg, 'A Strategy for Industrial Relations Research in Great Britain', (1974) 12 *British Journal of Industrial Relations* 91.

[5]*Ibid*, p. 95.

[6]*Ibid*, p. 96.

to be found in other countries.'[7] It is important to recognize and emphasize that each system of labour law is at least in some respects unique. Attempts to identify general trends, similarities and trans-national influences may nevertheless be made and this paper is concerned to look for these. But it proceeds from an analysis of the situation in Australia and Britain and is essentially confined to a consideration of the developments that may be foreseen in these two countries.

An analytical framework

Within these limitations this paper is concerned with the following question: can any trends in the development, nature and role of the law in industrial relations be identified which enable a valuable prognosis of the future of law in industrial relations to be made? To this end, a framework for analysing the role of the law in industrial relations is required. Reference may be made to analytical approaches that have been developed from two different standpoints.

Eugene Kamenka and Alice Tay have developed the view that a contemporary crisis in law and legal ideology exists, a crisis which can be demonstrated by recognizing the existence of three competing legal-administrative traditions, the *Gemeinschaft* type, the *Gesellschaft* type and the bureaucratic-administrative type. These traditions 'may and do co-exist within any one society and any one body of law, but . . . pull in different directions and . . . display themselves at different periods and in different places in varying strengths. [I]n the Western world there is no doubt that the immediate trend is toward the immeasurable strengthening and extension of bureaucratic-administrative strains at the expense of *Gesellschaft* and *Gemeinschaft* strains.'[8]

In contrast with this general theory of different types of law, Otto Kahn-Freund developed a theory of different types of law in analyses of the role of the law in industrial relations. He summarized it concisely as follows:

I suggest to you that [the law] can play three different roles: in the first place it can support the autonomous system of collective bargaining — by providing norms and sanctions to stimulate the bargaining process itself, and to strengthen the operation, that is promoting the observance of concluded agreements. I have called this the auxiliary function of the law.

It can secondly provide a code of substantive rules to govern terms and conditions of employment — a code designed to supplement that provided by the

[7]H. A. Clegg, *The System of Industrial Relations in Great Britain* (Oxford, 1970), p. 3.

[8]See E. Kamenka and A. E.–S. Tay, 'Beyond the French Revolution: Communist Socialism and the Concept of Law', (1971) 21 *University of Toronto Law Journal* 109, and their 'Beyond Bourgeois Individualism: The Contemporary Crisis in law and Legal Ideology' in E. Kamenka and R. S. Neale (eds.) *Feudalism, Capitalism and Beyond* (Canberra, 1975), pp. 126–44 where the theory is fully developed. The passages cited are from the latter article at pp. 135, 142. See also their opening contribution to the present volume, *supra*, chapter 1.

parties themselves. The importance of this regulatory function of the law will be inversely proportional to the strength and coverage of collective bargaining. That is, the more people are covered by effective norms and sanctions emanating from the autonomous process of collective bargaining, the fewer will depend on the regulatory function of the law, and, a point of immense practical importance, the richer in content collective agreements are, the less important the supplementary rules provided by legislation.

Thirdly, the law can provide the rules of the game, the Queensberry Rules of what is allowed and what is forbidden in the conduct of industrial hostilities. This the law must do so as to protect the parties from each other, above all to protect what is called the 'public', that is the interest of the community, of the consumers, of individuals whose interests may be affected.' [He calls this the restrictive function.][9]

Neither of these approaches is of itself, satisfactory. D.W. Rawson has demonstrated that the Kamenka/Tay analysis of the development of the law and the current crisis as involving a shift from *Gesellschaft* to administrative conceptions of law does not offer a convincing explanation of the more recent development of attitudes to the legal framework of Australian industrial relations. He argues that there is in fact a retreat from faith in bureaucratic-administrative regulation in industrial law in Australia and a move towards the contractual model of collective bargaining.[10] Kahn-Freund's theory when applied to Australian labour law is similarly unsatisfactory as the dominant compulsory arbitration legislation does not fall readily into any of the three categories of the law he describes. Although developed in the context of analyses of British labour law, Kahn-Freund's categorizations are also deficient when applied to the law embodied in the Industrial Relations Act 1971.[11]

However an adequate analytical framework may be developed by building on Kahn-Freund's view of the three different roles of the law and the three different legal-administrative traditions identified by Kamenka and Tay. It is suggested that to assess the impact of the law in industrial relations, it is necessary to examine the law from three standpoints. First, the nature of the legal processes involved must be examined, and the extent to which they are 'adversary' or 'investigative' determined. To this end the Kamenka/Tay theory is valuable. Second, the extent of regulatory law within a body of labour law has to be assessed. In this process, an important qualification to

[9]O. Kahn-Freund, 'Industrial Relations and the Law: Retrospect and Prospect', (1969) 7 *British Journal of Industrial Relations* 301, at p. 302. See also his *Labour Law: Old Traditions and New Developments* (Toronto, 1968) and *Labour and the Law* (first published, 1972, second edition, (London, 1977)). For a recent critical appraisal of Kahn-Freund's theory, see Roy Lewis, 'Kahn-Freund and Labour Law: An Outline Critique (1979) 8 *Industrial Law Journal* 202.

[10]D. W. Rawson, 'The Retreat from the "New Province for Law and Order" ', in A. E. – S. Tay and Eugene Kamenka (eds.) *Law-Making in Australia* (London and Melbourne, 1980), pp. 290 – 303. All future references to Rawson are to this paper.

[11]As he himself came close to admitting. See O. Kahn-Freund, *Labour and the Law* (London, 1972), p. 50.

the Kahn-Freund definition of the regulatory function of labour law needs to be made. Consistent with the Bain and Clegg definition of industrial relations, law which regulates the procedures by which the substantive rules governing terms and conditions of employment are made should be recognized as regulatory law. Given this categorization, a more accurate picture of the relative extent of regulatory as opposed to auxiliary law may be made.

The analysis must also take account of the distinction between law which is optional and law which is obligatory. While obligatory law provides for penalties where its substantive content is not observed, optional law does not. The application of optional law depends on the willingness of those with the right to invoke the law on their behalf to do so. The attitude of the courts may also be important. The degree to which they are able and prepared to extend the application and impact of the law may be a key factor in determining its character. If there is a general reluctance on the part of the courts to extend the application of the law in industrial relations, the law will have but a limited role to play, whatever its character. This third analytical viewpoint indicates that the analysis must also take account of the attitudes of the parties to industrial relations. These will depend to a significant extent on the context in which they operate. In this, the historical background of industrial relations is a factor of great relevance. It is perhaps these attitudes which are the most important factors in explaining the difference between the place of the law in industrial relations in different countries.

II

Australia

The dominant characteristic of Australian labour law is compulsory arbitration legislation. Its enactment at federal level and in four of the six states in the early years of this century was in marked contrast with the previous imitation of the British 1870s trade union legislation in all six states. The reasons traditionally given for this uniquely antipodean development are first, the defeats and consequent weakening of the trade unions in the 1890s strikes and second, their subsequent willingness to turn to political activity and seek their ends by the method of legal enactment.[12]

The development of Australian industrial relations and the law in the first half of this century is characterized first and foremost by general acceptance of this legal framework. That acceptance was certainly at times less than wholehearted. In 1933 the International Labour Organization commented that 'so far as can be seen, at almost any time there is a strong feeling against

---

[12]See J. E. Isaac and G. W. Ford, *Australian Labour Relations Readings*, second edition (Melbourne, 1971), pp. 324 – 5. For a detailed account of these events see J. T. Sutcliffe, *A History of Trade Unionism in Australia* (first published 1921, reissued Melbourne, 1967), and B. C. Fitzpatrick, *A Short History of the Australian Labor Movement* (first published 1940, second edition, 1944, reissued Melbourne, 1968).

the actual system in operation, coupled with a fairly persistent faith in compulsory arbitration as a method', and it has been suggested that that view has retained its validity.[13] Thus, while experience of the federal system when Higgins J. was President of the Arbitration Court was generally favourable to trade unions and therefore less well received by employers, employers gradually came to see the system as a means to effect restraints on the unions. Trade union disenchantment with the system during the depression grew to such an extent that in 1934 the ACTU called for unions to withdraw from the system. But that never occurred.

The continuing decline in trade union respect for the system is cogently explained by Rawson. His forceful critique may be contrasted with the almost unqualified admiration for the Australian system expressed by two British academics in 1971. Although they were writing after the O'Shea case, both had an eye on the imminent radical changes in British labour law, maybe to the extent that they wanted to demonstrate that regulatory labour law could be an integral part of a successful industrial relations system. Phelps Brown concluded that the Australian system demonstrated that public agencies established by law which provide a means of determining the pay of workers through most of the economy were practicable.[14] C. Grunfeld was more explicit. The arbitration system had 'great achievements to its credit', including 'a public awareness of wage and salary determination as a matter of national and not merely sectional concern'. But in his view the credibility of the system and its achievements depended substantially on the existence of residuary sanctions and the possibility of their enforcement. The profound change of character that the system would undergo if they were abolished would lead to a situation where industrial power became the real arbitrator.[15]

These views are in marked contrast not only to Rawson's appraisal of the state of the system at that time. After the O'Shea case, criticisms of the legalism of the system, like that by Woodward to which he refers,[16] were more readily understandable than the glowing approval of Phelps Brown and Grunfeld. Further in 1956, some time before the conflict over the enforcement of bans clauses, Bob Hawke, later to become president of the ACTU, concluded an extensive survey of the role of the federal arbitration court as it was then, by asserting that it was unrealistic in the extreme to repose the fundamentally important legislative powers of an economic character that it

---

[13]K. F. Walker, *Australian Industrial Relations Systems* (Cambridge, Mass., 1970), p. 4.

[14]E. H. Phelps Brown, 'Industrial Relations and the Law: Lessons of Australian Experience', *The Three Banks Review*, Mar. 1971, No. 89, p. 3 at pp. 27–9.

[15]C. Grunfeld, 'Australian Compulsory Arbitration: Appearance and Reality' (1971) 9 *British Journal of Industrial Relations* 330, at pp. 348–50.

[16]A. E. Woodward, 'Industrial Relations in the "70s" ' (1970) 12 *Journal of Industrial Relations* 115. Cf. J. H. Wootten commenting on this paper in 'The Role of the Tribunals' (1970) 12 *Journal of Industrial Relations* 130.

possessed, in a legal tribunal.[17] More recently in a considered appraisal of the role of the law in Australian industrial relations, Isaac concluded that it might be a cause for rejoicing that the new province for law and order had had its day, in that the arbitration system had led, through the development of trade unions to an Australian type of collective bargaining and relegated the law to its proper place.[18]

It is thus clear that for well over a decade there has been an increased questioning of the role of the law in Australian industrial relations caused at least in part by the increasingly apparent demise in respect for the sanctions of compulsory arbitration. What then is the place of the law at present? First, the law has a continuing influence on matters which are fundamental to industrial relations. The dominant element is the compulsory arbitration process, procedures which are the product of a body of regulatory law. While this law does not — and indeed at federal level cannot — regulate the substantive content of terms and conditions of employment, it has established a mechanism by means of which at least certain basic aspects of terms and conditions are determined. It is now easy to ridicule the simplistic assertions of Higgins concerning the achievements of compulsory arbitration, and his conclusion in 1922 that minimum wage laws and tribunals for industrial disputes were generally accepted, certainly requires qualification.[19] But over half a century later there does not appear to be any general desire to abandon the framework that his idealism helped to construct.

Certain fundamental notions, e.g. work value and comparative wage justice are the creatures of this framework and through them the compulsory arbitration procedures have placed an indelible stamp on the processes of wage determination as a whole. It has also been argued that through supply of the judicial model, the drafting, analytical and advocacy skills of the lawyer and his ability to remove the prejudices of his client through his role as confidant and counsellor, lawyers make an invaluable contribution to industrial relations through the arbitration system that should be retained whatever the sanctions it contains and the degree of respect for them.[20] This opinion of the value of lawyers is contentious. What is not is that the whole arbitration structure is the creature of the law. The detail of the procedures the law has created may be questioned, but there is no general desire or expectation that they should or will be abandoned.

Indeed the institutions of compulsory arbitration may be developing a

[17]R. J. Hawke, 'The Commonwealth Arbitration Court — Legal Tribunal or Economic Legislature?' (1956) 3 *University of Western Australia Annual Law Review* 422, at p. 474.

[18]J. E. Isaac, 'Lawyers and Industrial Relations', a paper presented to the Seminar on 'Australian Lawyers and Social Change', Faculty of Law, Australian National University, Canberra, 1974.

[19]H. B. Higgins, *A New Province for Law and Order* (first published 1922, reissued London, 1968), p. 148.

[20]J. H. Wootten, Commentary on Paper by J. E. Isaac referred to in note 18.

fresh impetus as the forum where government policy on the growth of incomes may be reconciled with the competing claims of management and unions. Rawson suggests that over the past twenty years the emphasis has been on dispute resolution at the expense of any general pursuit of social justice or economic efficiency. But in the recent past the federal commission has been the means through which effect has been given to a form of incomes policy. This development was foreshadowed by J. E. Isaac in 1974. Some of his observations are particularly pertinent to an evaluation of the present state of Australian labour law. He suggested that in the context of a wages system unable to achieve both full employment and reasonable price stability 'the task of labour law is not so much to balance the bargaining power between employers and unions but rather to assist in promoting these objectives in the public interest. . . . [I]t is tempting to ask whether Australia, with its well established wage-fixing machinery and tradition of using such a machinery, may not have an institutional asset, lacking in many other countries, for providing the basis for dealing with this problem' (pp. 49 – 50). He concluded that if such use was made of this machinery it would mark a move in the direction of the Higgins concept. 'But its viability will be sustained not by the force of legal sanctions but, more effectively, by the pressures which the trade union movement and employers will bring to bear on transgressors' (p. 52). Isaac thought all this might be too Utopian. Nevertheless perhaps the present may be witnessing the beginnings of a new role for Australian arbitration tribunals and labour law.

With reference to the demise in respect for the sanctions of compulsory arbitration it has been noted that there has been a revived interest in tort proceedings in respect of industrial action. Rawson describes this as possibly 'an Australian revival to fill the gap' created by 'a partial collapse of bureaucratically oriented law'. It is undeniable that employer interest in resort to such actions has revived in recent years, though it is difficult to estimate the extent of the interest. But it is not a peculiarly Australian phenomenon. Such actions have also occurred in New Zealand and Canada, and there seems little doubt that a major factor in this revival has been the expansion of the ambit of the relevant liabilities in the English courts, an expansion in the 1960s and 1970s which was motivated by a desire to outflank the defences provided initially by the Trade Disputes Acts, and now the Trade Union and Labour Relations Acts.

Further the distinction between the nature of proceedings for enforcement of bans clauses in arbitration awards and the nature of tort proceedings in respect of industrial action can be overemphasized. Enforcement of bans clauses was no more automatic than initiation of tort proceedings. Institution of proceedings in both cases is at the discretion of the employer.[21] It is optional and not obligatory law. Also just as the object of enforcing a bans

---

[21]Tort liability may also be invoked by other parties affected by the consequences of industrial action.

clause was not to prevent or stop industrial action, so the aim of virtually all tort actions is to proceed no further than the stage of an interlocutory injunction to the same end. In short, present evidence is insufficient to justify the conclusion that there is a new trend developing through general resort to tort proceedings, especially given that the function of the law in such proceedings is essentially the same as in proceedings to enforce bans clauses.

The practices of Australian industrial relations remain inextricably bound to the compulsory arbitration system. This system, though optional and not of universal application, has been widely used and thus has a strong influence on procedures, an influence independent of the nature and use of sanctions designed to ensure compliance with determinations made according to them. In so far as these procedures are adversary procedures based on the traditional judicial model of common law legal systems, Australian industrial relations appears to be strikingly legalistic and, in terms of the Kamenka-Tay theory, an embodiment of *Gesellschaft* strains of law rather than bureaucratic-administrative characteristics. The arbitration systems contain important elements of auxiliary law, notably in the support they give to trade union organization, trade unions being essential to their functioning, but their overall impact is as an effective and dominant body of regulatory law.

It seems clear that the nature of the retreat from the province of law and order which Rawson identifies must be qualified to refer primarily to the residual sanctions of compulsory arbitration. It may be that these are an essential element of the system in that in the absence of any vestige of legal sanctions to encourage compliance with the determinations made under it, its ultimate logic disappears. But as noted, the all-pervasive influence of compulsory arbitration as a body of law regulating procedures with related areas of auxiliary law remains and seems sure to continue.

What of the future; has the retreat gone as far as it will go? The policy document on employment and industrial relations produced by the Liberal and National Country Parties while in opposition in July 1975 could be seen as indicating a desire to revive the law and order ideal by strengthening the legal sanctions of the systems and providing for their enforcement independent of the wishes of the parties. The theme of the stated policy on negotiation, conciliation and arbitration was the restoration of *authority*, the demise of which down to 1969 is traced by Rawson.[22] If certain of the proposals had been enacted in their original form and actively pursued, it could well have led to a return to the conflicts between organized labour and the law of the 1960s. However the legislation enacted in 1977 was essentially

---

[22]Thus the stated policy was 'aimed at restoring and extending the authority of the existing machinery for the prevention and settlement of industrial disputes. . . . The authority of the Conciliation and Arbitration Commission must be re-established as an essential protection to the average Australian employee and employer'. *The Government Policies. A complete guide to the official announced policies of the Fraser Liberal/National Country Party Government* which took office in Australia in December, 1975 (Canberra, 1976), p. 24.

a compromise. In the light of the futility of the 1960s experience and the contemporary need for governments to retain at least in some degree the confidence and cooperation of organized labour, it may be doubted whether it was ever seriously intended or likely that a tough law-and-order approach to industrial relations would be revived. Even the general tone of the 1975 policy document disclosed an awareness of the desirability of pursuing policies with the cooperation of the trade union movement, rather than in the face of its opposition.

The influence of the system is too deep for its continued existence to be in doubt. This is most clearly seen in the evident dependence of trade unions on it. Through registration under arbitration legislation to gain access to the tribunals, trade unions submit to extensive legal control of their internal management. They have thereby become to a significant degree creatures of the system.[23] While it is true that there are unions which are not subject to such constraints, e.g. unregistered state unions in Victoria, the overall majority of Australian unions are content to operate within the framework of a system within the confines of which they have developed.

The role of the law would be minimized if the function of arbitration tribunals became restricted to assisting in dispute resolution on a wholly pragmatic basis. Conceivably they might be reduced to an augmentary role, supplementing voluntarily agreed disputes procedures and active only when the machinery of what had become effectively a system of collective bargaining proved inadequate. Given the context of the history of Australian industrial relations, such a development is unlikely. They are more likely to develop as a means to representing specific aspects of what is seen as the public interest, e.g. the role envisaged by Isaac in the context of the operation of an incomes policy. A general move away from the sanctions of compulsory arbitration to the body of restrictive law contained in economic tort liabilities must be regarded as equally unlikely, given that British experience has demonstrated the very blunt nature of torts as weapons when used in industrial relations.

That this should be mooted indicates a tendency to see the law in too narrow a context, to see it as confined to what Kahn-Freund terms restrictive law and to ignore law of a regulatory or auxiliary nature. The efficacy of restrictive law as a countervailing force to bargaining power is now more generally questioned than hitherto. Thus part of the first reaction to proposals like those made by the Liberal and National Country Parties in 1975 is inevitably now to question their efficacy as a means to secure industrial peace through general acceptance of arbitration agreements and awards. But if the restrictive role of the law is now limited, the auxiliary and regulatory roles are not. The optional character of Australian compulsory

---

[23]Though not to the extent that they would justify the disparaging references made at the 1909 Congress of New South Wales Unions to unions formed in order to take advantage of state arbitration legislation as 'law made unions'.

arbitration leaves the parties free to abandon it, but this is unlikely. Its continued influence as a regulatory force in the conduct of collective labour relations seems assured because of the use that has been and continues to be made of it. The auxiliary provisions that are an integral part of it have been so successful that it is difficult to envisage either management or labour generally deciding that they can better operate wholly independently of it.

Britain

In recent years British labour law has been subjected to a series of radical changes which have fundamentally affected its nature and structure in different and inconsistent ways. This process of change has made an evaluation of the contemporary place of the law in British industrial relations more difficult than it would have been in the early 1960s. There are however, signs that the pace of change may be slowing down and that its direction may be settling into a consistent pattern which is unlikely to be suddenly altered. A prognosis of the future role of the law need not therefore be a matter of mere speculation.

It remains true that a proper understanding of British labour law must proceed from the reforms of 1871–1913. Against a hostile legal background, trade unions in Britain nevertheless developed to a position of some strength by 1870, and they were able to exert a significant influence on the nature of the reforms which followed.[24] By 1875 they thought that they had achieved all that was required of the law. In the words of the TUC Parliamentary Committee, 'the work of emancipation was full and complete.' Their achievements lay in the 1871 Trade Union Act, later amended in 1876, which established no more than a legitimate legal status for trade unions but imposed no restraints or controls on them, and the 1875 Conspiracy and Protection of Property Act which effectively removed the criminal law from the industrial relations arena. But in the 1890s the unions faced judicial hostility to their activities, expressed in the development of civil liabilities known as ecomomic torts. The Trade Disputes Act 1906 was passed to remove the possibility of these liabilities being invoked in industrial disputes. The further threat posed by the House of Lords decision in *Amalgamated Society of Railway Servants* v. *Osborne* in 1910,[25] which by comparing a trade union to a statutory corporation limited its legitimate activities to those referred to in the statutory definition of a trade union, was removed by the Trade Union Act 1913, which enabled a trade union to pursue any lawful object.

---

[24]The illegality of trade unions and trade union activities before 1871 and some of the background to the reforms is described by O. MacDonagh, 'Pre-Transformations: Victorian Britain' in this volume, *supra*, pp. 117–132. On the development of British labour law generally see Roy Lewis, 'The Historical Development of Labour Law' (1976) 14 *British Journal of Industrial Relations* 1.

[25][1910] A. C. 87.

By 1913, British labour law exhibited all the features of its distinctive 'abstentionist' character as part of a system of industrial relations dominated by voluntary collective bargaining. Law regulating the substantive terms and conditions of employment and the procedures by which they are determined, 'regulatory' law, was little in evidence. However, 'auxiliary' law buttressing voluntary collective bargaining was already present: the Conciliation Act 1896 providing voluntary conciliation facilities, the Trade Boards Act 1909 to regulate employment in the sweated trades and the House of Commons Fair Wages Resolution 1891. Law restricting resort to industrial action, 'restrictive' law had been confined in its application to situations falling outside the area of legitimate industrial activities delimited by the 1875 and 1906 Acts.

The essentially negative character of these reforms makes it debatable whether the 1870s saw a transformation of the law in this area through the rejection of freedom of contract and its subjection to mass power and collective bargaining.[26] Indeed because of its abstentionist legal framework, British collective bargaining has been described as a form of collective *laissez-faire*. In retrospect this period may be seen as a 'revolution' in the sense that it established a basis for British industrial relations essentially devoid of legal regulation, a transformation of the law in that it marked the withdrawal of the *common law* as an *active* factor in the structuring of industrial relations.[27]

Over the next half century, this basic legal framework remained unchanged. The maintenance of abstentionism was not due to trade unions forming an irresistable pressure group. It was rather a combination of their preference for abstentionism, development of a favourable attitude to voluntary negotiation by employers, (a development with roots in nineteenth-century *laissez-faire* liberalism) and general social, political and economic circumstances.[28] Thus the overriding consideration behind the recommendations of the Whitley Committee in 1917 was stated to be the 'advisability of continuance as far as possible of the present system whereby individuals make their own agreements and settle their differences themselves.'

Even judicial attitudes changed to an extent reflected in the remark of Lord Wright in the *Crofter* case in 1942 that 'the right of workmen to strike is an essential element in the principle of collective bargaining.'[29] The

[26]See MacDonagh, *supra.*, fn. 24. On the character and effect of the reforms see K. W. Wedderburn, 'Labour Law and Labour Relations in Britain' (1972) 10 *British Journal of Industrial Relations* 270.

[27]Through the limitations on the availability of criminal proceedings and tort actions, the development of collective bargaining and of legislation auxiliary to it. The same comment is equally valid when applied to Australia, because of the introduction of a new body of comprehensive legal regulation, i.e., compulsory arbitration.

[28]See H. D. Pelling, *A History of British Trade Unionism*, third edition (London, 1976), Part III.

[29]*Crofter Hand Woven Harris Tweed Co. Ltd.* v. *Veitch* [1942] A. C. 435, at p. 463.

reluctance of the judiciary to intervene as they had done in earlier years has been attributed to 'an era of self-aware reflection by the judiciary itself'[30] in the 1920s followed by a period in the pre-second world war years when trade unions were weaker. On this view that reluctance started to diminish when in the 1950s trade unions were given new power by a period of full employment. 'Then middle-class opinion changed.'[31] Thus the seeds for the development of recent years were sown as the second half of the century began. For whatever reasons, it is significant that the only lasting modifications to the basic legal framework in the period were additions to the body of auxiliary legislation.

In the recent past significant developments in industrial relations have occurred, several of which concern the law. Most publicity has been given to the pattern of industrial conflict with the prevalence of unofficial unconstitutional industrial action and the increases in the number of stoppages and working days lost. It was this factor which provided the greatest motivation for proposals for radical reform of the law. Pressure for industrial relations reform grew during the 1960s and the role of the law was a prominent feature of the debate that developed. The principal incidents of that debate are well known. The report of the Donovan Royal Commission in 1968 concentrated on the substance of industrial relations and broadly approved retention of the abstentionist legal framework. However, the Conservative Government elected in 1970 preferred to pursue the line of legal intervention established in its pre-Donovan policy statement 'Fair Deal at Work', which represented a reversal of the approach of Conservative governments in the 1950s. The experience of the Industrial Relations Act 1971 was in many ways traumatic. The implacable hostility of a united trade union movement led to dramatic confrontations involving sequestration of union property, the jailing of shop stewards and confrontations between unions and non-union mavericks. At a level unnoticed by newspaper headlines, it probably achieved little in the way of fundamental change before its repeal in 1974.[32]

What these events may have obscured are two independent and in some ways contradictory legal developments over the last ten to fifteen years. The first is the renewed willingness of the judiciary to intervene in a manner that recalls the period at the turn of the century. The battle of wits between the judges and the legislature that was the feature of that period was renewed in the decision of *Rookes* v. *Barnard*[33] in 1964 and the Trade Disputes Act it

---

[30]Wedderburn, *op. cit.*, p. 276.

[31]*Ibid*, p. 277.

[32]For a considered appraisal of the effects of the Act on industrial relations see B. Weekes, M. Mellish, L. Dickens and J. Lloyd, *Industrial Relations and the Limits of Law* (Oxford, 1975).

[33][1964] A. C. 1129.

produced in the following year. The battle continues today[34] and judicial revival of tort liabilities has, as noted, evoked a response in other countries, notably Australia.

The other development is of greater long-term significance for it demonstrates a now almost unchallenged realization of the total inadequacy of the contract of employment based on the notion of a freely negotiated individual bargain between employer and individual employee as a framework for individual labour relations. Legislation starting with the Contracts of Employment Act 1963 has developed the rights of the individual worker to the extent that some commentators now speak of legal recognition of the rights of a worker in his job. This law may be characterized as auxiliary in the context of a voluntary collective bargaining system, for it provides a floor of rights on which the collective bargaining process can — and does — build.

The current state of the law and British industrial relations may be summarized as follows. The Trade Union and Labour Relations Acts 1974 and 1976 have effectively restored the abstentionist framework that existed for a century before 1971. That is not to say that industrial relations are characterized by a total absence of law, but rather that there is little regulatory law, restrictive law does not operate against pursuit of legitimate industrial purposes and most of the legislation is designed to promote a system of voluntary collective bargaining.[35]

However an important caveat must be entered concerning the present position, which points to uncertainty for the future. First, the influence of government incomes policies on collective bargaining no longer appears to be a short-term matter. Whether or not they are reinforced by legislation they inevitably qualify the 'voluntary' nature of the bargaining process. Second, the extent of the legislative floor of rights for the individual worker was radically extended in 1975 by the Employment Protection and Sex Discrimination Acts. The latter is to some extent distinct from other parts of this floor as, like Race Relations legislation, it involves considerations beyond the sphere of industrial relations. The individual rights now consolidated in the Employment Protection (Consolidation) Act 1978 may be seen as the ultimate recognition of the demise of the common law notion of the contract of employment as the regulator of individual labour relations as a matter of *law*. As a matter of *fact*, the individual contract has long since ceased to be of importance. While the expansion of individual rights may be seen as auxiliary to voluntary collective bargaining, it is also prompted in part by the failure of collective bargaining to establish adequate standards on

[34]The reinforced 'Trade Disputes Acts defences' in s. 13 of the Trade Union and Labour Relations Act, 1974 are unlikely to pre-empt the result in all cases. See the decisions noted in (1976) 39 *Modern Law Review* 715; (1978) 41 *Modern Law Review* 63, 80, 470; (1979) 42 *Modern Law Review*, 458, 701; (1980) 43 *Modern Law Review*, 319, 327.

[35]On the legal framework established by the 1974–76 legislation and the contradictions in it, see K. W. Wedderburn, 'The New Structure of Labour Law in Britain' (1978) 13 *Israel Law Review* 435.

certain issues which could no longer be overlooked. To the extent that the encroachment over what have traditionally been management prerogatives is the result of legal rights it may be that it is and will become increasingly misleading to characterize such law as purely auxiliary to voluntary collective bargaining. Whether this happens will depend on future experience which may demonstrate a movement towards increasing legal regulation by increased reliance on the legislative floor as the norm.[36] But equally future practice may be a reflection of disappointment with the failure of the law to achieve the goals at which it aimed.

Any projection of the future must demonstrate an awareness of the different types of law that can form the legal framework of industrial relations. The failure of the Industrial Relations Act stemmed in part from a failure to appreciate that abstentionism does not mean total absence of law. The foundations of the floor of rights laid by legislation in the 1960s were not a breach of abstentionism which the extensive regulatory procedures and restrictive unfair industrial practices and emergency procedures of the 1971 Act could logically build.[37] Nor was there a vacuum, a total failure to provide a regulatory structure for industrial relations which only the law could fill.[38] It is highly improbable that the future will see any repetition of the policy of seeking change through comprehensive regulatory legislation, or that any similar body of regulatory law would be more successful if it were enacted. For there is now evident a much more general questioning of the usefulness of the law to promoting desired ends. Thus notwithstanding their political impact even the changes in the law proposed by the new Conservative government in 1979 do not involve an essential role for the law as policeman and are generally cautious with respect to any major legal changes.

While the future is unlikely to see any more 'Industrial Relations Acts' it is nevertheless possible that the law will be a more potent influence and have a more lasting impact than in the past. The continued demise of the common law as a regulatory influence can be foreseen not the least because recent revivals of activity in criminal law, tort and contract have further exposed its limitations. Resurrection of the criminal law in the area of picketing has only served to highlight its inadequacy as a means of control consistent with a viable right to picket or, more generally, with industrial reality. The erosion of contract as the determinant of individual rights and obligations between employer and worker is demonstrated by the extension of the 'statutory

---

[36]See Roy Lewis, 1976, *op. cit.*, p. 19 for the view that the ever-increasing extent of the legal regulation of the British system of industrial relations is 'the one indubitably fundamental and irreversible trend'. Possibly such a development would be the 'favourable experience of legal support' which on one view is necessary for the erosion of voluntarist traditions. See A. D. Flanders, 'The Tradition of Voluntarism' (1974) 12 *British Journal of Industrial Relations* 352, at p. 369.
[37]*Cf.* E. H. Phelps Brown, 'Unofficial Strikes and the Law', *The Three Banks Review*, Sept. 1969, No. 83, p. 3.
[38]See generally Wedderburn, 1972, *op. cit.*

floor', even though, paradoxically, this embodies and relies heavily on the contractual nature of the individual employment relationship as its basis. The scale of government intervention in industry in furtherance of economic policy makes the maintenance and probable further extension of such legislation possible as a means to protect the individual against the sudden changes in expectations involved and generally the unpredictability of modern employment. This points to a further and possibly crucial factor concerning the future of labour law: the encroaching influence of legislation not primarily or solely motivated by industrial relations considerations. Incomes policy legislation is a clear example of this. So too will be any legislation concerning 'industrial democracy' even though it may be structured as a reform of company law.[39]

The precise nature of changes in the law in these areas is uncertain. More uncertain is the actual impact any such reforms will make. The long term impact of past experience of statutory incomes policies on collective bargaining has yet to be determined. However, it is clear that that experience revealed the limitations of legal constraints and the law as an agent of change. The same may prove to be equally true of industrial democracy legislation, the impact of which is particularly indeterminate, and the provision of a comprehensive floor of legal rights for the individual.

These areas are matters of speculation. At present the tendency seems to be for the law to develop as a real influence within the traditional abstentionist mould. However, the extent of law auxiliary to the collective bargaining process is being increased.[40] Where this flows over to the level of individual relations, the extent of the provision is so great as to provide a considerable regulatory code of rights. Whether this becomes so important in practice as to change the whole balance and character of the law is perhaps the greatest imponderable of all.[41]

III

The primary conclusion to be drawn from this survey of the law and industrial relations in two countries with widely differing labour law, is that the key characteristic of the current situation is a more questioning approach to the efficacy of the law in achieving policy goals. The future role of the law will depend on how this questioning process is resolved and that will of necessity, differ from country to country.

[39]See 'Report of the Committee of Inquiry on Industrial Democracy' (the 'Bullock Report'), Cmnd. 6706, January 1977 and 'Industrial Democracy', Cmnd. 7231, May 1978. The 1979 Conservative government is unlikely to adopt any of the proposals in either of these.

[40]*Viz.* the procedure for assisting in resolving disputed claims for union recognition and the provision for disclosure of information by employers to representatives of recognized unions in the Employment Protection Act, 1975, ss. 11–21.

[41]The experience of the late 1970s suggests that this is a real possibility. See too Wedderburn, 1978 and Lewis, 1979, *op. cit.*

Recent British and Australian experience makes it easier to say what functions the law cannot fulfil successfully and therefore probably will not be required to attempt to discharge. It has disclosed first the inefficacy of penal restraints as a means of achieving a balance of power in collective relations. Second, British experience in particular continues to reveal the inability of the common law to adapt to the realities of modern industrial relations. In general the inherent values of the common law embody too great a bias in favour of individualism to be reconcilable with the realities of collective labour relations.[42]

On the positive side, there are some pointers to the development of the role of the law, some of which presage movement towards greater similarity in the experience of different countries. The area in which, perhaps more than in any other, the experience of one country influences others is the search by governments for viable incomes policies as part of the general strategy of economic management. This inevitably raises questions concerning what role, if any, the law can effectively play in such policies. Isaac has suggested that in the institutions of its arbitration system, Australia may possess an asset uniquely suited to resolving this question. This may or may not prove to be the case. In Britain, by contrast, in keeping with the voluntarist tradition, the search is for a mechanism which, formally at least, impinges little if at all on the traditions of free collective bargaining, and that implies minimal legal involvement. Whatever form of incomes policy is applied it inevitably has an influence on the structure of industrial relations.

This is also becoming increasingly true of government economic and social policies generally, where actions not primarily motivated by industrial relations considerations may impinge greatly on the procedures and substance of these relations.[43] For Britain, membership of the European Community inevitably implies greater use of the method of legal enactment to fulfil social policy goals to meet the requirements of Community Directives. The first instance of this, the requirements of obligatory notification of redundancies and consultation with trade unions before they are effected,[44] is a clear illustration of use of the law to implement a policy that traditionally, in Britain, would have been pursued only by voluntary methods.

Greater use of the law to develop rights for individuals qua workers is already well established and likely to continue. This is the clearest illustration of the demise of contractual regulation of the employment relation-

---

[42]As Kahn-Freund has noted with reference to the Industrial Relations Act, 'The Industrial Relations Act 1971 — Some Retrospective Reflections' (1974) 3 *Industrial Law Journal* 186, at p. 199.

[43]E.g. the provisions for disclosure of information to representatives of recognized trade unions in the British Industry Act, 1975 (under Part IV), although these have never been used.

[44]Employment Protection Act, 1975, ss. 99–107. The Equal Pay Act, 1970 and Sex Discrimination Act 1975 similarly reflect the requirements of Article 119 of the Treaty of Rome and the Directives on Equal Pay and Equal Treatment for men and women.

ship in favour of a legislated status, a move consistent with the current trend of development of the law identified by Kamenka and Tay. This use of the law is likely to become more widespread as it is most easily reconcilable with a range of industrial relations systems, e.g. legal frameworks as different as those in Australia and Britain. In Australia there has long been a fruitful interaction between state legislation and arbitration awards which has extended the rights afforded to the individual worker. Recommendation 119 of the International Labour Organization on dismissals provided that effect could be given to its provisions through laws or regulations, collective agreements, works rules, arbitration awards or court decisions or in such other manner consistent with national practice as might be appropriate under national conditions. Even in Britain resort was ultimately made to legislation on unfair dismissal to implement this recommendation, and use of the law to promote and protect the rights of the individual in employment is now more generally consistent with national practice in most western societies.

Two other features of the modern world suggest that there may be greater uniformity or cross-fertilization between the role of the law in industrial relations in different countries. The first is the increase in the number and influence of multinational corporations. The relative impotence of national law in general and labour law in particular in seeking to exercise the degree of regulation of their operations thought to be desirable has already been exposed. As the search for some form of international response extends to industrial relations, and there is already considerable evidence of this,[45] so it inevitably produces a common influence on industrial relations in the countries concerned. The extent of this in shaping industrial relations in each country is difficult to assess and may be overemphasized, but that it is and will continue to be a significant influence is beyond question.[46]

The other issue is of equal or greater long-term importance: industrial democracy. This phrase is used to embrace many variants of a very amorphous subject ranging from more extended consultation to fundamental questions relating to ultimate control of economic activity. At its deepest this may be said to represent a crisis, as yet probably more potential than actual, in the contemporary structure of business enterprise. It is generally assumed that at any level beyond superficial extension of management-labour consultations this carries implications which involve major legal issues. If this is so, they certainly affect industrial relations. This is an

---

[45]E.g. the cooperation of trade unions in Western Europe in negotiations with the Ford Motor Co. See also the ICFTU report on multi-national corporations, 1975. The activities of the International Chemical Workers Union have made a significant impact in some areas. See generally B. C. Roberts and J. May, 'The Response of Multinational Enterprises to International Trade Union Pressures' (1974) 12 *British Journal of Industrial Relations* 403.

[46]See K. W. Wedderburn, 'Multi-national Enterprise and National Labour Law' (1972) 1 *Industrial Law Journal* 12 and O. Kahn-Freund, 'A Lawyer's Reflections on Multinational Corporations' (1972) 14 *Journal of Industrial Relations* 351.

issue in all Western countries, though so far only a peripheral one in most of them.[47] In the long term it may change basic social and economic structures within these societies and in that process revolutionize the nature of industrial relations. Within a shorter perspective changes in national law concerning business enterprise and collective labour relations are foreseeable in many countries.

What must remain indeterminate is the effect such changes in the law will have. This perhaps better than any other issue serves to emphasize the central issue concerning the place of the law in industrial relations. Recent British and Australian developments reveal a body of wide-ranging experience and changes in the law. This has quite naturally provoked comments like those of Rawson in his conclusion that industrial relations may continue to vary a good deal from some other aspects of social activity, not least in the extent to which the law in whatever form is accepted can be effectively applied. The future may well see extensive changes and developments in industrial relations law in the directions outlined above. In assessing the likely effect of these it is as well to bear in mind not only the appropriateness of different forms of legal regulation, which will undoubtedly vary from country to country, but also the extent to which the law has a function at all. In considering this, it may be wise to bear in mind the following words of Kahn-Freund:

> Many people have something like a magic belief in the efficacy of the law in shaping human conduct and social relations. It is a superstition which is itself a fact of political importance, but a superstition it is all the same.[48]

[47]Greatest attention has been paid to West German experience of co-determination. See T. Ramm, 'Co-determination and the German Works Constitution Act of 1972' (1974) 3 *Industrial Law Journal* 20, and W. Däubler, 'Co-Determination: The German Experience' (1975) 4 *Industrial Law Journal* 218. More recently see E. Batstone and P. L. Davies, 'Industrial Democracy, European Experience', (London, 1976).

[48]O. Kahn-Freund, 'Labour Relations and the Law: Retrospect and Prospect' (1969) 7 *British Journal of Industrial Relations* 301, at p. 311.

10

Landlord and tenant: the British experience

Martin Partington

Introduction

Housing in England today falls into three main tenure groups. At the end of 1977 there were some 16.8 million dwellings, of which 54 per cent were owner-occupied; 31 per cent were rented from public housing authorities (including 1 per cent from housing associations); and 15 per cent from private landlords.[1] However, this tenure pattern is of comparatively recent origin. In 1914, of a total of some 7.9 million dwellings, the vast majority (7.1 million) were rented from private landlords; about 0.8 milion were owner-occupied; and only 20,000 were provided by public authorities.[2]

The predominance of privately rented accommodation as the basic form of housing tenure in Victorian times is an essential basis for understanding how housing policy has developed since World War I.[3] Although legal theory may have defined the landlord-tenant relationship in terms of a contract based on a freely negotiated agreement entered into willingly on both sides, the social reality of that relationship was based on fundamental inequalities of power. Constant shortages of available accommodation, particularly for the very poor, meant landlords could dictate the terms on which they let to their tenants.[4]

Government intervention in the housing area may thus be seen as attempting to eliminate or at least reduce the potential for exploitation.[5]

---

[1]Department of the Environment, *National Dwelling and Housing Survey* (London, 1979), p. 13, para. 4.

[2]Department of the Environment, *Housing Policy Technical Volume I*, (London, 1977), p. 38, Table 1.23. The detailed figures are often quoted but very unreliable, for reasons discussed, *ibid.*, p. 37, para. 90 – 1. Nonetheless, it is quite clear that the predominant tenure was rented accommodation.

[3]The starting point of this policy had begun to emerge well before that period; see e.g. E. Gauldie, *Cruel Habitations* (London, 1974).

[4]See, e.g. the contemporary accounts in the *First Report of the Royal Commission on the Housing of the Working Classes* [C. 4402] (London, 1885).

[5]Department of Environment, *Housing Policy Technical Volume I. op.cit.* p. 10, para. 25.

Three main strategies have been used:

  (a) the encouragement of owner-occupation;
  (b) the direct provision of housing to let by 'social landlords' — public authorities and, now, housing associations;
  (c) the imposition of controls on private landlords.

This paper does not purport to analyse the successes or failures of housing policy as a whole,[6] or offer suggestions for improvement or changes in that policy. Indeed, it should be emphasized that I do not regard questions of law and law enforcement as *central* to the fundamental problems of housing policy.[7] Whether there are enough houses of adequate standard to accommodate people in the places where they wish to live and at prices they can afford,[8] involves decisions relating to the allocation of resources and the settlement of priorities that are essentially political tasks, not legal ones.

The sole purpose of this chapter is to discuss heading (c) above: the imposition of legal controls over private landlords. The approach adopted is as follows: in Part I, some of the controls which Parliament has sought to impose on private landlords are identified, and the extent to which such controls have affected the behaviour of landlords is discussed; Part II looks at some of the more frequently made suggestions for making the law more effective; in Part III I present criticisms of the limitations of this mode of analysis and offer suggestions for alternative approaches. In doing this, I hope that this chapter may make some contribution to the development of more general theories on the ability, or lack of ability, of the law to control economically powerful groups in society.[9]

It should also be stressed that this particular essay is not the product of a specifically designed socio-legal enquiry aimed at exploring the effect of landlord-tenant law. Rather, the arguments in this chapter are based on the interpretation of data and findings made in other published reports, in which the efficiency and efficacy of the law were not necessarily the primary concern.

---

[6]There is an already extensive, largely critical, literature on this topic, see e.g. F. Berry, *Housing: The Great British Failure* (London, 1974); S. Lansley, *Housing and Public Policy* (London, 1979).

[7]See too Community Development Project, *Limits of the Law* (London, 1977), esp. Chs. 4, 6 and 8.

[8]To paraphrase the cornerstone of Government housing policy: *Housing Policy: A Consultative Document*, Cmnd. 6851 (London, 1977), p. 1, para. 1.1. Though drafted under a Labour Government, it seems such an unexceptionable statement that doubtless the present Conservative Government would endorse it as well.

[9]Cf. work already done in other fields in Britain. W.G. Carson, 'White Collar Crime and the Enforcement of Factory Legislation', (1970) 10 *British Journal of Criminology* 383, and 'Some Sociological Aspects of Strict Liability and the Enforcement of Factory Legislation', (1970) 33 *Modern Law Review* 396; N. Gunningham, *Pollution, Social Interest and the Law* (London, 1974), and R. Cranston, *Regulating Business: Law and Consumer Agencies* (London, 1979).

I

A   The Meaning of Control: Instrumental Definitions

The very task of writing an essay on 'law and social control' is likely to be founded on the premise that the sole, or a primary function of law is in some broadly instrumental way to control the behaviour of people in society. (The validity of this premise will be questioned in Part III of this paper.) Here I wish to stress that even an instrumental analysis may be more complex than at first appears. A simplistic analysis of the legislative process may suggest that legislation is passed when a legislator has determined that there is a particular activity that he wishes a landlord to engage in (e.g., repairing a dwelling) or refrain from engaging in (e.g., putting up rents). Such a decision will define the apparent objective of the legislation. The measures that the legislation seeks to impose on the landlord in order to alter his behaviour to meet the defined objectives of the legislation may thus be described as *direct controls*. However, this simple picture may be complicated by the fact that the enactment of legislation may well result in consequences that were not designed or even envisaged. A landlord may be encouraged by the legislation *not* to behave in the way intended, but to act in some quite unintended fashion (e.g., by getting out of the private rented sector altogether). In such cases, the law has had an impact on and, in this sense, controlled the behaviour of the landlord but in a secondary or *indirect* manner. Any discussion of law and social control must therefore start by considering both the direct and indirect control functions that law may have.[10]

B   Direct Control Measures

It would be impossible in a chapter of this length to analyse all the possible examples of 'direct control' measures which the law contains.[11] I shall restrict the account to five topics:

(i)   Rent limits;
(ii)   Rent books;
(iii) Security of tenure;
(iv)   Unlawful eviction and harassment;
(v)   Housing conditions.

(i)   *Rent Limits*

The most direct challenge to the landlord's 'freedom' to dictate the terms on which he lets property is to limit the level of rent that he is permitted to ask,

---

[10]Cf. the 'latent' and 'manifest' functions of law reform: R.K. Merton, editor, *Social Theory and Social Structure* (New York, 1968), Ch. 3.
[11]For further details see e.g. M. Partington, *Landlord and Tenant*, (London, 1975), second edition forthcoming.

thereby keeping it below what he might have obtained in the free market. Broadly speaking, two different formulae have been used in Britain: (a) a relatively rigid system of *rent control* (first introduced in 1915) and (b) a more flexible system of *rent regulation* ('fair rents', introduced in 1965). This second scheme involves making an application to a rent officer to fix a 'fair rent' which is, in effect, market rent less the amount by which such rent is inflated because of scarcity.[12]

Little is known about how rent control actually operated. Much of the literature assumes it worked just as envisaged without question or abuse by landlords. However there is little direct evidence that this was so;[13] and as data on the operation of the 'fair rent' scheme suggest that its impact has not been what might have been expected, there must be some doubt, at least, that the rent control legislation was rigidly adhered to.

Regarding the fair rent system, the evidence shows there has been a steady increase in the numbers of applications for a fair rent to be registered. In 1969 rent officers in England and Wales received 54,017 applications and registered 48,665 'fair rents';[14] by 1978 the figures were, respectively, 251,570 and 248,297.[15] These figures might at first sight suggest that, after a slow start there has been gradual public acceptance, and thus use, of the scheme as a means of controlling rent levels. However, the rise in the figures is largely due to two major increases in the categories of lettings within the rent officers' jurisdiction,[16] rather than to increased public awareness of the scheme.

Indeed there are a number of indications that the fair rent system is not working as its originators might have expected. In the first place, much of the initial publicity suggested that the scheme would be used by tenants to protect themselves against exorbitant rents. In fact, from very early days the vast majority of applicants to rent officers have been landlords.[17] Secondly, while these figures may suggest that substantial numbers of landlords (and some tenants) are now using the scheme, by no means all are. The Francis Committee reported[18] that of 1.2 million potentially regulated tenancies

[12]Rent Act, 1977, s. 70. The effect of this formula has not been analysed in great detail. The Francis Committee found that rents were reduced by an average of 20 per cent; but the basis for this conclusion is weak, and was in any event subject to great variation throughout the country. *Report of the Committee on the Rent Acts,* Cmnd. 4609 (London, 1971).

[13]The failure of governments and researchers to ask adequate questions about the operation of housing laws at that period has been criticized: e.g. M.J. Barnett, *The Politics of Legislation* (London, 1969), pp. 56–60 and D.V. Donnison, *The Government of Housing* (Harmondsworth, 1967), Ch. 11.

[14]Department of the Environment, *Housing and Construction Statistics,* 1st quarter 1974 (London, 1974), Table 44, p. 54.

[15]*ibid.,* 4th quarter 1978 (London, 1979), Table 45, p. 59. The rise has not been steady; the figures for 1978 are lower than for 1976 but higher than those for 1977.

[16]As a result of the Housing Finance Act, 1972 and the Rent Act, 1974.

[17]Department of the Environment, *Housing and Construction Statistics,* 3rd quarter 1978 (London, 1979), Supplementary Table XV.

[18]Francis Committee Report, *op.cit.,* p. 11.

existing in 1969, applications for 'fair rents' had been made in respect of only 14 per cent of them. A more recent study by Paley[19] of densely *privately* rented areas of England and Wales[20] shows that, of the sampled lettings, 12 per cent appeared to have their rents controlled; 36 per cent had rents regulated by the rent officer;[21] but in 52 per cent of cases the rents were agreed privately.[22] In this last category, some lettings were clearly outside the jurisdiction of the rent officer; nevertheless, a substantial proportion of these lettings were potentially within his jurisdiction. Not surprisingly, 58 per cent of landlords stated that they preferred to agree the rent privately rather than go to the rent officer; only 31 per cent preferred to go to the rent officer.[23] Thirdly, even where a fair rent has been registered, the result of this process is not what might at first appear likely. The Francis Committee found that many tenants paid more rent than the limit set by the registration, some paying much more.[24]

Of course, these figures cannot reveal the extent to which landlords whose rents have not been registered have nonetheless reduced the sums they would otherwise have demanded. Paley did show that a number of landlords, particularly resident landlords, were not interested in maximizing their profits.[25] However it must still be concluded that the system of fair rents has not had the effect of controlling rent levels in the way that was originally intended.

(ii) *Rent Books*

Under the Landlord and Tenant Act 1962[26] landlords renting property where the rent is payable weekly are obliged to issue their tenants with a rent book. Failure to do so is a criminal offence, which may be prosecuted by local authorities. The purposes of these provisions are clear: a rent book will contain many of the terms on which the property is let; it will provide a record of rent payments made; and, as a result of statutory developments,

[19]B. Paley, *Attitudes to Letting in 1976*, Office of Population Censuses and Surveys, Social Survey Division (London, 1978).

[20]For definition and rationale of this classification, see *ibid.*, p. 5.

[21]Or by the Rent Tribunal, the distinction need not be explained for the purposes of this paper.

[22]Paley, *op.cit.*, p. 16 and Table 3.2(a). Detailed figures show that where the tenant had an individual landlord, the chances of the rent being agreed privately were considerably higher than where the landlord was a company, a charity, or housing association.

[23]*ibid.*, p. 19 and Table 3.7. Again the figures show that individual landlords were much more reluctant to use the Rent Officer service.

[24]Francis Committee Report *op.cit.*, p. 117 and *Tenant's Survey* (Appendix 1), p. 241, Supplementary Table II(6) at p. 259. It was suggested, *ibid.*, p. 256, para. 2.11 that part of the reason for this was that many tenants who had been through the fair rent procedures were nonetheless unaware of the effect of the registration.

[25]Paley, *op.cit.*, pp. 24 – 6.

[26]Replacing the Increase of Rents and Mortgage Interest (Restrictions) Act, 1938, s. 6. D.C. Hoath, 'Rent Books: the law, its Uses and Abuses', (1978 – 9) *Journal of Social Welfare Law* 3.

special forms prescribed by Government should be printed in them giving tenants some information about their rights, including the amounts of rents they should be paying where these are controlled or where fair rents have been registered.[27]

Empirical evidence on the working of these provisions, such as it is, indicates that they are widely ignored. The Tenants' Survey conducted for the Francis Committee found that, in London, 39 per cent of weekly furnished tenants in areas of great housing stress had no rent book; and in the conurbation as a whole, 55 per cent were without rent books.[28] While, according to the same survey, nearly all unfurnished tenants did appear to have rent books,[29] the rent stated in the book was frequently incorrect as compared with rent levels that had been fixed by the rent officer.[30]

(iii) *Security of Tenure*

Under the Rent Acts, tenants have security of tenure unless and until they come within the grounds for eviction prescribed therein,[31] and a county court makes an order for possession. Under these provisions a county court is sometimes able in its discretion to order possession; in other circumstances the court is obliged to order possession. Requiring a hearing can be justified on a number of grounds: it may stop landlords taking matters into their own hands and causing a breach of the peace; it can give an opportunity to the court to consider whether an order for possession should be granted; and more generally it can allow the court to review the validity of the proceedings, which, given the complexity of the legislation, may in some cases be invalid.

In the last six months of 1977, 6348 applications for possession orders on grounds contained in the Rent Acts were determined by county courts in England and Wales; of these 3610 were applications based on the discretionary grounds contained in the Rent Act. Those statistics may seem to indicate substantial use of court procedures. However, in only 78 cases did the county court fail to exercise its discretion in favour of the landlord. Two studies indicate[32] that possession cases are dealt with at great speed; that parties are frequently unrepresented; and that possible points of law or other

[27]See now Rent Book (Forms of Notice) Regulations, 1976. (S.I. 1976 No. 378).

[28]Francis Committee Report, *op.cit.*, p. 292. For further evidence of evasion of rules, see Select Committee on Race Relations and Immigration, Report on Housing Vol. I. (H.C. 508–1, 1970–1)(London, 1971), para. 177 and D. Caplan, *People and Homes: an Independent Study of Landlord and Tenant Relations in England, 1974–5* (London, 1975) para. 5.17.

[29]Francis Committee Report, *ibid.*, pp. 254–5.

[30]*ibid.*, p. 256 and Table 8. This may go some way to explaining why some tenants paid more rent than the limit registered by the Rent Officer.

[31]Now Rent Act, 1977 s. 98 and Schedule 15.

[32]M. Cutting, *Tenants in the County Court* (London, 1975); M. Leevers, P.Nee and J. Rogers, *A Fair Hearing? — Possession Hearings in the County Court* (London, 1977). Both studies were based on participant observation in a small number of cases.

arguments are not presented. While the research on which these findings are based was limited to London courts, and thus cannot be generalized throughout the country, they do suggest that the rules are not operating so as to satisfy the objectives stated above.[33] Furthermore, there is no evidence on the numbers of tenants who leave their accommodation without having first gone to court, though one may guess that substantial numbers do not take advantage of the statutory procedures.

(iv) *Harassment and Unlawful Eviction*

To reinforce the rules relating to security of tenure, the Protection from Eviction Act 1977[34] makes it a criminal offence for a landlord to evict a tenant 'unlawfully', i.e., without first obtaining a court order; it is also a criminal offence for a landlord to harass a tenant, e.g., by cutting off essential services, or doing acts 'calculated to interfere with [his] peace or comfort . . .'

There is a dearth of evidence on the extent of unlawful eviction and harassment, and much of what exists is anecdotal. Nonetheless, the Milner-Holland Report, 1965[35] found that, in London alone, 790 cases of abuse were reported to a number of agencies within a 3-month period; this would have given an average of at least 2000 – 3000 cases a year.[36] Indeed it was this evidence that contributed to the enactment of the Protection from Eviction Act, 1964. Yet the Francis Committee in 1971 reported that in the first 6 years of the operation of the Act there had only been in England and Wales as a whole a *total* of 614 prosecutions for unlawful eviction and 684 prosecutions for harassment.[37] Furthermore, the penalties imposed in cases where a conviction was obtained were usually small fines; only 5 cases resulted in the imposition of prison sentences.[38] Despite increases in the maximum penalties that may be imposed,[39] evidence that abuse continues,[40] and the occasional judicial condemnation of the tactics of harassment,[41] levels of

---

[33]E.g. in the study by Leevers *ibid.*, it was shown that the validity of a notice to quit was frequently not considered (pp. 33–4) despite detailed provisions of law relating to such notices (Notice to Quit) (Prescribed Information) (Protected Tenancies and Part IV Contracts) Regulations, 1975 (S.I. 1975 No. 2196) and the principle that a notice to quit that is not formally valid is of no effect.

[34]This replaced and consolidated earlier legislation dating from 1964. A detailed description of the law is to be found in A. Arden and M. Partington, *Quiet Enjoyment*, forthcoming, Ch. 5.

[35]See the Milner-Holland Committee Report, *Report of the Committee on Housing in Greater London*, Cmnd. 2605 (London, 1965).

[36]*ibid.*, p. 255 see also A. Harvey, *Tenants in Danger* (Harmondsworth, 1964).

[37]Francis Committee Report, *op.cit.*, Table 39, p. 104.

[38]*ibid.*, Tables 39 and 40.

[39]Criminal Justice Act, 1972 s. 30. See Department of the Environment Circular 15/73.

[40]Partington, first edition, *op.cit.*, pp. 342–4; Caplan, *op.cit.*, paras. 5.11–5.16; Law Centres' Working Group, *Rent Act, 1977* (London, 1978) pp. 32–3.

[41]e.g. *Drane* v. *Evangelou* [1978] 2 All E.R. 437.

prosecutions and penalties have remained extremely low.[42]

(v) *Housing Conditions*

The American Bar Association once claimed that 'the first object of Land-lord-Tenant Law should be to encourage the making of repairs and the general maintenance of property'.[43] Data on rented housing in Britain suggests that this principle has been wholly inapplicable in this country. Whereas it has been estimated that in 1976, less than 3 per cent of owner-occupied housing and 1 per cent of local authority housing was statutorily unfit for human habitation,[44] almost 15 per cent of housing in the privately rented sector was so classified.[45]

A number of strategies have in recent years been adopted by governments in attempts to improve and maintain the standard of housing conditions. Most of these have involved direct action on the part of local authorities.[46] In addition there have been two statutory obligations imposed on landlords which have the effect of requiring them to carry out repairs in certain cir-cumstances.[47] There has been no systematic study of the extent to which these two provisions have been utilized. There is some evidence that a number of housing advice bodies, law centres, and other agencies, have taken cases against landlords (often public landlords) using these provisions. Nonetheless, it is clear from the data on the state of British housing, that these provisions have not been effective in forcing landlords to maintain their properties.

C Indirect Control

(i) *The Decline of the Private Rented Sector*

The most marked effect that the legislative measures discussed above are often alleged to have had is to be found in the overall decline of the private rented sector of the housing market. The crude proposition that the Rent Acts have been the *sole* cause for the shrinking of the private rented sector is not correct. Many other factors have contributed to its reduction.[48] Indeed,

---

[42]Arden and Partington, *op.cit.*, Ch. 1.

[43]Quoted in L.N. Brown, 'Comparative Rent Control' (1970) 19 *ICLQ* 205, at p. 215.

[44]The definition of unfitness is to be found in the Housing Act, 1957, s. 4 (as amended).

[45]Department of the Environment, *Housing Policy Technical Volume III* (London, 1977), p. 109, para. 47. In numerical terms, the numbers of dwellings were, respectively, 263,000; 46,000; 334,000.

[46]See now Tom Hadden, *Compulsory Repair and Improvement* (Oxford, 1978).

[47]Now Housing Act, 1957, s. 6; Housing Act, 1961, s. 32. These provisions have the result of shifting the legal obligations for repairs, which would normally be placed on tenants, onto the landlord. Even when tenants were typically responsible for such repairs, the actual enforcement of repairing covenants was very limited. Political and Economic Planning, 'The Future of Leasehold' (1952) 18 *Planning* 201, at p. 204–5.

[48]Perhaps the best of many discussions of this question is to be found in *Housing Policy Technical Volume III*, *op.cit.*, Ch. 9, paras. 8–23; see also N. Finnis, 'The Private Landlord is Dead but he Won't Lie Down' *Roof* July 1977 p. 109; and D. Eversley, 'Landlords' Slow Goodbye' *New Society* 16 January 1975, p. 119.

possibly the most remarkable finding in the recent study on attitudes to letting by Paley[49] is that 61 per cent of landlords sampled stated that they would relet their accommodation if it were to become vacant,[50] and a number of landlords anticipated that they would increase their holdings of rented accommodation within the next three years.[51] Further, 'despite the fact that the landlords of many of the lettings made by resident individuals said they did not intend to relet if the letting became vacant, it was not necessarily the case that this sector of the letting market was in decline. From the survey evidence, it seems likely that it was simply subject to considerable turnover, and that it had been only marginally affected by the operation of the Rent Act.'[52] Nonetheless, there is little doubt that the provisions of the Rent Acts, or what are perceived to be their provisions, have caused many landlords to give up the business of letting.

(ii) *Rent Act Evasions*

Another mode of response to regulatory legislation is to arrange one's affairs so that they are not caught by the relevant legislative provisions. The Rent Acts, and the other statutory provisions discussed above, have never been exclusively pro-tenant. Whatever the political rhetoric may claim, detailed study of the legislation shows that there are always special categories of letting that have been treated differently by or exempted wholly from the legislation. Thus, in addition to genuine cases, there have always been landlords who have sought, artificially, to place their lettings in the exempt categories.[53]

To give some examples: it was never the intention of the Rent Acts to cover hotels and boarding houses. Thus if 'board'[54] is provided, the accommodation will not be Rent Act protected.[55] Landlords have been known to provide tenants with instant coffee, packets of cereal and other comestibles, so that the letter, if not the spirit, of the exemption is satisfied. Again, landlords who provided accommodation for the purpose of a holiday were never intended to be covered by the Rent Act.[56] Now it is not uncommon to find 'holiday lettings' being offered in insalubrious inner city areas, where no-one would realistically be likely to take a vacation.[57] Since companies cannot 'reside' in premises, they cannot be statutory tenants under

---

[49]Paley, *op.cit.*, at p. 33.

[50]*ibid.*, p. 33 and Table 45. 98 per cent of charitable landlords stated that this was their intention.

[51]*ibid.*, p. 40, Table 4.19(a). The bulk of these were charity/housing association landlords; but other landlords were also proposing such increases.

[52]*ibid.*, p. 37, col. 1.

[53]The analogy with reactions to tax legislation is striking.

[54]Not defined, but intended to include the provision of meals.

[55]Rent Act, 1977, s. 7.

[56]Rent Act, 1977, s. 9. and s. 19 (7).

[57]Such arrangements are difficult to challenge: *Buchmann* v. *May* [1978]2 All E.R. 993.

the Rent Acts[58] and thus effectively have no security of tenure; casual empiricism[59] suggests that it is often companies who are favoured tenants, rather than private individuals. A more sophisticated evasion stems from the principle that the Rent Acts only apply where accommodation is 'let'. This has been held to mean that a true, common law tenancy, giving tenants the right to exclusive occupation of premises, must have been created. It is now common to find groups of tenants, who are sharing accommodation, living there under 'non-exclusive occupation agreements'.[60]

The extent to which these and other evasive devices are being utilized throughout the country as a whole has never been comprehensively studied. But there are sufficient case studies and reports to suggest that such evasions of the Rent Acts are widespread.[61]

D Summary

The evidence presented above shows that while some landlords have acted within the spirit and intention of the law and followed its procedures, many others have not observed the statutory rules which attempt to regulate the landlord-tenant relationship. Equally, there is evidence of deliberate action frequently being taken to evade the legislation altogether.

Recognition of the gap between legislative intention and legislative achievement may be interesting, but by itself is hardly surprising. (After all, it is seventy years since Roscoe Pound distinguished between law in the books and law in action.[62]) The existence of such gaps has been increasingly acknowledged, even in Britain. Thus in the second part of this essay, I wish to go beyond description to discuss why the gaps exist, and to look briefly at suggestions that have been made for closing those gaps.

II

Much of the existing literature suggests that the main, if not the sole, reason for the gap is the result of various malfunctions in the existing law and modes of its enforcement. These 'functional causes' will be discussed first; reform proposals which have derived from such analysis will be noted later.

A Functional Causes

1 Unwillingness to Use the Law

One possible explanation for the 'gap' is that, while landlords or tenants may

---

[58]Rent Act, 1977, s. 1(1)(a).
[59]Reading the lettings columns of the London evening papers.
[60]There are conflicting Court of Appeal decisions as to whether such arrangements are an effective method of evasion or not: see M. Partington, 'Non-Exclusive Occupation Agreements' (1979) 42 *Modern Law Review* 331.
[61]See e.g., Garratt Lane Law Centre, *Laws that Leak* (London, 1977); Weir, 'Landlords Exploit Rent Act Loopholes', *Roof* October 1975, p. 11; Francis Committee Report, *op.cit.*, Ch. 15.
[62]R. Pound, 'Law in Books and Law in Action', (1910), 44 *American Law Review* 12.

be fully aware of the legal position, they are unwilling to let their landlord-tenant relationship be framed by the law. The Francis Committee suggested that many tenants did not go to the rent officer because they were happy with their rent, or felt that they ought to stick by their agreements.[63] More generally, Professor Cullingworth argued, in his study of landlordism in Lancaster[64] that, particularly where the landlord was an individual or a resident landlord, a legalistic approach to the landlord-tenant relationship was regarded as irrelevant. 'Responsibility for the upkeep of the houses was often shared between the landlord and tenant on the basis of an informal understanding. The legalism of the Rent Act was quite foreign to this loose social situation.'[65]

While this may go some way to explaining perceptions of landlord-tenant relationships in relatively small provincial towns, or in intimate social situations, it would not seem to apply in areas of social stress where landlords and tenants are often overtly in dispute and may be very dependent on the law to resolve their conflicts. (Indeed, it is interesting to observe that in the public authority sector of the landlord-tenant relationship, where legal regulation had been noticeably absent, the assumption being that as 'model landlords' local authorities would always act in the best interests of their tenants, this assumption has now effectively collapsed, and a relatively detailed legal framework is currently being created which it is intended local authorities shall observe.[66])

2   Ignorance of the Law

The most obvious reason for the failure of the law to achieve its apparent goals is that both landlords and tenants are ignorant of their rights and obligations under the law. There is substantial evidence to support this view.[67] It has been suggested that such ignorance may be the result of a lack of legal services.[68] The extent to which lawyers are actually utilized by either landlords or tenants is not known. Statistics on the operation of legal aid

---

[63]Francis Committee Report, *op.cit.*, pp. 16 and 17.

[64]J.B. Cullingworth, *Housing in Transition* (London, 1963).

[65]J.B. Cullingworth, *Essays on Housing Policy: The British Scene* (London, 1978), p. 64. In passing it may be observed that although this essay is focusing on law as a means of social control, Cullingworth's comment indicates that frequently non-legal norms play a much greater role in controlling social behaviour.

[66]The process was begun by the Housing (Homeless Persons) Act, 1977 and is being continued in the Housing Bill, 1979.

[67]M. Zander, 'The Unused Rent Acts' *New Society* 12 September 1968, p. 366; Francis Committee Report, *op.cit.*, *Tenants' Survey* p. 241, Ch. 7 at p. 303; *Landlords Survey* p. 317, para. 3.7 at p. 334 and Supplementary Tables III (13) to III (15) at p. 346; Paley, *op.cit.*, Ch. 4.2.

[68]E.g. B. Abel-Smith, M. Zander and R. Brooke, *Legal Problems and the Citizen* (London, 1973), pp. 120–4; see also *Royal Commission on Legal Services* Vol. 2, Cmnd., 7648–1 (London, 1979) 'Users Survey', pp. 258–60.

show that solicitors do relatively little work in the landlord-tenant area under the legal aid scheme.[69] The overwhelming demand for legal advice on housing problems at the few neighbourhood law centres that have so far been created[70] is, however, an indicator of the failure of the traditional legal profession to meet this particular need. Similarly, it has been argued that the creation of more housing advice centres[71] and other advisory agencies would help to educate landlords and tenants about their rights and obligations.[72]

A second cause for ignorance, which also emerges from the studies[73] is that people may have some idea of what the rules are, but that the information that they have is misconceived. The causes for this have not been adequately investigated, but a number may be suggested. First, much of the legislation has been enacted in an atmosphere of intense political debate in which the governments which have promoted the legislation have been seeking electoral credit for their actions. Labour Party initiatives tend to be publicized as pro-tenant and Conservative ones as pro-landlord. Such crude descriptions of legislative provisions may well be far removed from what the legislation actually provides. Similarly, my impression of discussions of landlord-tenant law in the mass media is that they are almost invariably wrong, often seriously so. Again casual empiricism suggests that the quality of much legal advice on housing law matters is often inadequate, which may in turn prevent either landlords or tenants from getting an accurate statement of their legal position. A fourth point relevant here is that many people have no chance of clearly comprehending the law since it is so complex.

3 Inconsistency of Policies Embodied in the Law

A third set of functional defects may lie in the policies behind the law. Given the haphazard way in which housing laws have developed, often as short-term responses to immediate political crises rather than as part of a carefully considered strategy, it would not be surprising if such internal inconsistencies were found to exist. Perhaps the best documented example is the tension that clearly exists between rent controls, designed to keep rents low, and the imposition of repairing obligations which may entail considerable expense but which landlords may claim they cannot afford. The introduc-

[69]The Legal Advice and Assistance scheme was used in 5 per cent of 226,320 cases in 1977 – 78: *28th Legal Aid Annual Report* (H. C. 5, 1979 – 80) (London, 1979), p. 23. Legal aid certificates were issued to 1179 legal aid applicants for proceedings in court on landlord-tenant matters out of a total of 118,596 certificates issued, *ibid.*, Appendix 8, pp. 28 – 30.

[70]See, e.g. A. Byles and P. Morris, *Unmet Need: Case of the Neighbourhood Law Centre* (London, 1977), p. 30.

[71]e.g. the Seebohm Committee's Report on Social Services, *Report of the Committee on Local Authority and Allied Personal Social Services*, Cmnd, 3703 (London, 1968), para. 391.

[72]See, e.g. R. Brooke, *Information and Advice Services* (London, 1972) and more recently, National Consumer Council, *The Fourth Right of Citizenship: A Review of Local Advice Services* (London, 1977).

[73]See above, note 67.

tion of 'fair rents' in place of rent control, and an increase in the range of grants available to landlords to repair and improve their property may have done something to ease the position; but until these relatively recent changes, it may be conceded that the interaction of these two different sets of rules did help to prevent the achievement of intended social objectives.

4 *Judicial Attitudes*

Another set of reasons for the mismatch between the letter of the law and the achievement of its policy objectives is argued to derive from judicial attitudes. In a highly polemical article, Andrew Arden has castigated a number of judicial statements on the Rent Acts which were clearly hostile to the legislation.[74] It is argued that such statements have the effect of creating an atmosphere in which statutory interventions are seen as undesirable and to be enforced by the courts only in the most restricted circumstances.

There are two problems with this line of argument. First, although hostile remarks have been made or decisions taken which appear contrary to the purpose of the legislation, there are also judicial remarks made that do reveal some understanding of what the legislation is about.[75] The judges are by no means consistent in their hostility. Secondly, although lawyers may be concerned and influenced by every dictum that falls from a judge's lips, it is by no means certain that the public at large is so affected. Despite these difficulties, certain of the Rent Act evasions have received at least qualified judicial support and this must have at least encouraged some additional use. Further, it is also clear that housing law experts are often hesitant to challenge other evasive devices in the courts for fear of an unfavourable ruling. To that extent, the judges may be said to have contributed to the inability of the legislation to reach its defined objectives.

A more generalized complaint, of which judicial statements are merely an overt example, is that those whose task it is to decide housing cases — county court judges, rent assessment panel members, as well as high court judges — have no real understanding of problems facing tenants in the private rented sector and tend to exercise their judgements favourably to landlords and against the interests of tenants. The social and class background of the judges is said to make them more sympathetic to landlords than to tenants. This is exacerbated by rules of evidence which do not permit adequate discussion of the general social background to cases in this area.

---

[74]A. Arden, 'The Rent Acts — A Personal View' (1976) 126 *New Law Journal* 319. See too his, 'High Court Guerrillas', *Roof*, May 1979; pp. 78–82. Also J. I. Reynolds, "Statutory Covenants of Fitness and Repair: Social Legislation and the Judges' (1974) 37 *Modern Law Review* 377. This area is regrettably omitted by J. A. G. Griffith in his *Politics of the Judiciary* (Manchester, 1977).

[75]D. W. Pollard, ed., *Social Welfare Law* (London, 1977), para. A.208. Also M. J. Robinson,' "Social Legislation" and the judges: a Note by Way of Rejoinder' (1976) 39 *Modern Law Review* 43.

5 *Ineffectiveness of Enforcement Agencies*

A fifth set of arguments highlights the failure of the appropriate agencies adequately to enforce the relevant law. For example, as a matter of policy, the police refuse to intervene in harassment and unlawful eviction cases, even though, as we have seen, they are criminal offences.[76] From the operational viewpoint of the police, this may be highly justifiable, but it does have the result that the official disapprobation which is generated when the police act to suppress certain patterns of behaviour is missing from this aspect of the enforcement of the criminal law. To compensate for this lack of police activity, many local authorities now employ tenancy relations officers, or anti-harassment officials. (Many of these are ex-policemen.) Their approach to their work is primarily concerned with conciliation and compromise, rather than confrontation. Thus they will frequently attempt to negotiate settlements[77] rather than take offenders to court. Even where they do wish to institute court proceedings, they may then find officials in local authority legal departments unwilling to allow a prosecution to proceed.[78]

B Suggestions for Reform: Responses to the Identification of 'Functional Causes'

Many of the points made above have been used as the basis for various, rather obvious, suggestions for reform: improving legal aid and offering better legal services; creating more housing advice centres; offering better education to lawyers and housing advisers; establishing a housing court, or housing tribunal, that would have special knowledge of housing law and housing issues; employing more harassment officers; and so on. Such proposals have been made with a view to making the law 'effective'.

However the adequacy of these lines of analysis has come under increasing attack. Doubts are growing as to whether the *mere* provision of information, or the creation of more experts, or detailed changes in the law, or the appointment of different adjudicators will have any more than the most marginal impact on the community at large. Unfortunately, rather little work has so far been done to assess the value of improvements in legal or other services of the kind mentioned above, reflecting, no doubt, a belief that all such developments are, *ex hypothesi*, beneficial.[79] One study of a neighbourhood advice centre has stressed the difficulty it had in getting itself across to the people in its 'catchment area'.[80] Experience in many agencies

[76]Francis Committee Report, *op. cit.*, Ch. 14.

[77]An often ineffective procedure: J. Lambert, C. Paris and B. Blackaby, *Housing Policy and the State: Allocation, Access and Control* (London, 1978), p. 44.

[78]Arden and Partington, *op. cit.*, Ch. 1.

[79]M. Zander's description of *Legal Services for the Community* (London, 1978) is wholly premised on the proposition that developments in legal services are an unqualified human good.

[80]J. Baker, *Neighbourhood Advice Centre: Community Project in Camden* (London, 1978), p. 194.

has shown that a commitment to offer advice or assistance to every individual who comes through the door can, paradoxically, become a vicious treadmill which effectively prevents any work from being done. These examples indicate that the impact of such developments may be limited. This is not to say that they will not be useful; the provision of advice and assistance to individuals will frequently be of great value. What is doubtful, though, is whether simply increasing that kind of assistance will, by itself, do much to close the perceived 'gap' discussed above. Indeed, to frame the issue in this way may divert attention from consideration of rather more fundamental questions.

III

If explanations of the 'gap' in terms of the functional causes identified above and the value of resultant reform proposals are to be regarded as inadequate, it is necessary in the final part of the chapter to ask whether there is an alternative approach which may help us to understand why the 'gap' exists, which may in turn lead to greater understanding of the potential for landlord-tenant law to act as a measure of social control. Here we enter an area of discussion that is inevitably more speculative. Nevertheless, it is important to try to offer such an alternative, so that it may be exposed to criticism and refinement, or even rejection.

For such an analysis it is necessary, first, to be reminded of the economic context of housing provision. The history of housing policy, briefly alluded to at the start of this essay, shows that government, responding to social and political pressures, intervened in housing by providing legislative and policy cosmetics to disguise what might otherwise have been described as the unacceptable face of landlordism.[81] But, unlike other areas of social policy, such as education, or health, or social insurance, where what was originally provided privately came to be taken over predominantly by government, housing has remained the one area of social policy in which the private sector of the economy has continued to dominate. Although about a third of homes have been provided by local authorities, the ideology of private property, and those whose interests were protected by that ideology, have helped to ensure that there should be no serious challenge to the predominance of the private sector. (Indeed the current commitment of both major political parties in Britain to extensions of home ownership suggests that any radical change in the means of housing provision is unlikely, at least for the foreseeable future.) Thus, governments' attempts to make landlords socially

---

[81]Or as in the Minority Report of the first Ridley Committee, *Report of the Inter-Departmental Committee on the Rent Restriction Acts* [Cmd, 5621] (London, 1937) put it: ' . . . we consider that control of some kind is desirable as a permanent feature of the housing service. . . . We cannot agree that housing is a fit subject of commodity economics but rather hold the view that, so long as it is left to private enterprise, its management should be subject to public utility principles . . . a social service of such extreme importance ought to be controlled'.

responsible by use of the kinds of legal form discussed above are analogous to their attempts to use the law to make employers respond more readily to the interests of their employees, or manufacturers to the interests of consumers. Seen in this light, the 'gap' between the social objectives of housing law and their achievement is revealed as yet another manifestation of the problem of attempting to use legal forms to control the activities of the economically powerful.

Expressed thus, many would argue that attempts to use the law in this way are either futile, or irrelevant. For example there are those on the right who argue that most, if not all, attempts at the regulation of 'natural' economic forces by government are doomed to fail since it is the untrammelled operation of the private market that will optimize the allocation of scarce resources in favour of the overall public good.[82] The experience of history, together with alternative economic analyses,[83] convinces me that the right's case against intervention is simply misconceived; but nonetheless the point is frequently made.

For the left, even to discuss questions of controlling landlords by law is to miss the point. 'To transcend [the limits of bourgeois law], even to the smallest extent, requires the political perspective of a movement aiming at the total transformation of social relations'.[84] More specifically, some argue that although the examples of law discussed above might *appear* to be examples of attempts to control the behaviour of landlords (the premise that was adopted at the start of Part I of this paper), this view must be challenged, for it disguises what might be described as the 'ideological control' function of law. That is to say, by offering tenants 'legal rights' this helps to control the behaviour of *tenants* by diverting their attention from making more strident demands for fundamental changes in the forms of wealth-holding that currently exist in society.[85] While these analyses are valuable as critical counterbalances to the usual perceptions of law as an instrument of social control, I am not persuaded that, on their own, they offer a completely satisfying explanation of the social function of law.

Thus the position adopted here is that it is worth continuing to discuss the question of law and social control in the context of the landlord-tenant relationship, but that such analysis and any policy implications that may arise from it must take account of the imbalance of power that exists in that relationship. The essential conflict between the interests of the majority of landlords who are anxious to maximize their profits and the social needs of tenants, often poorly paid and inadequately educated and thus in a weak bargaining position, must be admitted and not ignored.

[82]D. Stafford, *The Economics of Housing Policy* (London, 1978).

[83]S. Lansley, *Housing and Public Policy in Britain* (London, 1979), Ch. 1.

[84]S. Picciotto, 'The Theory of the State, Class Struggle and the Rule of Law', in B. Fine, editor, *Capitalism and the Rule of Law* (London, 1979).

[85]P. Beirne, *Fair Rent and Legal Fiction: Housing Rent Legislation in a Capitalist Society* (London, 1977); Z. Bankowski and G. Mungham, *Images of Law* (London, 1976).

This position is by no means free from difficulty. But it is a position that is attracting increasing attention. For example an extensive body of literature has begun to develop on the crisis of law and legal ideology,[86] in which concern and doubts are being expressed about the functions that law may or should have in developed (or late) capitalist society. A number of studies in other areas have already indicated[87] that attempts by legal means to change patterns of behaviour of the economically powerful have had, on their own, limited results. Thus attempts to use the law as a measure for controlling the behaviour of landlords is but a specific illustration of this more general question.

A key factor, limiting the effectiveness of law, is that the whole emphasis of the common law has been directed to the solution of individual disputes. Individual issues are treated as isolated incidents which therefore need not affect the generality of behaviour. Where patterns of behaviour of the economically powerful have been changed, this has occurred because those exploited, either in fact or potentially, have acted collectively and have used or threatened to use their collective power to produce change. The obvious example is in the field of labour relations; but the same point can be made about consumer affairs, or environmental issues. I have recently argued elsewhere[88] that in the landlord-tenant context an important development in the law and legal process might be to build on a number of current developments regarding tenants' organization, and to give greater legal recognition to collective action by both tenants and landlords. In this way, the imbalance of power between the weak and the strong might at least be brought into the open, and more effective methods of correcting that imbalance than exist under the present system of law could thus be encouraged.

Related to this, it is beginning to be suggested that the form in which legal disputes are presented to courts and tribunals should take greater account of the broader social realities which lie behind the dispute, and should not simply focus on the facts of the individual case.

Whatever changes in law and legal process may occur, however, the limits of the law must be constantly stressed. Law is only one of many ways in which patterns of behaviour may be controlled and influenced. The powerful are only going to alter their behaviour if the general social and political climate generates the pressure to force them to alter it. Law may contribute to the creation of that climate. To that extent, looking at the objectives of

---

[86]One of the earliest of such studies was W. Friedmann, *Law in a Changing Society*, first edition 1964, second edition (London, 1972), esp. Ch. 3; see also Lord Scarman, *English Law: The New Dimension* (London, 1974); an attempt to put the issues raised in a more theoretical context is found in Eugene Kamenka and A. E. S. Tay, 'Beyond Bourgeois Individualism: The Contemporary Crisis in Law and Legal Ideology' in Eugene Kamenka and R. S. Neale (eds.), *Feudalism, Capitalism and Beyond* (Canberra, 1975), p. 126 and in Eugene Kamenka, R. Brown and A. E. S. Tay (eds.), *Law and Society: The Crisis in Legal Ideals* (London, 1978).
[87]See above, note 9.
[88]M. Partington, *Urban Law and Policy*, forthcoming.

legislative provisions and asking to what extent they have been fulfilled may be useful. But it is only part of the picture. More generally, discussion of issues of law and social control must not be allowed to divert attention from more fundamental political questions relating to the distribution of material resources in society.[89]

[89]And see R. L. Abel, Book Review, 'Law Books and Books About Law' (1973) 26 *Stanford Law Review* 175, esp. pp. 184 – 9.

Contributors

Shlomo Avineri is Professor of Political Science in the Hebrew University of Jerusalem and a former Director of that University's Levi Eshkol Institute for Economic Social and Political Research. Born in Silesia in 1933 and educated in Israel, he took his doctorate in the Hebrew University in 1964. He has served as Dean of the University's Faculty of Social Sciences (1974 – 6) and as Director General of Israel's Ministry of Foreign Affairs (1976 – 77) and has held visiting appointments at Yale University, Cornell University and in the History of Ideas Unit of the Australian National University. He has published numerous articles on Marx, on Hegel and on social and political developments in Israel; his books include *The Social and Political Thought of Karl Marx* (1968), *Hegel's Theory of the Modern State* (1972), the selection *Karl Marx on Colonialism and Modernization* (1968) and a Hebrew translation of Karl Marx's early writings. He has also edited and contributed to *Israel and the Palestinians: Reflections on the Clash of two National Movements* (1971), *Marx's Socialism* (1973) and *Varieties of Marxism* (1977).

John Dyson Heydon was born at Ottawa in 1943 and educated at the University of Sydney and University College, Oxford, where he was Vinerian Scholar for 1967. He has held an Official Fellowship at Keble College, Oxford (1967 – 73), taught at the University of Ghana in 1969, and been Professor of Law in the University of Sydney since 1973 and Commissioner of the New South Wales Law Reform Commission from 1975 – 8. He served as Dean of the Faculty of Law in the University of Sydney in 1978 – 1979. He has published articles on the law of contract, torts, equity, evidence, and restrictive practices. His books include *The Restraint of Trade Doctrine* (1971), *Economic Torts* (1973), 2nd ed (1978), *Trade Practices Law* (1978, with B. G. Donald) and the 2nd Australian edition of *Cross on Evidence* (1978, with J. A. Gobbo and D. M. Byrne). He has prepared, collected and edited *Cases and Materials on Evidence* (1975) and (with W. M. C. Gummow and R.P. Austin) *Cases and Materials on Equity* (1975).

Eugene Kamenka is Foundation Professor of the History of Ideas in the Institute of Advanced Studies of the Australian National University and was in 1978–79 Visiting Fellow in Trinity College, Oxford, and Visiting Professor in the Max-Planck-Institut für ausländisches und internationales Privatrecht in Hamburg. He is a Fellow of the Academy of the Social Sciences in Australia and Fellow and Secretary of the Australian Academy of the Humanities. Born in Cologne in 1928, Professor Kamenka was educated in Australia in the Sydney Technical High School, the University of Sydney, and the Australian National University. He has also worked and taught in Israel, England, Germany, the United States, Canada, the USSR and Singapore. His books include *The Ethical Foundations of Marxism* (1962), *Marxism and Ethics* (1969) and *The Philosophy of Ludwig Feuerbach* (1970); he has edited *A World in Revolution?* (1970), *Paradigm for Revolution: The Paris Commune 1871–1971* (1972), *Nationalism — The Nature and Evolution of an Idea* (1973), with R. S. Neale *Feudalism, Capitalism and Beyond* (1975), and with A. E.–S. Tay *Law-Making in Australia* (1980). He is general editor of the Edward Arnold series, 'Ideas and Ideologies', in which he has co-edited and contributed to *Law and Society* (1978), *Human Rights* (1978), *Bureaucracy* (1979), *Intellectuals and Revolution* (1979) and *Justice* (1979), and is a member of the editorial boards of *History of European Ideas, The International Journal for the Sociology of Law, Political Theory* and *Sociological Theory and Practice*.

Martin Krygier is Lecturer in Jurisprudence in the University of Sydney Faculty of Law, a solicitor of the Supreme Court of New South Wales, a member of the editorial board of the Australian monthly journal of letters and ideas, *Quadrant*, and editor of the Bulletin of the Australian Society of Legal Philosophy. Born in Sydney in 1949, he graduated from the University of Sydney with degrees in Arts (Government) and law and gained his PhD in the History of Ideas Unit of the Australian National University with a thesis on 'Marxism and Bureaucracy'. He has co-edited and contributed four chapters to *Bureaucracy* (this series, 1979) and contributed to *Socialism and the New Class* (1978, edited by Marian Sawer).

Oliver MacDonagh is W. K. Hancock Professor of History and Head of the Department of History in the Institute of Advanced Studies of the Australian National University. Born in 1924 in Carlow, Ireland, Professor MacDonagh was educated at University College, Dublin, and King's Inns, Dublin (called to the Irish Bar, 1946), and at the University of Cambridge where he took his doctorate in 1952. He was Fellow in History at St Catherine's College, Cambridge, from 1952 to 1964, when he moved to Adelaide to become Foundation Professor of History and Foundation Chairman of the School of Social Sciences at the newly-founded Flinders University of South Australia. From 1968 to 1973 he was Professor of Modern History at Cork, and during 1970 Visiting Professor of History at

Yale. Professor MacDonagh is a Fellow and former member of the Executive of the Australian Academy of Social Sciences, a Fellow and current Council member of the Australian Academy of the Humanities and Chairman of the Management Committee of the Australian Bicentennial History Project. He has lectured and given seminars at many universities in North America as well as in Great Britain and Ireland. He is author of numerous articles in learned journals and essays in volumes of collected work, and had edited and introduced the volume of Emigration (1973) in the Victorian Social Conscience Series. His own books include *The Pattern of Government Growth, 1800 – 1860* (1961), *Ireland: The Union and its Aftermath* (1968, revised and extended, 1977), and *Early Victorian Government* (1977). At present he is working on late eighteenth-century social legislation and reform.

Martin Partington has been lecturing in Law at the London School of Economics since 1973. Born in 1944, he studied law at Cambridge University. He held appointments at the University of Bristol and Warwick before moving to London. He has taught landlord and tenant law for a number of years and is author of *Landlord and Tenant* (2nd ed. forthcoming, 1980) and is at present also working with a barrister on a legal practitioner's text on housing law. From September 1980 he will be Professor of Law at Brunel University. He is also interested in social security law and legal services. In 1976 he was Visiting Professor at Osgoode Hall Law School, York University, Toronto.

P. H. Partridge was Professor of Social Philosophy in the Institute of Advanced Studies of the Australian National University from 1951 – 75 and Director of its Research School of Social Sciences from 1961 – 68, and is now an Emeritus Professor of that University. A Fellow of the Australian Academy of the Humanities and of the Academy of the Social Sciences in Australia, he is currently Chancellor of Macquarie University, Sydney. Born in Hornsby, New South Wales, in 1910, he was educated at Fort Street Boys High School and the University of Sydney, where he was Lecturer and Senior Lecturer in Philosophy from 1934 – 43, Senior Lecturer in Moral and Political Philosophy from 1943 – 46 and Professor of Government and Public Administration from 1947 – 51. He has served as President of the Academy of the Social Sciences and of the Australian Council for Educational Research, as Chairman of the Australian Advisory Committee on Research and Development in Education and as a member of the Australian Universities Commission and the Australian Press Council. He has published numerous articles on philosophy, politics and social theory; his books include *Society, School and Progress in Australia* (1968) and *Consent and Consensus* (1971).

Robert Simpson is Lecturer in Law in the London School of Economics and Political Science. Born in 1944, he was educated at the London School of Economics. He has lectured at Sheffield University and been Research Fellow in the Department of Law of the Institute of Advanced Studies of the Australian National University. He is co-author with John Wood of *Industrial Relations and the 1971 Act* (1973) and is currently working on a new edition of this appraisal of the role of the law in British industrial relations. He has also written on aspects of the role of law in British industrial relations in *Modern Law Review* and the *Industrial Law Journal*.

Alice Erh – Soon Tay is Professor of Jurisprudence in the University of Sydney, an Associate Academician of the International Academy of Comparative Law, Paris, a member of the Australian National Commission for UNESCO and its specialist Committee for the Social Sciences and was, during 1979, Visiting Professor in the Max-Planck-Institut für ausländisches und internationales Privatrecht in Hamburg. Born in Singapore in 1934, she was educated at Raffles Girls' School, Singapore, Lincoln's Inn and the Australian National University, where she took her doctorate with a thesis on 'The Concept of Possession in the Common Law'. She has practised in criminal law and lectured in law in the (then) University of Malaya in Singapore and the Australian National University, spent 1965 – 66 and part of 1973 as a visiting research worker and professor in the Faculty of Law in Moscow State University and in 1978 visited Kiev and Yerevan State Universities and the Academy of Sciences of the USSR. She has also been Senior Fellow at the Russian Institute and the Research Institute on Communist Affairs of Columbia University, New York, and in the East-West Center of the University of Hawaii. She is the author of numerous articles on common law, jurisprudence, comparative law, Soviet Law and Chinese law, and of several contributions to the *Encyclopedia of Soviet Law*, besides being co-author, with her husband, Eugene Kamenka, of two forthcoming books, *Marxism and the Theory of Law* and *Sowjetische Rechtstheorie*. In this series, she has co-edited and contributed to *Law and Society, Human Rights* (both 1978) and *Justice* (1979) and co-contributed to *Bureaucracy* (1979); she is also co-editor and co-contributor (with E. Kamenka) of *Law-Making in Australia* (1980). She is a member of the international executive council of the International Association for Philosophy of Law and Social Philosophy and served as President of that Association's Extraordinary World Congress held in Sydney and Canberra in 1977.

Klaus A. Ziegert is Senior Research Fellow in the Research Unit on Sociology of Law in the Max Planck Institute for Foreign Private and Private International Law, Hamburg and, in 1980, Visiting Lecturer in the Department of Jurisprudence of the Faculty of Law, University of Sydney. Born in Marienburg, West Prussia in 1944, he was a cadet and trainee officer in the West German Navy, commissioned in 1966. He then studied sociology, economics, law and history in the University of Frankfurt and sociology and Nordic and Slavonic languages in the University of Münster. Awarded his Dr. Phil. *cum summa laude* in 1974, he has held research and teaching positions in the University of Bielefeld and in the Institute for the Sociology of Law in the University of Lund, Sweden, and worked as a visitor in the Centre for Socio-Legal Studies in Wolfson College, Oxford. His doctoral thesis, *Toward Effective Sociology of Law: The Reconstruction of Society through Law*, was published in Stuttgart, in German, in 1975; he has contributed articles on law and sociological theory, and detailed studies on the workings of bankruptcy law, labour law and family law to journals and books in Europe and North America.

Index